Unz

Dress, Body, Culture

Series Editor: **Joanne B. Eicher,** *Regents' Professor, University of Minnesota*
Advisory Board:

Books in this provocative series seek to articulate the connections between culture and dress which is defined here in its broadest possible sense as any modification or supplement to the body. Interdisciplinary in approach, the series highlights the dialogue between identity and dress, cosmetics, coiffure and body alternations as manifested in practices as varied as plastic surgery, tattooing, and ritual scarification. The series aims, in particular, to analyze the meaning of dress in relation to popular culture and gender issues and will included works grounded in anthropology, sociology, history, art history, literature, and folklore.

ISSN: 1360–466X

Previously published in the Series

Unzipping Gender
Sex, Cross-Dressing and Culture

Charlotte Suthrell

Oxford • New York

First published in 2004 by
Berg
Editorial offices:
1st Floor, Angel Court, 81 St Clements Street, Oxford, OX4 1AW, UK
175 Fifth Avenue, New York, NY 10010, USA

Berg is the imprint of Oxford International Publishers Ltd.

Library of Congress Cataloguing-in-Publication Data
A catalogue record for this book is available from the Library of Congress.

British Library Cataloguing-in-Publication Data
A catalogue record for this book is available from the British Library.

ISBN 1 85973 720 X (Cloth)
     1 85973 725 0 (Paper)

Typeset by Avocet Typeset, Chilton, Aylesbury, Bucks.
Printed in the United Kingdom by Biddles Ltd, Guildford and Kings Lynn

www.bergpublishers.com

Contents

List of Illustrations

Preface and Acknowledgements

Some years ago, Dr Emily Kearns, a friend who knows of my interest in the somewhat odd combination of India, mythology, gender issues and menstruation, sent me a postcard from Thanjavur in Tamil Nadu. It said: 'No menstruation here but a very interesting puja near Trichy (Tiruchirapalli) where the priest of the Goddess dresses as the Goddess to worship the God – remarkably impressive and "ritual transvestism" does no justice to the theological complexities!' This, in conjunction with the discovery that there was surprisingly little within material culture studies on that most everyday and important artefact, clothing, was the start of my interest in a subject which first became a D.Phil thesis and then this book. (It is interesting to note that the gap in research on dress and identity has been rapidly filling up in the intervening years.)

Although for me personally the roots of the notions discussed in this study began with India, this work, whilst not primarily an ethnography, is principally concerned with transvestites in the UK and the strong contrast provided by the hijras of India, the two groups with whom I did fieldwork.

These are just two instances of cross-dressing, a phenomenon which occurs in a wide range of cultures and contexts. This work uses clothing and cross-dressing to illustrate a network of topics, in particular the convoluted web of discourses on sex, gender and sexuality and its divergent perceptual and conceptual structures

Many of those who have written on transvestism make the explicit or implicit assumption that it concerns only men dressing as women and not vice versa. Although it is clear that female to male transvestism certainly exists and in a wide range of contexts, in this thesis I have continued (somewhat reluctantly in many ways) the trend of focussing primarily on male to female cross-dressing. There are several further themes which have either had to be excluded altogether or have only been grazed in the interests of avoiding the confusion of too many concerns. It has often been frustrating to have to bypass these engaging branch lines in the interests of keeping on the main track but transvestism is, I would suggest, a cultural signifier which can illustrate several key anthropological motifs. During the course of research and uncovering, I realised there were many areas I could pursue but the themes which began to emerge above all the others, as well as being of particular interest, were those of sex, gender and sexuality coupled with material culture and these therefore form the main focus of this study.

There are numerous people who have contributed in large and small ways to this work, particularly my doctoral supervisor, Marcus Banks, who gave invaluable pointers and guidance over the years, his predecessor, Howard Morphy (now basking in the Australian sun) and my examiners, Drs Roger Goodman and Alison Shaw, whose pointers contributed greatly to the ideas in the final chapter. Within the Department of Ethnography at the Pitt Rivers Museum I would most like to thank Schuyler Jones and Donald Tayler. Mark Dickerson, at the Balfour Library and his counterpart at the Tylor, Mike Morris were both endlessly patient and helpful with my queries (and overdue books). I also owe great thanks to many of my fellow anthropology students, especially Christina Brannemark, Lorraine da Luz Vieira and Lennox Honeychurch. Sarah Coulson also deserves a special mention. She had chosen to do a short project on transvestites and we started some of the UK fieldwork together; I valued her company and help with this initial, potentially tricky stage very much.

My thanks go to countless people at Trinity College who provided solace, information, sounding boards and inspiration, but especially Matthew Steggle, Bryan Ward-Perkins and Jan Martin. I would also like to thank both Trinity and the Rajiv Gandhi Foundation for grants which assisted research both here and in India considerably.

I owe grateful thanks to many people who provided assistance along the way – Michael Yorke, Janett Scott of the Beaumont Society and the many UK transvestites who took the time to reply to my questionnaire or to come and be interviewed, especially Shelly, Gina and Sandra. Shelly has been an wonderful source not just of her own information and reflections but also of newspaper cuttings and other helpful material, of discussion and of thoughtful gifts. Also to many friends who have given support and succour, Margaret Simon, John Carpmael, Allegra Wint, David Frost, Pam and Ken Bean, Carol and Philip Houseman, Jeff Allen and David Peat, Susan Simpson and Julie Nasmith, to Pamela Howard for keeping up my spirits in that aspect of material culture with which this thesis principally deals, and especially to Mairead Devlin for the gift of some life-changing information.

In India, I am very much indebted to the Gurjar family from Anopura, a village outside Jaipur, especially Kajod, Hanuman and Hari. Also to Shambu Singh, all at Diggi House and particularly Sanjay and Priya Sharma and their family for their help with a great deal. All of them have contributed in immeasurable ways and much of the research could not have happened without them.

In particular, gratitude is also due in great measure to Peter Cozens for being prepared to read my drafts and give the most helpful assistance, and to my sister Jenny Suthrell and to Mark Bean for their thoughtful and steady succour.

Most of all, my thanks and love are due to my parents for their support – not only financial, without which this would not have been imaginable – but in immeasurable and wonderful ways, and especially for being prepared to believe that this was possible. This book is dedicated to my mother, who died in April 2001; I wish she could have seen it.

Introduction

In the 1962 film of *To Kill a Mockingbird*, there is a scene in which it is the first day at school for Scout, the daughter of Atticus Finch. In every previous scene, Scout (also Jean Louise) has appeared in a boy's shirt and dungarees, like her brother. But school demands that she wears a dress and at breakfast her father and Jem, her brother, are at the table with a neighbour who has come especially to see Scout on her first day. Scout is conspicuously absent and eventually, after she doesn't respond to being called, has to be lured out by the housekeeper, Cal. She makes her entrance with great uneasiness, clearly feeling resentful and stupid in this new garb – a pretty dress. Her brother laughs and points at her, her wise father is comforting and encouraging, the neighbour tells her she thinks the dress is 'mighty becoming' and smiles a knowing smile. Scout says, 'I still don't understand why I have to wear a darn old dress'; the neighbour purses her lips into another sly smile and replies, 'You'll get used to it'. Later, at school, Scout starts a fight in the playground and her brother – who has not been bothered by this before – stops her, telling her she is wild and stupid. The message is clear; it is time to stop acting like her brother, to put off her tomboyish ways and to start the process of becoming a woman, the main part of this being symbolised by her dress.[1]

Forty years later, some things have changed but others have stayed determinedly the same. A modern Scout would almost certainly not have a problem going to primary school in trousers and a shirt. Her road through childhood and adulthood is equally unlikely to be peopled by knowing female smiles of complicity and directives not to engage in boyish behaviour or, when the time came, masculine activities or professions. Jem, however, would incur considerable mockery should he choose to associate himself with any feminine behaviours – dolls, knitting or, most disturbing of all, the wish to dress in female clothing.

The subject of this book is transvestism, specifically male to female transvestism, apparently a backwater activity, engaged in by a minority group commonly perceived as dubious and ridiculous – and thus possibly suggesting research which is equally nugatory. (When I began this research, many friends, both in the UK and in India, expressed their surprise that I should want to study such a bizarre group, with their undertones of under-ground-verging-on-deviant lifestyles.) I am proposing, though, that through the use of a significant piece of material culture – clothing – trans-vestism highlights key areas of the ongoing discourses on sex, gender and sexuality, and that a study of cross-dressing, particularly one which looks at more than one cultural context, is in fact as mainstream as is possible because it illustrates how fundamental aspects of our lives – the lived real-ities of men and women – differ, and why it matters. Transvestism and transgenderism occur in a wide variety of contexts, both historically and geographically and, as will be seen, different cultures deal with them in very different ways. Although this study is particularly concerned with the position of transvestites in the UK, I would suggest that it is the juxtaposi-tion provided by cross-cultural context which really highlights the full implications of the cultural response to cross-dressing in Britain and furnishes the most useful insights.

The knot of cultural notions which constitute and inform any one culture's concepts of sex, gender and sexuality are unusually difficult to unravel, partly because they are so seldom questioned, so integrated into societal structures, so taken for granted that it is almost impossible to uncover them without recourse to another means. (Strathern, for example, achieves this in her work *The Gender of the Gift*, 1988.) In asking 'why' – do some cultures treat transvestism so very differently from others? – we are launched immediately into the heart of that knot. The process of unravelling is still not straightforward, though, because we have to do that almost impossible thing – to stand apart from our own ethnocentric view and all the cultural 'truths' and givens which have inevitably been swal-lowed during socialisation.

This entails moving in a terrain which has proved slippery and trouble-some for many, one which continually shifts underfoot and which even Henrietta Moore, a highly regarded academic theorist in this area, admits to finding 'terrifying': 'I find my relations with these terms to be strenuous, nuanced and unrelentingly complex.' (1994:2) I therefore acknowledge some trepidation in adding to the work in this field, particularly since the acquisi-tion of gender identity continues to be a enigmatic compound of features which is far from being fully understood. Within this knot, however, it begins to be apparent that the cultural discourses of any society – which include ideologies of the person, cosmology, folktales, 'common sense' and many others – are a crucial part of how a society is informed, in our notions regarding sex, sexuality and gender and how these can be dealt with.

Clothing is unusual in artefactual terms because it allows us to play – temporarily or permanently – with identity and self-image. It can fix us into the gendered space we occupy on a daily basis as we get dressed or, in the transition from male to female, it can function as the means by which gender is slipped on and off. Clothes are also a tangible indicator of normative structures which are so taken-for-granted, so obvious, they can remain almost invisible if they stay within permitted 'common-sense' boundaries. We seldom notice clothing unless it is particularly flamboyant or outlandish. But once it crosses into the world of blurred genders and unacceptable wearers, it moves intensely into focus and thus acts as a very material marker of ideas, notions and theories. Without such material items, issues of sex, gender and sexuality can be perplexing and difficult to theorise in the abstract but clothing can function as an objectification of these problematic questions. Transvestism, the act of putting on the clothes of the opposite biological sex, is an act as deliberate and intentional as that of making a pot or a fish trap. As a signifier, it carries profoundly different meanings and it is viewed very differently in different cultures. It forms an excellent subject for study because whilst it is obvious that gender is the source of the main binary divide in nearly all societies, and that gender polarities are often seen as the opposite ends of a continuum, the central space on that continuum may be occupied or perceived in a number of quite different ways and transvestism is an important one of these ways.

Fieldwork

Starting research in the field cannot help but begin with some preconceived ideas and prepared research plans – they form the basis for the study. Quite often, these notions receive some challenge or disruption during the course of the research, and this was certainly true for me. Even in the early stages of fieldwork I found I had different sets of expectations with regard to each of the two groups with whom I did primary research. My initial intentions involved studying both groups roughly equally but I was strongly advised that it would be better to consider one group as the primary one and the other as a secondary comparison and this very quickly began to make more sense to me also. I therefore focused primarily on the UK with India as a comparison – and there are a number of reasons why the UK fieldwork was able to delve more deeply, which are described in the fieldwork chapters. From the reading I had done, my expectations about the hijras were mainly regarding their spiritual aspect within Indian society. I understood them to be a special category –perhaps with an aspect of difficulty and adversity but also with compensating positive qualities, in particular their ability to heal and to bless. Once in India, I began to realise that although this has been true – and within living memory – it is a situation in the process of change.

With regard to the main part of the fieldwork with UK transvestites, I had in my mind already divided those I would study into at least two fairly firm groups: transvestites (TVs) and transsexuals (TSS). It is not hard to see why this framework emerged so clearly in my thought, since most of the work that does refer to transvestism and transsexuality does exactly this (as indeed I have done in parts of this study.) I imagined that although the boundary between the two might be somewhat blurred in the centre, for the most part it would be quite easy to distinguish between them. I now realise that it should have been quite obvious to me that this was unlikely to be the case. As Woodhouse states, 'How do we categorise the person who has periodically cross-dressed throughout his life and then decides, in his sixties, to have sex reassignment surgery? And when the outcome is not a happy one, the label broadens.' (1989: 37)

One of the main conclusions I had already reached was that in most matters concerning sexuality and gender, there are not so much binary divisions as points on a route between A and Z (or, as I began to imagine, more like markers on an abacus with not one but several lines or indices). So I should not have been surprised to discover that there are not *these men* who only dress in women's clothes and *those men* who would actually like *to be* women; but a range of different positions on not just one continuum but several, so that in the end there are probably almost as many positions as there are people. Bornstein (1995) states – and most transvestites seem to agree – that every transvestite and transsexual has different experiences, needs and desires from every other TV/TSS, in the same way that we all do as human beings; and in the same way that we habitually divide people into male and female, there is the convention of dividing transgenderism into transsexuality and transvestism.

UK transvestites are a thought-provoking group for an anthropologist. The decision to cross-dress is their own choice – and yet it appears to derive from a compulsion, arguably as an outlet for emotions which they perceive to be inapplicable to their own male life and character. This brings into question whether emotions and behaviours are more strictly gender-coded than would at first seem to be the case in British society – as the transvestites believe them to be. In common with the gender-coded clothing, it would seem that the traffic is one way and that it is particularly difficult for men to allow themselves to experience feelings perceived to be female – particularly the 'silly' ones – the desire to be elegant and sensual, to take care over their appearance, to appreciate beauty, to be vulnerable and protected, to be tender and caring, to be coy and flirtatious, or liberated and wild. (See Appendix D for a list of adjectives used by transvestites to describe aspects of their perception of femininity.) Transvestites do something apparently quite harmless and yet are vilified. They are a very small minority group and yet attract large headlines when 'discovered' since transvestism is arguably more of a guilty secret than, for example, having an affair or being a wife-beater. This cannot help but arouse curiosity and inevitably leads to questions about sex and gender within society and what Ramet calls 'gender culture'.

The Doctrines of Gender

As Ramet points out, it is necessary to have an understanding of *gender culture* in order to perceive how it is crossed and becomes gender reversal. (1996:1) Such conceptual frameworks were part of what I wanted to investigate during fieldwork. What I noticed led to further reflection on how these are informed by 'certitudes', often based on belief systems, even if these are no longer predominantly those of the majority of the members of a society. They may have been replaced by new and different ideas and ideologies, but prevailing frameworks of ideologies and doctrines of what is 'natural' and 'normal' are reflected in and rein-forced by, for example, literature, art, ceremonies and rituals (whether at a secular or religious level) through to newspaper articles and pub conversations. Potential factors which shape gender culture will be explored in the final chapters.

Because this study relates so closely to issues of gender – which itself lies at the intersection of culture and biology – it starts by examining the ongoing debates and discourses on sex, sexuality and gender. With the possible exception of performance cross-dressing (which is excluded from this study for this very reason) transvestism seldom receives cultural approval. It demonstrates that boundaries highlighted by gender specific dress are seldom crossed lightly or without intention, and that issues of gender are clearly illustrated by clothing, sometimes in surprising ways.

From these hypotheses, three main elements evolve: first, that of clothing as material culture, as an artefact which can be subject to categorisation; second, that of issues of sex, gender and sexuality as expressed by clothing and attitudes towards them; and third, how it is possible through a cross-cultural perspective to demonstrate the way in which these issues are influenced by prevailing attitudes, beliefs and cultural ideologies. The outward and visible manifestation of transvestism – of its building blocks – is the material culture of clothing but the deeper directions and inner motivation are inevitably to be found in cultural issues of sex and gender. The debate over these has been running for some decades and will be explored throughout, but particularly in Chapter 2.

Whilst this work is not intended as an ethnography, it does use primary fieldwork to illustrate issues of sex, gender and sexuality. This was carried out amongst transvestites and transsexuals in the almost wholly secular culture of the UK, described in Chapter 3, contrasted with the Indian hijras, described in Chapter 4. Hijras have held and to some extent still hold, an attributed place within Indian culture, within but apparently not bound by either of the two predominant religions of Hinduism and Islam and, some have argued, function beyond the binary divisions of sex and gender so as to constitute more of a third gender category. The hijras will be considered with reference to other groups who have also been assigned to this category.

The Prevalence of Transvestism

Transvestism is both a global and historical phenomenon. Descriptions of reversals of gender-coded dressing seem ubiquitous, throughout cultures and ages.[2] James Frazer, renowned author of *The Golden Bough*, cites numerous examples of cross-dressing in widely disparate parts of the world in his chapter entitled 'Priests dressed as women':

> In the Pelew Islands it often happens that a goddess chooses a man, not a woman, for her minister and inspired mouthpiece. When that is so, the favoured man is often regarded and treated as a woman. He wears female attire, he carries a piece of gold on his neck, he labours like a woman in the taro fields . ... The pretended change of sex under the inspiration of a female spirit perhaps explains a custom widely spread among savages, in accordance with which some men dress as women and act as women through life. These unsexed creatures ... are regarded sometimes with awe and sometimes with contempt, as beings of a higher or lower order than common folk. Often they are dedicated and trained to their vocation from childhood. Effeminate sorcerers or priests of this sort are found among the Sea Dyaks of Borneo, the Bugis of South Celebes, the Patagonians of South America and the Aleutians and many Indian tribes of North America. In the island of Rambreem off the coast of Aracan, a set of vagabond 'conjurors' who dressed and lived as women, used to dance round a tall pole ... Male members of the Vallhaba sect of India often seek to win the favour of the god Krishna, whom they specially revere, by wearing their hair long and assimilating themselves to women; even their spiritual chiefs, the so-called Maharajas, sometimes simulate the appearance of women when they lead the worship of their followers ...

The list continues to include the Congo, North America, Sauks & Omahas, the Ibans, the Chukchees of North-Eastern Asia, Teso of Central Africa and Uganda and a number of others (1906: vi: 257–8); many other anthropologists or recorders writing in the late nineteenth and early twentieth century (Bastian, Monier Williams, W.H. Keating, for example) noted examples of transvestism, as well as much earlier writers such as Plutarch, Apollodorus and Catullus. Clearly, Frazer was not the first to observe that the donning of opposite gender garments existed, since he was collating material recorded by others, but he was perhaps the first to put all the accounts together and categorise them thus.

There are numerous examples of transvestite/transgender categories of people being sometimes accorded 'special' status, both in history and ethnography. Examples are transglobal and some are described here to give an idea of the range of contexts. They include the 'two-spirit people' or berdaches of Native American Indian culture, the cross-dressed shamans of Siberia and Central Asia, and, in rather different ways, the Travestis of Brazil, the Bantut of the Philippines and the Xanith of Oman. Transvestism may also occur in a ceremonial or ritual context, such as the Naven ceremony of Papua New Guinea, in which most members of a society dress as the opposite sex at some time in their lives. The notion of a third gender has been discussed by many and in widely varying contexts. In the cultures described in Chapter 6, the travestis of Brazil and the two-spirit people (or berdaches) of Northern America, like the hijras described in Chapter 4, are instances in which men have chosen to dress or to live as women. (Also, although they do not appear here, there are recorded instances of women who have been assigned to this category.) As Whitehead comments, this kind of research cannot fail to highlight that 'ways of thinking about the sexes' are to be 'found to be rooted both in a wider set of cosmological premises ... Furthermore, it is often the "offbeat" (to our eyes) sexual and sex-related practices ... that help to bring the native theory most closely to the fore, probably because, being unclouded by obvious utilitarian aims, their 'symbolic' nature stands out more boldly.' (1981: 82)

A study of cross-dressing cannot help but consider concepts of sexual orientation, polarity, and attributes of maleness/femaleness. Other factors which inevitably come into play include ideologies of personhood and the importance of 'individuality' within a society, relationships of power, dominance and inequality, notions of the place between the polarities of gender, and the role of gendered deities. In any work, however, there are naturally many connected themes which have to be excluded. The three most important of these considered exclusions here are, firstly, female to male transvestism, which is touched on but not explored in any depth;

secondly, the area of transvestism as performance usually known as 'drag'; and finally, UK transsexuals; both of these last two are referred to, but there is no empirical material on them. Regarding transsexuals, they may seem in some respects to be a more directly comparable group with the Indian hijras, in that both have altered genitalia. The reason for not including them chiefly pertains to the goal of the research – the crossing of gendered clothing – and arguably, transsexuals no longer do this because once they have changed sex, it is fairly automatic that they would necessarily change gender and thus clothing. In India, the hijras provide an interesting contrast in that they also use clothing, hair, adornments and so on to define themselves as feminine and, in a culture in which there would seem to be no exact category of comparison with UK transvestites, this is the accepted form which cross-dressing takes. The stories of the hijras themselves demonstrate that whilst there are some who would no doubt fall into the transsexual category in a UK context, there are others who would almost certainly have become transvestites and would not have undergone surgical changes.

Clothing as Gender Landscape

Does transvestism involve a single choice – to cross-dress – or many? In Western culture, most transvestites dress in the clothing of not only the opposite sex but also their own, and are therefore in some sense choosing to create a second identity. Perhaps the appeal is not only of *another* identity but of passing through forbidden (and therefore exotic) portals into the world of the opposite. Clothing is the clue and the passport to this because it acts as such a significant marker. To enter into the clothing of the opposite sex is as close as one can become to *being* one of that sex; to participating in activities which would otherwise be proscribed. George Sand deliberately adopted male clothing in order to engage fully in Parisian literary society because it allowed her to behave as a man, with all the associated freedoms of masculinity.

In *Cross-Dressing and Re-Dressing: Transvestism as Metaphor*, Gilbert and Gubar remark that both Violet Trefusis and Vita Sackville-West wrote about their experiences of there being more than one possibility of opposite genders:

> In 1920, when Vita Sackville West looked back on her exuberant impersonation of the wounded soldier, 'Julian' during the height of her post war love affair with Violet Trefusis, she was bemused. She had experienced herself, she remembered,

as inhabited by several sexes: 'I hold the conviction that as centuries go on ... the sexes (will) become more nearly merged on account of their increasing resemblances'. (1989: 324–5)

Clearly, this has not happened; three quarters of a century on, although there is practically no proscription on women wearing items of men's clothing, we would certainly not appear to be moving towards a gender-free, multi-gender – or even gender-balanced – climate, despite having been through a phase where 'unisex' clothing and hairstyles were all the rage. Why, in early twenty-first century Britain, is it still more acceptable for a man to carry a flick knife than to wear women's clothes – and why is it still so clear that those *are* women's clothes?

This book aims, through the lens of clothing, to examine why gender-related exclusions persist in Western societies[3] which purport to be egalitarian and where there have been major shifts in men's and women's roles. More importantly, it will question why in the West it is possible to cross the gender barricades in one direction but not in the other or rather, why climbing them in one direction leads to success and preferment but in the other to derision. (And for those who would dispute that transvestism *is* still treated with mockery, I would refer them, for example, to the popular 1992 film, *Sleepless in Seattle*, starring Meg Ryan and Tom Hanks, in which transvestism is referred to amongst a list of seriously socially undesirable attributes. Meg Ryan's character is considering a meeting with the as yet unknown 'Sam'. Her friend Becky is anxious for her and says: 'the guy could be a crack-head, a psychopath, a flasher, a junkie, a transvestite, a chainsaw murderer or someone really sick.')

Are such gender-crossing intolerances found to be true of other societies? This text will look at the other possible options, as well as proposing some reasons for the underlying sources of such norms and strictures. In particular, the question of Western notions of society, where being 'an individual' is not only allowed but applauded and 'destiny' is largely believed to be of that individual's own making, will be considered – and contrasted with India, where rather different social perceptions hold sway.

Chapter 2 will introduce transvestism in relation to the principal themes of material culture, the discourses of sex, gender and sexuality and the theoretical framework of cross-cultural categories. Chapters 3 and 4 are concerned with the fieldwork in the UK and India and describe the two primary groups studied; their differing ways of life are then contrasted in Chapter 5. The final section outlines the dominant themes uncovered and discusses what is gained from the key threads. Chapters 6 and 7 consider cultural conceptualisations of sex and gender and whether these are inevitably yoked to ideologies of personhood and the relationship in a given society between self and role. The construction of individuality, the discourses and life histories created by the UK transvestites are demonstrably different from those of the Indian hijras and it is interesting and valuable to observe how crossing clothing shows up the relationship between these and the prevailing cultural concepts of sex, gender and sexuality.

As anthropologists notice the roles, beliefs and rituals of the cultures and peoples that they study, apparent 'contradictions' can arise, particularly from cross-cultural comparisons. The case of transvestism is an excellent illustration of such contradictions, not only in terms of its own contrary quality, the 'contradiction' of dressing in the clothes allotted by culture to the opposite gender, but also in terms of the startling differences in the use and perception of transvestism in different cultures. It holds possibilities for many key anthropological themes and yet it would appear that, certainly until recently, there have been few studies of clothing as a marker or cross cultural category. There are fewer still of transvestite groups or communities, in both the industrialised and the non-industrialised worlds and those studies that do exist are entirely or primarily monocultural. And yet, perhaps in the same way that Marcuse saw great art – as contradictory, troublesome and illogical and therefore a valuable element in our society – transvestism is also a necessarily chaotic and creative influence.

Notes

1. The film is referred to because, intriguingly, this scene does not appear in the book.

2. One of the more famous European examples is the Comte de Beaumont, Chevalier d'Eon, after whom the Beaumont Society (an organisation established in London in the 1960s for transvestites) was named, as well as Havelock Ellis's concept of cross-dressing which he termed 'eonism'. Beaumont was born in France in 1728 and is alleged by some to have started dressing as a woman when he was engaged on behalf of the French government to spy in Russia. Whether this was the true reason or whether it just suited his purpose, he became so famous for his ability to perform both gender roles that when he was later sent to London, a dispute raged as to whether he was a man or a woman. The London Stock Exchange even took bets on his gender and Beaumont became frightened that he would be summarily kidnapped by those who wanted to discover 'the truth'. No doubt the persistence of his notoriety into the 21st century rests partly on the continuing fascination for mystery, particularly in the area of gender.

3. Although the term 'Western' or 'the west' is, arguably, contentious, it has been used in this work as a shorthand term to denote the dominant, primarily white, protestant cultures of northern Europe and North America.

2

Clothing Sex, Sexing Clothes: Transvestism, Material Culture and the Sex and Gender Debate

The Importance of Sex and Gender

After the birth of a baby the first question of interest seems almost always and inevitably to be with regard to its sex and it seems likely that this has been the first question not just for centuries but for millennia. Alison Shaw bears this out:

> 'What have you got?', the midwives persistently asked me, at the birth of my third child. Dazed and amazed, by having just delivered a healthy and very red-looking baby, it took me some minutes to work out why they kept asking me this question. I had not even thought to look at the baby's genitals. It seems that in all societies, when a baby is born, its sex – whether it's a boy, or it's a girl – is, almost universally, the first statement that is made about it. We would expect this to be the case in societies where gender has considerable social significance, in parts of India and Pakistan, for example, where the birth of a son is cause for greater celebration than the birth of a daughter, and in societies where gender distinctions inform political rights, systems of punishment, and inheritance rules, and so on. But it seems that a newborn baby's sex is also proclaimed in societies in which biological sex differences make relatively little social and economic difference, such as among various peoples of South East Asia. Perhaps this is because, to offer a 'common sense' type of explanation, the sex of a newborn baby is one of the few things – perhaps the only thing – apart from who its mother is – that can be known about it for sure – but ... there may be more to it than this. (Unpublished paper, 2001)

So deeply does the gendered divide run through our understanding and interpretation of forms of life that it comes even before the questions about fingers and toes, grandmother's eyes, and so on. From then on, having ascertained the sex, the process of gender begins, or at least this is how the story – of sex and gender as theoretical models – was posed until relatively recently. Work in this area has, however, moved on to question how universal these categories are and anthropology has provided some key evidence in the debate, particularly through its discourses over 'difference' (for example Moore, 1988a: 9). Further than that, even biologists would admit that a child born 'intersexed' is still viewed as a combination of the two binary categories of male and female. More than those, versions of them or pluralities, do not exist – in most cultures, at least.[1]

Transvestism provides an eye-opening link in this research between two theoretical fields – material culture and gender – because it lies at the intersection of the two. For many decades now, sex and gender have been popular and well-studied topics and the implications, which certainly affect our lives in a multiplicity of ways, both directly and indirectly, have been of particular interest to academic research and to feminism. In addition many authors have written about or with particular relevance to the subject of those who cross the sex/gender/sexuality barriers, and there has begun to be a growing literature on the sexed and gendered significance of dress and textiles. Very little of this latter research has, however, put these two together or related directly to cross-dressers and it is in bringing these two topics together that this book can contribute to thinking in this area. It accentuates, in particular, the issue of individual agency as linked with culturally inherited forces. Clothing as an artefact, with its clear gender divisions, illustrates, as few other things can, the socially constructed nature of gender which goes beyond biological sex.

Dress and Identity: Transvestism and Material Culture

In their preface to *Fashioning the Frame*, Warwick and Cavallaro ask, 'should dress be regarded as part of the body, or merely an extension of, or supplement to it?' (2001; xv) Although the obvious answer would seem to be the latter, since we are not born into the world with clothes, in most parts of the world we acquire them very soon after and, in public at least, are seldom without them again. One reality is therefore that they do become part of our bodies as well as an extension to them. We also use dress, consciously or unconsciously, as one of the ways in which we project ourselves, the self we wish to present to the world, the group with which we desire to be associated. It is a strong and visible part of our need to assert identity – perhaps in Western society particularly, with its lack of clearly stated hierarchies and boundaries – and thus forms part of our individuation. It materialises the process of separation and aggregation in the process of becoming an autonomous self, whilst at the same time holding an element of ambiguity with regard to where the self (body) ends and dress begins, for everyone to some extent but for transvestites in particular. The dress itself may be seen continually renegotiate its relation to the body and the world.

Clothing may be functional but, apparently everywhere, it is much more than that, denoting for example, status or economic standing, age group, respectability and attitudes, including the desire to conform or rebel. As Barnes and Eicher state in their introduction to *Dress and Gender* (1992), clothing and body decorations have formed part of the way that humans have interacted with the world and each other in all recorded cultures. Decorations may also serve a function, perhaps to indicate allegiances or membership of a particular group, but are often worn even when they do not.

Although clothing is one of the most obvious, ubiquitous and yet multi-form of material culture items, for much of the last century anthropologists have rather neglected it as something which imparts significant cultural information and which, in particular, can show up the boundaries which surround and delineate these cultural markers. Tarlo's work on dress in India (1996) suggests that, following the advent of fieldwork as a primary anthropological technique, the study of clothing and material culture in general was generally dropped in favour of social customs, networks and structures, perhaps largely because clothes were considered a 'feminine issue' and thus too frivolous to be of interest to the academic or serious-minded. Over the last decade, however, as the interest in material culture has increased and become more comprehensive, so there has developed a growing literature on clothing and dress; but little of this has focused on transvestism as a significant aid to understanding issues of dress, gender and sexuality.

What we wear on our bodies becomes part of the transactional relationship we have with the world. Clothes function, as Ardener has observed, as a 'sheath', 'as the least of all possible spaces, and also the purest kind of egocentric territoriality'. (1987: 114) It is hardly surprising that artefacts, as objects created and interpreted by people, embody many principles of the ways in which humans organise life processes and can therefore function as pointers in the quest for greater understanding of social environment. Clothing is generally the artefact of greatest physical proximity to us, and therefore most closely linked to notions of the body. The body is of importance, not only because of its connections with anatomy, gender and sexuality but because it is what we present to the world. Even more than our objects, dress mediates between the individual and the world and is a key element in the constructed image that says 'I belong'. One could question, then, why clothes are used in a manner that sometimes signifies just the opposite; the act of not belonging, or belonging to an 'anti-category'.

Clearly, in order to 'cross-dress', there must be a gender based dress code. The use of dress as a form of visual identificatory code is described particularly clearly by Eicher in her introduction to *Dress and Ethnicity*, as a 'coded sensory system of non-verbal communication that aids human interaction in space and time.' (1995: 1) Significantly, gendered clothing and decorations would appear to exist in practically every culture. Some have suggested (Mellen, 1981, for example) that this may be because the biological imperative to be gender specific, both in dress and in roles, has on the whole encouraged demarcated and distinct sex and sexuality due to its survival advantages.[2] This seems probable and would seem to be even more true of consumer capitalist societies where gender is a well-defined part of the conscious – and unconscious – activity of shopping.

Transvestism, particularly in a Western context, deals with fantasy identities; in previous centuries, folk tales and ballads were legion of women who went to look for their long-lost husbands or lovers and needed to dress in male attire in order to sail the seas or go to war. This is borne out by research which reveals, in the period from the late sixteenth century to the nineteenth century, many examples of females cross dressing to enable a more outdoor or exciting lifestyle from the one ordained for them as women, whether as buccaneers, soldiers, doctors or refugees from the law.[3]

Although this work does not include female to male transvestism, such accounts demonstrate only too clearly how important clothing is to identity. It is the means by which transformation and a different life, a different set of values, characteristics and activities is acquired and supported. Bourdieu's concept of *habitus*, which speaks very much to the artefactual world, is a useful concept in that the wearing of a particular set of clothing can create an entire social world (arguably, for the ordinary user as much as for the transvestite.) Our clothing choices are themselves a cultural construction which has all too obvious roots in the way in which selves and personal choices are themselves part of the social world. In a small-scale society, the type of clothing worn by users may demonstrate, for example, the village from which they come, their ancestry or place in the social hierarchy. In Western, industrialised societies, clothing preferences are far more eclectic and difficult to place in easy, immediate categories but, arguably, they are almost always indicative of choices both consciously and unconsciously made, including reference to aspects of the wearer's social status. The clothing choices made by transvestites may be more specific in that they have been selected for their ability to transform a male person into a female but they still reflect the wider preferences of a group within one society.

Transvestism in all contexts uses items of material culture of a very personal and individual nature to cross both sex and gender boundaries – and it is perhaps helpful here to define the term 'transvestism' since the word itself can be value-laden and polemical. The *Oxford English Dictionary* (1976) gives the definition of 'transvest' and subsequently, transvestism as 'clothe (usually oneself) in other garments, especially those of the opposite sex'; and this meaning would appear to be universally accepted – that 'trans' = a/cross and 'vest' = 'dress'. *Cross*-dressing (*trans*-vestism) must also imply that there must be some movement across, a place of coming from and a place of going to which is between the worlds of gender polarity, otherwise a person would simply be getting dressed. And these in turn involve the notion that they are moving from the place trans-gendered individuals 'naturally' inhabit, dictated by birth-sex and gender. (Such assumptions regarding the polarisation into only two sex/gender categories will be discussed later.) I would define transvestism as the delib-erate and conscious wearing of clothes which, in that particular society, are perceived as the domain of the opposite sex, usually to knowingly create an image of the self as a person of the opposite sex.

Clothes are an everyday part of the creation of an image. We are all familiar with the dress codes required by certain situations; clothes may enable a person to look like an executive during the week and a rave-goer at weekends – and the two sets of clothes are seldom interchangeable, although there may be single items which are. Similarly, in Western culture, many items of clothing have become 'unisex' but there are few 'insiders' who, if questioned, would not be able to identify which items could not be worn by the opposite sex, particularly female items which are not available to men, although it is interesting to speculate how intelligible these notions would be to an 'outsider', or indeed how easy it would be to explain such shifting, personal and unwritten codes.

Within the binary framework of sex and its associated cultural, gendered expectations transvestism reveals much about these issues; clothing becomes a world of intelligible metaphors once one understands the local codings and signifiers. Clothes allow us to play, temporarily or perma-nently, with our identity and self-image. (For most women, it is probably no surprise that there are at least some men who wish to 'play' with women's clothing because its range in terms of colour, style and possibility goes so far beyond men's.) Although in the West, with its cult of the individual, clothing is used to express personality, there can be few examples of cultures where clothing is not similarly performative in creating identity. Once we start to ask questions about how clothes are used and why, it is clear that clothing is crucial to identity. We use clothes as visual markers to identify ourselves to others and this also works in reverse, as Virginia Woolf describes it in *Orlando*: 'there is much to support the view that it is clothes that wear us and not we them ... we may make them take the mould of arm or breast, but (clothes) mould our hearts, our brains, our tongues to their liking.' (Woolf, 1928: 188)

In the case of transvestism, both in Western and non-Western contexts, dress is used much more specifically to create an illusion both for the user and the observer in order to make a particular point – that the wearer wishes to be seen as a member of the opposite sex – and for most transvestites it is important that the clothing is used in such a way as to make the illusion as real as possible. The male transvestite must disconnect from man-world with its masculine properties and re-establish his identity in woman-world, exchanging the gender indicators in a deliberately fashioned manner. Particularly for the hijras, there are links also with Van Gennep's notion of 'limen' as a threshold stage within the process of *rites de passage*, since the movement across boundaries must involve the traversing of the margins which usually confine.

Although these boundaries are mostly not palpable, there are some situations where they are. One example, as Ardener has discussed, is in terms of 'space'; some of my UK interviewees suggested that 'women's space' in this society is, for example, particular areas of some shops, especially the parts which sell hosiery, perfumes, cosmetics, women's clothing, and so on, whilst 'men's space' might be the garage or old-fashioned type of DIY store/ironmonger. Those structures may be considerably more relaxed than a few decades ago but, arguably, women are still more at ease in a restaurant, wine bar or café, whilst men find that male refuge, the pub, more comfortable.[4] But beyond the actual physical structures of buildings, there are socially constructed spaces which are less tangible:

> Societies have generated their own rules, culturally determined, for making boundaries on the ground, and have divided the social into spheres, levels and territories with invisible fences and platforms to be scaled by abstract ladders and crossed by intangible bridges with as much trepidation or exultation as on a plank over a raging torrent. (Ardener, 1981: 11–12)

The contrast between transvestites and hijras depicts some of these constructions which comprise gender crossing. For transvestites who wish to cross over one of these invisible (but only too real) bridges into the world of the feminine, clothing is an essential component of their scaling and spanning equipment; arguably it is the one without which they would not gain any kind of entry, either to the internal or external parts of woman-world. This applies particularly to the cross-dressers of the UK who wish only for a temporary pass to this other country but it is also crucial for the hijras, the long-term immigrants, since clothing is part of their being accepted as the separate category of 'neither man nor woman'.

The study of dressing and cross dressing as a tool for understanding can also venture beyond the artefactual environment to look at issues of identity, agency and intention and desire. As will be further discussed towards the end of the book, emotions can play a very strong part in the motivation of UK transvestites in particular. Themes of identity, agency and intention have been the province of philosophers for centuries but have more recently attracted the attention of anthropologists and are most illuminating here, especially when viewed as a contrast between the two major fieldwork groups. The difference in attitude towards and perception of individual agency in England and India will also be discussed later.

'Is Gender to Culture as Sex is to Nature?'[5]: Transvestism and the Discourses of Sex and Gender

Stereotypical gender difference may be currently accepted (particularly within the social sciences) as largely a matter of social processes, but for most of the twentieth century and now into the twenty-first, there continues to be debate and controversy over the 'real' differences between men and women, and disagreement about why these seem to exist (albeit in widely variant forms) in every culture that has been explored and written about. Particularly in the last few decades scores of anthropologists, as well as academics from other fields, have been engaged in work on gender, together with its partners, sex and sexuality. It could be argued that these are three threads which are so twined around each other that it may be impossible to untangle them, particularly since each attempt at untangling either reveals further knots beneath or undoes itself as the theory progresses. Certainly it would seem more valuable to look at cultural models of sex/gender as a plurality of discourses rather than a single model, however multiform.

It is hardly surprising, though, that these three raise such interest when they carry implications which go far beyond the nomenclature 'male', 'female', 'masculine' and 'feminine'; beyond our personal relationships and into society and culture at large which interprets almost everything through the dialects of gender, with all their indicative associations such as dominance and submission, exterior and interior, energy and quiescence. Gender, like identity, is a very broad and generalised notion and has led to much debate, particularly since cultural notions regarding gender are demonstrably dynamic; they change from society to society and over time. But, in the same way that each generation is said to have 'invented sex', each also has its prevailing notions about what men and women do and are. As several authors show (Herdt, 1993, for example), philosophers and medical theorists as far back as Aristotle and Galen discussed differences between men and women, both as constituted in biology and in their philosophical and moral attributes. It was considered 'natural' that male and female were binary polarities.

Throughout the changes in every field which have taken place since classical times and have become ever more discussed and challenged during the last century, arguments have raged over the nature of sex and gender, and whether and how much there is an essential component of masculinity and femininity. On the one side – the farthest end of these arguments – are the biological determinists who would argue that there is a fixed core of traits belonging rigidly to each sex, immutable and unaffected by societal constructions, with any who do not fit into these descriptions (homosexuals, for example) perceived as deviant and unnatural. On the other side are ranged the arguments of social constructionism which, at their most extreme, would suggest that nothing is biologically determined and that all gender associated behaviour is brought about by societal pressures.

In between are those who suggest that first, there is likely to be a balance between nature and nurture, biology and culture, and second, we are unlikely to ever be able to know the configuration or patterning for sure. Even those rare examples of (for example) boys brought up as girls, because of indeterminate genitalia or penises severely damaged in early childhood, are hardly conclusive evidence for either biology or culture, partly because there are so few of them and partly because they do not by any means all tell the same story. The medical techniques for 'fixing' or 'creating' sex are relatively new and the implications in the early stages of being documented.[6] Furthermore, the multi-layered and complex nature of both biology and social construction suggest that the question of biology/culture is one which cannot ever really have pure answers. Margaret Mead argued over half a century ago that gender based roles are not biologically but culturally assigned, that they are inevitably limiting for both sexes, and that their cultural grip is exceptionally strong. One result of her work – and that of others – is that the biological determinist model now holds little sway and is used as a model by few anthropologists. It is largely recognised that being born male and female creates difference, but how this difference is constituted, why the widely divergent cultural constructions arise and why they continue to be practised in such a pervasive form is still very much an ongoing debate.

Corporeality and the Politics of Sex

My body became my enemy at an early age. And since the brain is a more important organ than the penis, it became necessary to change my physiology. A male body, with or without clothes, was an inept device for expressing femininity. (Griggs, 1998: 10)

Sex has conventionally come to mean the differences between the biological patterning of males and females whilst gender is seen as the social and cultural attributes of masculine and feminine which may differ considerably from one society or culture to another. The difference between sex and gender and the formation of ideas and theories regarding both (gender in particular), have marked a move away from a biologically determinist viewpoint and allowed for the separation of the two. One outcome of this is that more recently, historians, sociologists and anthropologists have started to question whether either sex or gender is as determined as we believe them to be. Foucault's work in particular (1981), exposes the shifting and piecemeal nature of gender identity and has been crucial to the development of ideas in the areas of sex, sexuality and gender, since it probes many of the fundamental and valuable 'why' questions regarding constructions of femininity and masculinity.

The body of knowledge in sex and gender has been considerably expanded and informed by work in the parallel and connecting areas of lesbian and gay studies, or 'Queer Theory'. These studies have questioned many assumptions, as have Masculinity Studies and Cross-Cultural Studies. Together they have explored themes of sex, gender and sexuality in politics, history, philosophy, economics, art, literature, religion and more[7] – and the perspective of biological determinism has been contested by many of them. Into the 1990s, academic discourses have begun to explore the possibility that sex is not the defined and constant category it has always been assumed to be. Thomas Laqueur's *Making Sex* (1990) argues that sex may be as socially constructed as gender and challenges our 'taken for granted' attitudes about, and notions of both, whilst pointing out the repercussions of the almost entirely male perspective in how these perceptions have evolved. He suggests that ideas about sex and sexuality have changed fundamentally, together with our consciousness of ourselves and our bodies. Caplan writes that 'gender ... is not so much ascribed on the basis of physiological sex as of achieved sex, and a vital part of that achievement is sexual behaviour and identity'. (1987: 2) (And this notion is echoed in many popular songs – 'He made a woman out of me ...', etc., the implication presumably being that 'I may have been female before but it took 'him' to create/authenticate the 'real' woman'.)

Judith Butler, whose ideas have done much to fuel current thinking in this area, points out that in many ways, although the early distinction between sex and gender may have been a necessary part of the conceptu-alisation process, it is not without its problems and difficulties as a theo-retical model. She goes on to question where the 'given-ness' of sex comes from anyway – chromosomes? anatomy? hormones? And how much it is affected by history (whose? – And is it the same history for all sexes and genders?) Neither can we assume any more that the two go hand in hand:

> Originally intended to dispute the biology-is-destiny formulation, the distinction between sex and gender serves the argument that whatever biological intractability sex appears to have, gender is culturally constructed: hence gender is neither the casual result of sex nor as seemingly fixed as sex. ... If gender is the cultural meanings that the sexed body assumes, then a gender cannot be said to follow from a sex in any one way. Taken to its logical limit, the sex/gender distinction suggests a radical discontinuity between sexed bodies and culturally constructed genders. ... When the constructed status of gender is theorised as radically independent of sex, gender itself becomes a free-floating artifice, with the consequence that man and masculine might just as easily signify a female body as a male one, and woman and feminine a male body as easily as a female one. (Butler, 1990: 9–10)

Anthropology has considered such issues for a some time; Strathern's *Gender of the Gift* (1988), for example, discusses them with great insight, using both her own and others' fieldwork to demonstrate the difficulties and absurdity of regarding sex and gender as intractable properties inherent in a fixed sex body, producing images which do not accord with a Western model and have the possibility of crossing or alternating between a number of points on the sex/gender boundaries.

This has led some commentators to question whether a simple, sexual binarism is simplistic and over-reductive. Some (Yorke (1991), Herdt (1993), Whitehead (1981), Wikan (1977) and others) have posited a third sex or third gender category, whilst research among the Native American and Central Asian Indians suggests that cultures have existed (even if they do not now) who have accepted and allowed for up to nine categories. Laqueur for one would seem to support this need for greater possibilities of variance: 'Indeed, if structuralism has taught us anything, it is that humans impose their sense of opposition onto a world of continuous shades of difference and similarity.' (1990:19) Marjorie Garber has further contributed to this debate, exploring whether the issue of 'the third' is in itself simply another reductive category or whether it has uses in terms of a 'space of possibility'. (1992: 11) Revealingly, the third sex has been designated sometimes as primarily male territory and sometimes female; in either case, it generally continues to perceive the individual as an 'original' male or female who has 'gone wrong'. Caplan notes that although Western societies show antipathy to male homosexuality because it 'threatens male solidarity and superordination', and likewise female homosexuality because lesbians do not 'need' men, 'Sex-change operations ... do not appear to be condemned; it is as though surgery removes not only organs but also anomalies, making a correct fit between sex, gender and sexuality'. (1987: 2) (I would argue that this feminist perspective on gender re-assignment surgery may make a very valid point, but hardly takes into account the very real experience of those who feel condemned to a life-time of feeling a misfit. Which in turn, raises again the social partitioning of expectation.)

I would suggest that the inability of Western cultures to see that 'space of possibility' is deeply rooted in the philosophy which is part of our rich inheritance from the classical cultures – in the West at least, it is so conditioned that it is almost impossible to try to forsake dichotomous conceptualisation in this area and that it is inseparable from the notion which came along with it – that of the essential inferiority of women. Men who choose to dress in women's clothes and adopt female mannerisms and behaviours have been censored for both components of this, for dressing as the inferior sex and for transgressing the binary rule, for blurring the boundaries.

Clothing the Brain

I am suggesting here that transvestism is a particularly dextrous tool in the sex and gender analysis kit because it is *of* both and will not fit into either category alone, in addition to supporting the familiar dictum that the brain is the biggest sex organ, since it is our minds we dress to please, more than our bodies; transvestites demonstrate this very clearly. In addition, transvestism also links to one of the most significant material culture items we have and is therefore objectifiable – and it would appear that some persons, male and female, have always found it possible, and even imperative, to act or behave in the role opposite to their own biological gender, however strong the local gender-coded norms.

This is of particular importance given Henrietta Moore's assiduous explorations into the question of the division between 'sex' and 'gender', whether and how they can be split. As Moore puts it:

> Is it appropriate to separate 'Sex' from gender? ... This question becomes particularly crucial in the light of the previous argument that sex as well as gender must be understood as socially constructed. The result is that the analytic distinction between sex and gender seems very blurred. At least in the context of cross-cultural analysis, it seems that the attempt to uphold a radical distinction between sex and gender will not necessarily help us to gain an improved theoretical perspective'. (Moore, 1994b: 819–21)

This cross-cultural study of transvestism can be seen on one level as lending support to Moore's position that a radical distinction between sex and gender cannot be upheld. I would even suggest that a key significance of transvestism is that it is not possible in practice to make a clear distinction between the discourses of 'Sex' (with a capital 'S' to distinguish it from 'sex') and gender in considering this subject. (The inter-relationship between sex, Sex and gender, as posited by Errington, is discussed further in Chapter 6.)

All societies and cultures experience sexual digression – a variety of sexual behaviours and inclinations. Internal and external suppression means that the evidence from some cultures, societies and eras is tantalisingly fragmentary but there is no lack of historical and anthropological evidence to indicate that it is so. All societies need in some way to 'manage' this sexual deviance/aberrance and evidence suggests there can be wide variations in the types of behaviours and inclinations permitted and suppressed. Is transvestism simply a form of sexual digression? The fieldwork evidence suggests that it is more than this, also being a form of gender digression. The particular importance of transvestism is that it transgresses the sex/gender boundary and indeed cannot be satisfactorily accounted for except in this holistic way. In addition, the material culture aspect of transvestism has the capacity to make inner states and behaviours material and observable – it is about the presentation of the body together with embodiment in material culture. In dressing in clothes of the other gender/sex, most transvestites are seeking both to emulate and to be the other gender/sex – at least temporarily. What we are exploring here, then, are the complexities of gendering and gendered difference using the perspective of the iconography of transvestism, since they both highlight gender markings *and* operate within a 'no-man's land', the space of possibility, between the biological opposites.

In academic fields, we continue to interrogate issues of sex and gender. Much of this greater exploration within sex, gender and sexuality has – perhaps inevitably – led to greater confusion, due in no small part to the essentially slippery nature of all three. It is probably only when confronted with another culture's practice regarding something in this area that our instinctive and 'common sense' grasp of what is normal and natural is jolted sideways. The cross-cultural perspective is crucial to this study since it points up the often unseen differences in both attitudes and stereotypes, especially those cloaked in habitual and taken for granted places. The development of individual perspective and critical reflection is valuable but can only be taken so far – and seeing cross-culturally and applying categories of whatever kind is one of the crucial applications of anthropology. It is the ethnographic fieldwork, with its descriptions of 'doing it differently' which allow theories such as those within the sex and gender debate to question and re-model ideas.

One of the primary problems in categorising is the delineation of boundaries. In an abstract world, it is possible to fashion categories. In a human and real world, expecially when attempting to define something as mutable as transvestism and gender-marked clothing or ornamentation, those boundaries cannot help but become somewhat blurry at times. In terms of cross-dressing in a Western context, an example might be the wearing of clothes which are 'almost' gender neutral such as shirts/blouses, jeans and sweaters, for which the only difference might be the terms of the labelling.

This investigation considers both comparisons of perceptual experience of transvestites themselves (whilst accepting that entire debates exist around the problem of how to categorise experience), and the role of transvestism in some societies as a mediator, not only between the sexes as a binary opposition, but also between the secular and religious and ritual worlds. It is perhaps not entirely surprising that transvestites in their culturally perceived position as 'freaks' should also in some instances be assigned other roles. The desired order of things may include more than binary pairings. Clifford Geertz contrasts the very divergent treatment of 'intersexuality' in three different societies and concludes that the very different approaches and conclusions to individuals born neither clearly male nor female pose problems for biological science, but promote questions also for common sense, 'for the network of practical and moral conceptions woven about those supposedly most rooted of rooted realities:

maleness and femaleness. Intersexuality is more than just an empirical surprise; it is a cultural challenge ... [one] that is met in diverse ways.' (1983: 81)

Woodhouse's excellent book, *Fantastic Women* (1989), deals with quite similar material to the UK fieldwork in this one – and to some extent has a similar approach in that Woodhouse's work is also concerned with the implications of transvestism for the politics of gender – however, there are significant differences: this study explores issues which go beyond and beneath the politics of sex and gender and questions both the underlying beliefs which inform those power structures and how transvestism contributes to the current discourses on sex and gender. In both of these questions, the cross-cultural approach is central to the perspective and conclusions.

Transvestism, it will be suggested, is more than an individual experience of perversion or deviance, at least in some contexts and cultures, where it has an important role to play in both the secular world and the ritual or religious world. In these societies, like art and aesthetics, it is therefore an informative and interesting ingredient of the iconography of gender. In terms of material culture, like artefacts, it is both the alike-ness and the disparity of forms of cross-dressing which make this subject enlightening. In some cases, such as the industrialised West, these responses are almost entirely secular, but, as the ethnographic evidence will show, this is not always the case.

Gender-defined positions and relationships between men and women vary greatly cross-culturally, but it has been well-documented that in most societies, men tend to accord their activities with higher status and frequently devalue female spheres of activity.[8] Why then would men choose to devalue themselves by dressing themselves as women? As related in the opening quote to the Introduction from *To Kill a Mockingbird*, women who dress as men are obviously in a rather different position since, in the same way that the term 'cissy' for a boy is generally considered more insulting than 'tomboy' for a girl, women could be seen to be 'upgrading' themselves by dressing in men's clothes.[9] Posture, manner, gesture, and so on are social acquisitions, purposive though often unconscious. To dress in the garments of the opposite gender cannot therefore be an inadvertent act, it must be deliberate and intentional. Although transvestism is often viewed negatively, the reality is that there have always been some people who have functioned in the gender role opposite their biological sex. (Consider, for example, the Anakreontic vases, from 510–460 BCE which portray either adult men in women's clothes or women with false beads – and are still the cause of scholarly dispute. (Halperin et al, 1990: 212–17))

The act of crossing over or moving between gender-polarised worlds in many cases appears to confer the ascription of a special position in society, whether this is perceived as 'special-good' or 'special-bad'. It may result in regard, as conferring singular and auspicious powers of healing and blessing, or it may provoke contempt and odium. It may involve crossing normative social structures as well as symbolic boundaries. Transvestism, wherever it is found, is seldom of the ordinary or everyday world, hence the suggestion of a 'third gender category' to supplant the limitations of existing gender categories.

This forces a number of significant questions: 'Why do attitudes differ so radically?'; 'Why is transvestism institutionalised by some cultures and forced underground by others?'; 'How does this inform us about the culture from which these attitudes stem?'; 'In what way does this contribute to our understanding and analysis within the anthropological tradition, and in particular to our notions of cross-cultural categories, especially with reference to issues of gender and sexuality?'; 'Does transvestism encode an aspect of culture and enable us to see, for example, the projection of the feminine more clearly?' 'Can transvestism be regarded to some extent as a metaphor for the way that women are perceived?'

In deconstructing ideas of transvestism, both ritual and secular, and viewing it as a form of gender iconography, it is possible to unravel and reveal cultural models and ideas of male and female. Although the symbolic is hardly the only approach within the sex and gender discourses, (Leacock (1981), for example, promotes the importance of the social model), I agree with Ortner and Whitehead's argument that the symbolic approach is unusually powerful when considering sex and gender issues, since they open up the debate to a set of otherwise unasked and crucial questions. (1981: ix) The value of a study of transvestism is that it anchors these matters in the observable, artefactual environment and provides a window, a set of visual clues, which enhance our understanding of cultural notions in this arena.

Notes

1. Exceptions can be found – for example incidences of 'multiple genders' in Navajo culture until the end of the nineteenth century (see, for example, Thomas (1997: 157)) and these are echoed by Nanda's comment that according to ancient Hindu texts, there existed not only a third sex but sub-divisions into further categories. (1990: 21)
2. Lurie notes that 'one basic purpose of costume … is to distinguish men from

women. In some periods this separation is absolute: what is properly worn by a man cannot be worn by a woman and vice versa. As might be expected, at such times, the birth rate is usually high. In other periods, such as our own, many items of clothing are sexually inter-changeable and the birth rate is lower. Even today, however, most garments are recognisably male or female.' (213)

3. Ramet gives a particularly engaging example amongst numerous eighteenth-century women 'who fancied a life of adventure as a swashbuckling buccaneer [and] coped with sexual prejudice by donning false beards and moustaches and passing themselves off as men. In one such case, riddled with irony, a certain pirate, whose real name was Anne Bonny, cross-dressed as a male and fell in love with a handsome bearded pirate, only to find out that this pirate was herself a cross-dressed female by the name of Mary Read.' (Ramet; 1996: 9)

4. Clever promoters of modern drinking places have carried out market research to discover what is off-putting to women about traditional pubs and modelled their chains of bars on the results which, for example, revealed that large, clear windows which enable the passer-by to see what is going on inside appeal more to a putative female patron. (Report on BBC Radio 4, 1999)

5. 'Gender is not to culture as sex is to nature'. Butler, *Gender Trouble* (1990: 11)

6. Hendricks asks, 'Why do they assign most infants female?': 'You can make a hole, but you can't build a pole', quips one surgeon.' (1993; 10–16) And as Raymond, Fausto-Sterling and others have noted, modern, Western, interventionist societies have tended to 'fix' transsexuals through surgery, the implication being that it is not right for them to exist as they must be put into a 'sex' as soon as possible in order that the 'gender' processes are appropriate. Medical intervention may be 'forced' on babies born with indeterminate genitalia, whose 'fixing' is seen as a medical emergency (Shaw, 2001) to be carried out if possible in the first day of life, but their lives without this intervention and within a twenty-first century Western society are hardly likely to be happy.

7. That gender, sex and sexuality are more than just an academic debate is evidenced by the extent to which, in our own 'liberal' democracy, the state and its adjuncts of police and law, together with the media and the education system – and many other sectors of society – are prepared to participate and formulate, specify and uphold, argue about and fight over what exactly are the sexual politics, norms and mores which we would have in society.

8. There are many examples which demonstrate this, across a range of cultures. One instance is given by Strathern from her research in Hagen: 'The *noman* (mind, desire, consciousness) may be classified by gender. Thus through the different ways it works, females are held to be less capable than males of pursuing rational goals … The most salient and embracing is between the prestige-full (*nyim*) and the rubbish (*korpa*) … Males as a category have an aptitude for big-manship. Females, on the other hand, carry out worthwhile and necessary tasks, attaining prestige only when their activities are seen as contributing to male enterprises. In themselves they may be called 'rubbish'.' (1981: 175)

9. Although the acceptability of 'masculinised' women may seem to be a relatively recent occurrence in Western societies, it has in some manner been true for centuries; for example Saints Margaret of Antioch and Joan of Arc might have encountered some condemnation at the time but have been fairly approved of, particularly by their biographers, for dressing in male attire.

3

Transvestites in the UK: the Dream of Fair Women

Are those *Women's* Clothes?

As I began to write this section, the *Sunday Times* obligingly provided a most interesting cover to their 'Style' section; it showed a sultry looking man, with a fringe over his eyes, lipstick and a visible five o'clock shadow, wearing a lacy black top with a plunging front that reveals his modestly hairy chest. The accompanying banner footer reads, 'Strewth! Will blokes be wearing blouses?' (see Figure 1) The article inside, by Simon Mills, headed 'Boys won't be girls' declared that many designer names – Vivenne Westwood (skirts for men), Moschino (also skirts), Dolce and Gabbana ('transparent black lace blouses and figure-hugging slashed-to-the-navel batwing tops'), Jean Paul Gaultier ('jet embroidered floaty skirts for men, designed to be worn with battered leather jackets and motorbike boots'), Donna Karan (evening skirts to be worn to formal dinners) and Dior (a male corsage) – were currently showing versions of clothing typically seen as female among their collections for 2002 and commented that: 'Nothing, it seems, can dent the designers' enthusiasm for hetero transvestism – not even men's reluctance to buy any of it.' (2:xii:01; 11) Mills also stated that Gaultier had 'made a male bra the *pièce de résistance* of his spring/summer 2002 collection. In flame-orange silk and lace, it gives a lovely deep plunge to the pecs.'

The author commented that this is not the first time that designers have tried to introduce 'female' items into the male wardrobe – there have been fashion-statement skirts for men since the 1980s – but that they would probably fail this time as they have before. When he attempted skirt wearing in the mid 1980s, he took this very seriously:

I kept my face rigidly straight when builders wolf-whistled at me from scaffolding towers. I felt confident that I was pushing the sartorial envelope, challenging the sexual stereotypes and daring to be different. There was only one

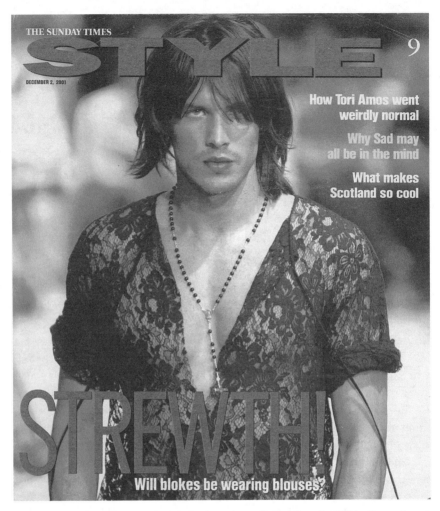

THE SUNDAY TIMES

STYLE

9

DECEMBER 2, 2001

How Tori Amos went weirdly normal

Why Sad may all be in the mind

What makes Scotland so cool

STREWTH!

Will blokes be wearing blouses?

Figure 1 Sunday Times 'Style' section cover, December 2, 2001. Reproduced with permission.

problem. I looked very, very silly. I also felt intensely self-conscious – not to mention cold – and if my memory serves me correctly, I don't think I ever 'pulled' while wearing it. Eventually I discovered that I, in common with most men, prefer wearing the trousers. ... The designers may dream, but today's men, it seems, would much rather be out chasing skirt than wearing it.'

Mills did not provide any analysis of why this should be so but if men who are prepared to try out such fashion statements still end up feeling 'silly' (a word which reveals much and which, like 'soft', explored further in Chapter 6, has very strong feminine connotations) – and to average eyes, the models pictured did look a little ridiculous – it does imply that attempting to put clothing habitually perceived as female into the male fashion world is unlikely to meet with much success.

One possible reason for this – and one which has often been put forward – is that male clothing is much more practical, easy to wear, warm, and that this is why the move towards opposite gender clothing has only happened in one direction. Indeed, the two particular moments in British history when women made great moves towards societal acceptance for their wearing trousers were during the two World Wars. There is therefore a straightforward association with male clothing and doing practical jobs in the Second World War primarily in factories and on the land. However this was hardly the first time that women had done such labour. Women had been working in factories since the Industrial Revolution and on farms for a great deal longer but this did not result in their donning trousers. The implication then, must surely be that there is something more at stake – arguably, that, until the wars brought about a greater burden of expecta-tion, responsibility and thus entitlement for women, they felt that they would incur significant social disapprobation if they put off their skirts. Further than that, there is the implication that skirts in themselves carry secondary, inferior, 'silly' social status, hence the difficulty that modern designers have in persuading twentieth and twenty-first century men to wear them – and a similar reaction from those who see them worn, even in a photograph. As Woodhouse states in *Fantastic Women*,

> masculinity is treated as a thing in itself, something to be achieved by all men. Those who do not evince a convincing image of masculinity have failed and, in the common parlance of insult, they become effeminate. It is no accident that transvestites are commonly thought to be homosexual; after all, any man who is effeminate cannot be heterosexual, there must be something 'wrong' with him.' (1989:136)

If skirt-wearing is perceived as going directly against the construction of masculinity, and more than that, as 'silly', it seems most unlikely that designers will succeed in convincing men that it is acceptable, still less advantageous.

Transvestites, however, long to be able to put on (for example) black lacy tops and flounced skirts *but* – they almost certainly would not consider doing this in public unless their aim was to go out entirely 'dressed' as a female (transvestites commonly refer to cross-dressing as simply 'dressing'), complete with wig, make up, etc. I doubt very much – and some of my 'research subjects' whom I asked confirmed this – that they would go out as a man in a skirt. Female clothing is reserved for the times in their lives when they want to feel like a woman, to become their own particular rendition of a woman (even if only temporarily) – and the clothing boundaries thus remain impermeable.

Fieldwork in the UK

How to begin research in the UK? How to find transvestites? My theoretical ideas and scholarly research were all very well but I was in my own country with no idea of where 'the field' as anthropologists call it, had its existence. My initial enquiries were through what, in the mid-1990s, was a new and amazing research tool, the world wide web. Through typing 'transvestism' into one of the internet search engines, I was able to find a list of contact phone numbers and helplines and to begin to compile a list of organisations that offer advice and assistance to transgendered/transvestite men, women and their families. After a number of telephone calls, I spoke to Janett Scott, the President of the Beaumont Society, a UK organisation founded in the 1960s to provide a forum for heterosexual transvestites. I found her to be an immensely balanced and helpful person without whose assistance the rest of this fieldwork would have been considerably less rewarding. (Janett herself was born male and spent several years as a part-time, male-to-female transvestite, but since her wife died and her children grew up, she has chosen to live full time as a woman, although she has not had any gender re-assignment surgery.) She reassured me that I would be completely welcome at the monthly social meeting of the Beaumont Society – in a pub in Soho – and that I would by no means be the first enquirer to come in the name of research.

In addition to attending several of these gatherings I went to visit her at home in Luton, both on her own and at the social evenings she holds there monthly. It is through these two social groups, combined with the many who got in touch with me following a research request advert in the Beaumont Society journal, that I met most of the transvestites and transsexuals with whom this research was carried out. Although I did meet a few transvestites who were not members of the Beaumont Society, the fact that most of those I met, and those who responded to the questionnaire were members of one particular organisation may inevitably give this study a certain bias. (It can be seen, though, from the list of occupations in Appendix E that the respondents are from a wide variety of occupational backgrounds.)

Most transvestites I have met in social groups (which in itself implies

Figure 2 Janett Scott

that they have made a positive choice to 'come out') are undeniably *feminine*, as opposed to *female*, something which some TVs are obviously aware of themselves, as one questionnaire reply put it, ' ...the inherent need to be feminine and not necessarily a woman. This is a feeling to which I can relate.' (QR (Questionnaire Respondent) 22, q.9)

My worries that they would regard an anthropologist observer in their midst as something akin to a psychologist studying forms of deviant human behaviour were completely unfounded; the reverse was true. After media coverage which portrays them as either disgusting perverts or an absurd joke, they were pleased to talk to someone about their real and valid experience. They were always friendly, never hostile, and most of all, they struck me as being considerably more thoughtful than the average individual about issues of gender and sexuality. This is hardly surprising, since they have had to inquire into, consider and process these matters much more deeply than the rest of us who hardly spare a thought, as we dress each morning in our gender-related clothes, for whether we are male or female, how much of each, and whether it matters. A transvestite's desire to cross-dress may involve lying, pretence and, in some cases, feeling deeply that whatever it is that he is, there is something profoundly wrong with it. Men who dress in women's clothes can be categorised in many ways but because of the derision with which they are often treated, I initially thought it might be difficult to find and meet research subjects.

In the spring of 1997, I therefore placed an advert in the Beaumont Society journal stating that I was doing research in the field of cross-dressing and needed 'research subjects'. The editor could not be exactly sure when the journal would come out but when I placed the advert (in April), she said that it would be at least two months until the next bulletin was printed. In the intervening weeks of term, I was busy and preoccupied with other pieces of research; the pending advert went to the back of my mind and I almost forgot about it. I need not have worried that it might be neglected. At the end of the first week of June, the phone started to ring almost without a break and continued to ring day and night for several weeks. I realised after the first few calls that most of those who had responded to my request were only too willing to talk, sometimes for several hours at a stretch and their stories often involved real pain that they had gone through, sometimes involving thoughts of suicide.

The criteria for those I eventually met up with were partly that I wanted to select representatives of different age groups if possible, and partly practical, based on proximity or willingness to travel; several of those I contacted did come to see me (and, to my wonder and relief, were happy to do so at their own expense). I left the decision to them as to whether they came in male or female clothing and some chose the latter whilst others chose the former but brought clothes to change into. Some interviews also took place by telephone.

The questionnaires were sent out through the Beaumont Society journal and were intended primarily to be of assistance for their narrative content as I realised that a written response from a wider variety of men – including that group of 'closet transvestites' who wished to remain anonymous – would be most helpful, as indeed it proved to be. Five hundred were sent out and around two hundred and forty returned a far better than average response, perhaps giving further proof that transvestites have a great wish to be 'understood'. (The questionnaire is given in Appendix A.) The English fieldwork was therefore carried out in a range of locations including pubs, bars, cafés and restaurants, the interviewee's own homes, my rooms, both in college and at home, and at gatherings/parties in a transvestite's home. It took place between 1996 and 1999, with the questionnaires being sent out in 1997.

Becoming Extraordinary: the Experience of the Transvestite in Western Societies

Because they (transvestites) see it so completely contrary to the behaviour expected by Society, they are frightened to death that someone will find out and, even in everyday life, it is always in the back of their minds. They may cross-dress for many years without even their closest family, mothers or wives finding out. When not dressing they try to forget it and pretend it isn't true, but little everyday happenings trip their memory and they get an unreasoning fear that, somehow, people can "know" them, like having the mark of Cain. Even dressing brings only temporary relief ... It is this society's most awful sin.

Bland: *The Dual Role Transvestite*

I'm an ordinary looking man who can be this extraordinary looking woman – it takes a lot more to be a woman – and you have a lot more decorations ... I think its far more exciting to be the best of both than to simply be one or the other.

Winston, compere of London Club Kinky Gerlinky,
Channel 4 documentary, *The Gender Bender*, 1995, Postma

While researching this work, I have periodically questioned people whom I have met about the image that comes into their head in response to the word 'transvestite' and their answers were remarkably similar. For most, the word conjured an image of a very obviously masculine man (several mentioned hairy legs, five o'clock shadows, broad shoulders and such like), dressed in women's clothes. For some, the man was much more feminine, probably homosexual, rather camp, but still clearly male (and, despite newspaper articles, television documentaries and other popular programmes which clearly state that most transvestites are heterosexual, there is still a widely prevalent notion that most transvestites are gay). The image then is one which confuses reality; if the man 'really' looked feminine, he would not cause comment because it would be assumed that he was a woman but it is the fact that his maleness is apparent underneath the veneer of female clothes which arouses attention.

Few statistics are available regarding the number or proportion of transvestites in Britain or America, perhaps because it is still a largely secretive activity, despite a perceptible broadening of attitudes in recent decades. One transvestite I met had read (in a survey of 5,000 men for *Woman* magazine in the early 1990s) that a quarter of all men cross-dress at some time, up to eight per cent dress regularly and many of these find it compulsive. In a recent television interview, a doctor who specialises in this field stated that one and a quarter per cent dress regularly (i.e. 300,000 in Britain), although the real figure may well be higher.

For many of these men transvestism is a profoundly difficult and painful experience. Statistics at British Gender Dysphoria clinics indicate that about 65,000 people are seeking help. Bland reports that:

> Some secret TVs are literally paranoiac about discovery and go to the most amazing lengths to hide their activities even from their closest relatives. Yet they always have the feeling that 'people can tell'. Between sessions, they wonder if they've got the lipstick off properly, or if they've remembered to put everything away. While dressing, they imagine that people can see through curtains, through walls. They jump at every creak of the floorboards. Thus, the release of cross-dressing is replaced by the fear of discovery, the guilt and the secrecy. They feel that social attitudes are such that they dare not speak of it to anyone. There is a feeling of loneliness in having to keep it to oneself. ... Efforts to control, like 'wardrobe burning', fail repeatedly. The person may attempt other escapes, through alcohol, drugs, tranquillisers, workaholism. He will tell lies and will become less 'present' for his family. (Bland: 1993: 12–13)

Not all transvestism is a negative experience, though. Many of the responses given to me during fieldwork, in interviews or from questionnaires, demonstrate that men who have come to terms with the fear find cross-dressing a pleasure and a release from the stresses of 'man-world'.[1] One even says that if he could choose what he would be in the next lifetime, he would be a male-to-female transvestite again. (QR167) The existence or not of a supportive partner – usually a wife – who not only condones but actually encourages the dressing and is helpful with, for example, buying clothing and cosmetics, makes a tremendous difference. But both men and women who cross-dress have stated that it gives them an experience of 'the other' in a culture in which the expectation is that gender roles are defined early and adhered to throughout life. Gender boundaries might seem to have become less solid in the decades since World War II, but only in one direction. Women may have more 'freedom' to act in traditionally male ways, but men are still discouraged from female behaviours, whilst male socialisation into stereotypes such as 'strong', 'hard-working', 'controlled', 'rational' and 'unemotional' retain their hold.

For gay men, it would seem that transvestism is more likely to be a 'fun' activity: to quote Winston again, 'Drag helps me feel better about myself; this is what I get my kick from ... I think drag is a way of having fun – there's a recession out there – what can you do? Put on a carnival, because that's what it is' (Postma:1995), whilst for at least some heterosexual men, it is much more liable to become a source of torment. For the homosexual man, this must in part reflect the existence of a supportive subculture of the kind which forms out of a sense of 'brotherhood in oppression'; he has already been forced to leave the ranks of 'regular' society . The 'normal man' has no such structures and is therefore considerably more anxious about what he perceives to be his own 'deviance', although the motivations to cross-dress are clearly multiple in any category.

Several transvestites of both sexes, both from my own fieldwork and reported interviews, have expressed the view that cross-dressing allows them to experience the differences of gender positions, to become more aware of both gender roles and thus to more fully appreciate their own and 'the other'. This is perhaps analogous to Stephen Greenblatt's study of cross-dressing on the Renaissance stage (1988), in which he argues that, in the parts of, for example, Rosalind and Viola, the characters are able to attain a fuller degree of womanhood through their temporary experience of living as a man; it is a stage of the development of a whole personality (with a twist, since in the context of the Renaissance stage, the actors at this time were all male.)

Cross-dressing may also be a therapeutic reaction to social pressures – male dual role transvestites often describe a feeling of relaxation and comfort when dressed in women's clothes, which they are unable to attain when in the male 'uniform'; releasing the male self from the regime of stereotypical male emotions through the outward and visible manifestation of wearing women's clothes can be a form of 'play'. The whole context of theatre and acting acknowledges the production of an illusion, in which clothing plays a crucial part; that the participant is not part of a 'real life' situation, thus opening doors which usually remain closed.

Much has been written on gender identity, how it is acquired and, in particular, the difficulty of separating this from how we learn to adopt gender specific behaviour. The age at which gender identity is formed and 'stable' is variously estimated at around three to five years old, certainly very early on in life. As discussed in Chapter 2, there has been much debate around whether this identity is formed by nature, nurture or culture but whichever of these is accepted as the fundamental causative principle, there has been insufficient research to be able to unequivocally state *why* the desire or compulsion to cross dress occurs. Psychologists such as John Money talk authoritatively of, for example,

> ... the loci of male/female dimorphism [which] have been discovered in the pre-optic area of the brain's hypothalamus but not yet in the cerebral cortex, which is where gynemimesis will definitely be eventually found to have some neuro-sexological representation. Presumably, this representation will be shown to be programmed into the cortex post-natally, chiefly by means of social learning and assimilation, the port of entry being the five senses'. (Foreword in Nanda, 1990: xiii)

But in reality, it seems clear that very little is clearly known or understood as yet. In the last decade, the research into the biological, endocrinological, hormonal, metabolic, molecular bases for sexed bodies have increased dramatically, provoking much controversy, as it becomes only too easy to attack previous thinking as over-simplistic which put forward notions that an infant was born into a frame of gender neutrality, or that sex and gender were primarily a cultural construction. As reports on radio, television and in newspapers become alert to the possibilities of hormones such as testosterone, the genetic issues which touch on the development of male/female characteristics continue to arouse much heated discussion.[2] Although biological determinism would still not appear to be the answer, there does seem to be increasing evidence which demonstrates that some traits are biologically hard-wired as male or female.

Bullough and Bullough discuss several theories of the physiological influences on gender identity, attempting to sum up the 'vast and growing literature documenting the hormonal influence on gender behaviour and the impact of prenatal hormones on the brain' (1993: 318) – and this literature has not diminished in the intervening decade. If anything it shows signs of becoming ever more well-researched and it is entirely possible that much more will be known in the next decade about why cross-gender behaviour occurs. The point is, however interesting these initial studies are of the neuro-biological bases for why transvestism is so widespread across cultures, they do not explain why the cross-cultural *response* to transvestism should be so different. The UK research examples which follow illuminate several underlying themes of the conscious construction of 'womanhood' in a Western context, as well as the perception of social pressure regarding transvestism.

Becoming 'the Other':

Dressing allows me to experience those things that I cannot allow into my male self. I am now a whole person, not a half one … . There are two of me but they make a harmonious whole.

Pauline, QR63: q18/20

I'm a little more extrovert when I'm dressed – maybe the dressing is a release from my normal introverted and boring self. It's probably also a release from a stressful job … my female role has an easier lifestyle than my male one.

QR50: q18

I keep trying to integrate my life. I keep trying to make all the pieces into one piece. As a result, my identity becomes my body which becomes my fashion which becomes my writing style. Then I perform what I have written in an effort to integrate my life, and that becomes my identity, after a fashion.

Bornstein: *Gender Outlaw*

Of all the pieces, articles, books, sections of books, written about transvestism and/or transsexuality, Kate Bornstein's *Gender Outlaw: On Men, Women and the Rest of Us,* (1995) contains some of the most interesting insights and these often ring true when contrasted with the experience of transvestites as described to me during the course of social meetings and interviews. Her statement that 'standing outside a *natural* gender, I thought I was some monster, and that was all my fault', echoes many of the accounts received whilst doing fieldwork with transvestites. It also portrays very clearly the situation which obtains for most of those who do not choose to live their lives wholly, or even partly, within the gender boundaries that society has prescribed for them. Through the fieldwork carried out I discovered, however, that there is also a large group of transvestites who, even if they have experienced a stage of feeling guilty or ridiculous, have come through this. By dressing and adopting the mannerisms of 'the other', they reach a point where they recognise that transgenderism gives them access to a different world not encountered by most men and they are profoundly appreciative of and happy about this, despite the problems it may cause them.

Cross-dressing and transvestism could be considered to be the same thing – especially since one is simply the Latin equivalent of the other – and therefore able to be used interchangeably, but they do appear to have slightly different meanings. Most transvestites I contacted would categorise themselves *as* transvestites, not cross-dressers (who may include, for example, drag queens and flamboyantly 'scene' cross-dressers). Nor would they associate themselves with female impersonators, even though they do desire to impersonate women, preferably as well as possible. Although there are those who wish to become women – a small-ish proportion of questionnaire respondents said that they would or had considered this and for them transvestism is a stage on this journey – many questionnaire responses vividly demonstrate that many transvestites definitely do not want to *be* women; they want to be men but, when they choose, to become a female aspect of themselves. The question of why they would want this, particularly when it involves assuming the guise of the secondary gender is very well explained by the transvestites themselves.

UK Transvestites: Interviews with Anthony/Suzanne, John/Joy, Dan/Shelly, Gavin/Gina and Simon/Sandra

My first interviewee was **Anthony**,[3] female name, **Suzanne**, 31 years old[4] and living about 25 miles from Oxford. He[5] timed his visit to me to coincide with one of his regular visits to Oxford. He talked about how he first came to start dressing and what a positive thing he generally felt it to be. He remembered a *Two Ronnies* sketch from when he was quite young, in which women ruled the world, and how very appealing he had found this, and also a film about prisoners of war escaping from Germany in which one had to dress as a woman and how this stirred his interest and desire. At around 14 years old, he thought how nice it would be to go out and buy skirts and realised how much he envied women for being able to wear them.

The first item he ever bought had to be as inexpensive as possible (he was still at school) and he went into Oxford to try to find something, although he quickly discovered that Oxford was not an ideal place to look because most of the shops tend to be branches of national chains such *as Laura Ashley, Next* and *Principles* and were much too expensive. He finally found his way into *New Look* where he bought a white mini skirt in a wraparound flippy style, quite like a tennis skirt. He would have liked to have found a top to go with it but could not, so he wore it with T-shirts. He now has several of these quite girlish, short, very flared style skirts and has realised that they are a particular favourite, but the most wonderful outfits he ever saw were typified by those worn by Emma Peel, played by Diana

Rigg, in the 1960s television series *The Avengers*.[6] He particularly remembers a dress that she wore which was very short and had a band of navy across the chest and a matching jacket in a firm but stretchy cream-coloured material. He added that he finds it quite interesting that transvestite men often seem to go for a 'power dressing look', since this would seem to have been created or suggested mainly *by* menswear. When he had acquired the beginnings of a wardrobe, he realised that this was probably going to be something that he would do for the rest of his life and that he could choose a female name. At first he selected one that was the female equivalent of his male name, but then realised that in fact he could choose anything, so he picked Suzanne because it is a very feminine name and he liked it.

He has never understood why women don't wear nice clothes when they go out doing quite ordinary things like shopping. When he does see an appealing woman who is well dressed, he finds that he is partly attracted to the woman and partly to the clothes but he cannot see why women, who can wear skirts, would choose to dress sloppily, and he particularly envies summer frocks. He almost never goes out 'dressed', as he is too worried that he might be seen and recognised. Anthony was the youngest transvestite I interviewed and, based on much research (Ekins (1997), King (1993), Woodhouse (1989) and others), together with the information I received from transvestites I met and interviewed, it is entirely possible that over the next few years, Anthony will find the need to go out 'dressed' stronger than his fear of doing so and Suzanne will develop much more as a personality. This transition is described in the next narrative.

John/Joy, my next interviewee, was much younger when he became interested in women's wear. He could remember exactly his first memory of wanting women's clothing. He was aged about seven and in a shop with his mother. He was so attracted by a soft fluffy cardigan that he eventually had to be banished from the shop. Some years later, at about fourteen, he was searching through his mother's underwear drawer (for an equally illicit copy of *Lady Chatterley's Lover*) and was fascinated by what was in the drawer. His mother was out and he could not resist the temptation to try on some of the contents; he was delighted by their softness and delicacy. He progressed to trying on a full set of his mother's underwear and then continued to dress in her clothes – a long, full-sleeved dress. After sashaying round the house for about an hour, he began to feel seriously guilty and took all the clothes off (but he was still so captivated by the lightness of the knickers that he weighed every pair and discovered that each one was less than an ounce in weight). He vowed to himself that he would not do this again, although he was less worried by the transgression of wearing women's clothes than that they were his mother's clothes.

He did not stop, however, and eventually became very worried about the risks, so he tried to limit the frequency. If he tried really hard, he could go without dressing for a fortnight but usually he was cross-dressing several times a week. However many times he actually did 'dress', the desire to do so was always present. He decided again that he must stop because he felt as if he was violating his mother's things and he made a conscious effort to stop by gradually weaning himself off it item by item but he found that in reality, however much he might want to try, he simply could not stop. (He was much more worried by what his mother would think if she found out than by the thought of having to face his father.) By this time he was eighteen, it was 1970 and he was still living at home which meant that he could not buy his own wardrobe, partly because he had very little money but chiefly because he had no private space and therefore nowhere to put the clothes and accessories. Added to this was the embarrassment of going into a shop to buy female clothing which he couldn't face. His parents started to be interested in ballroom dancing, which was helpful as far as John was concerned because it meant that they went out a great deal. He continued to feel desperate to spend time dressed but also to be terrified of being discovered. (He stressed that this was definitely not part of the enjoyment but detracted from it.)

In 1972 he finally managed to leave home and find his own bedsit. This meant the possibility of his own wardrobe of female clothing for the first time, but he had to build up the courage to go and buy it. He walked past shops again and again, wanting to go in and thinking 'if only'. As Christmas approached, he decided that he could pretend to be buying a Christmas present for his girlfriend. He managed to get through the door and was standing in the shop waiting to be served when the office cleaner from work walked in. He lost his nerve and left. He returned a few days later and found the assistant most helpful. He came out with knickers and a slip.

A year later he moved to a larger town and this caused some initial anxiety that his small collection of items would be found so he threw everything away. He did not feel that this was a waste of the things themselves, though, or the effort it had taken to amass them, partly because he was learning that the biggest thrill was in the whole process purchasing of them, the selection and choosing, the knowledge that although the shop assistant believed that the items were for his wife or girlfriend, he knew – and was excited by the fact – that they were really for him. (He added that if, at this point, someone had asked him if he was a transvestite, he would have categorically denied it. Only much later did he start to admit to himself that he was a transvestite.) For many years his dressing was confined to underwear and in 1985, he finally abandoned wearing men's underwear altogether and wears standard women's briefs all the time. Gradually, he progressed to further items of underwear – bra, suspenders, stockings and eventually to outer clothes. The softness and fineness of the fabric continued to fascinate him and to be the most important factor in selecting items for himself. In 1977, he went to British Home Stores in York and bought a skirt and top, followed by a trip to Birmingham to buy shoes (size 8, therefore still just possible within the regular women's range). He chose strappy sandals with a small heel as he is already quite tall. He had previously purchased a wig and some make up.

By the time he reached his mid-twenties, he wanted to go outside, to walk around the streets in his female wardrobe, just to experience being out there. He adopted a female name – Joy – because his father once shouted at his mother that he had wanted a girl and she would have been called Joy. He would go out particularly on summer evenings, because it was pleasant to be outside anyway, but especially so in women's clothes. He would not consider mixing masculine and feminine clothes but comes home from work, takes off all his male clothes, bathes and starts dressing from scratch. It takes more of an effort to wear female clothing but he would take the opportunity whenever possible because it might not come again for a week or so. In his late twenties he moved to Nottingham, by which time he had so much clothing that he couldn't just dispose of it all and had to send it anonymously by parcel to Nottingham station. When I asked him if there was any particular kind of clothing he liked most, he replied, 'I'll wear anything!', but he did then go on to define this more. He prefers sleeves to bare arms (in common with nearly every transvestite I talked to, generally because they cover up arms which are tellingly masculine and also possibly hairy) and skirts which are just above the knee. Much of this preference, however, has to do with the kind of shop that he has the courage to go into.

Several times he said that women's clothes were just so much nicer – so much more comfortable, soft, interesting, smooth. He often chooses women's casual wear now – jogging pants, T-shirts, cotton lawn blouses, as well as night-dresses in polycotton or silk. He remembers that his father used to buy his mother gifts of very beautiful underwear, as well as silky night-dresses and dressing gowns. He has realised that clothes are particularly associated with what one is doing, or which part of life they fit into, for example work clothing and play (casual) clothing and if for some reason he cannot put on clothes from his woman's wardrobe when he gets home, he finds that the tension really rises. He has therefore started to choose clothes which can be worn around the house and not arouse any comment if, for example, he had to open the door to the postman. He seldom wears tights because he finds stockings or hold ups much more comfortable and he enjoys most colours, though he prefers strong colours such as red to drab ones and really dislikes grey.

He sees transvestism as a problem but also a wonderful addition to his life in that it opens doors to a quite different sort of life; his world would be considerably less interesting without it.

Shelly/Dan:

I dress to look smart and well groomed, like a mature, sensible but sensuous woman and definitely not tarty or in bad taste. Certainly not fetish – leather, PVC, rubber or inappropriate items like fishnet stockings, 6-inch stilettos or blond hair down to my bum! I want to dress so as to make real ladies feel dowdy and unkempt when they look at me. ... I love the way that when I am dressed I have to think, move, walk, sit, bend stand, use my hands and even walk differently. That is why I love all the fiddly bits of being feminine that most real ladies find a nuisance. I love allowing my mind to be reminded constantly that it must think no more in a male way. I love to be able to say 'MY skirt', 'MY lipstick', 'MY stockings' and 'MY handbag'. I love it when I need to buy something feminine for myself like a new mascara.

QR180/q12/18

Shelly grew up as the only boy among four children. As a child, he was very like his father – intelligent and creative, quite shy and introverted – and surrounded by female energy. His first memory of wanting to cross-dress was in the month coming up to Christmas when he was about four or five years old and he desperately wanted Father Christmas to bring him a cowgirl outfit. (He didn't).

Through the following years, until he was about twelve, he regularly dressed in his older sister's clothes, or his younger sister's, if they would fit. He would take the clothes outside and change into them in the bushes. Sometimes, he came home from school in the lunch hour and put them on under his school uniform and then wore them for the rest of the afternoon. In his teens he regularly started to wear girl's underwear under his boy's clothes because 'it just was right'. Now, he tends not to bother with getting dressed unless he can do it for a whole day or at least most of it. He does not want to cross-dress for any sexual reason but to be on the same wavelength as a woman. He believes his wife appreciates this feminine side of him in some ways; that the reasons why he is kind and gentle are part of

Figure 3 Shelly

the same package and she loves him 'to pieces', but still wishes that he was not a transvestite, mainly because she can see that it causes conflict and unhappiness inside him.

When he goes out shopping he looks at women's clothing all the time, even if he is supposed to be shopping for something else. He assesses them, can sense how they would feel and is as interested in their softness to the touch as their colour or style. Usually, if he is going shopping for clothes, he will go as Shelly because it gives him more freedom to look at and touch the clothes. (He thinks that he 'passes' about 60–70 per cent of the time.) Shop assistants have usually been perfectly pleasant, especially in 'the better establishments' and are not shocked even if they do realise that he is a man; he likened it to how they would probably treat someone who is disabled.

Later, in his questionnaire, in response to the section on the particular types of clothing he favours, he replied:

I like all that is feminine. Outerwear: Mostly skirts and blouses/sweaters. I have a couple of dresses and would like more but it is finding them that fit well enough. I like all kinds of skirts – full ones that swirl and move around my legs and straight ones that limit my movements. I have a few jackets. I like to mix and match but love suits – skirts and jackets. ...

Underwear – is very special to me. Men don't have the same range as women. And for some women it isn't important either, but I relate to those women for whom it is. Not surprisingly therefore I never wear tights or popsocks or go bare-legged. I love my stockings and suspenders. My favourite Aristoc black Tango 100 per cent nylon stockings are not made any more (they are non stretch, make your legs as smooth as glass and rustle when you rub one leg against another). At the moment I wear a corselette because of the need for a means to hold in place my hip pads and to trim my waist, but my intention is to have a special foundation garment made so that I can wear the separate items of bra, briefs/french knickers and a suspender belt. I want pretty undies too and to be able to go out and have the enjoyment of buying them. I can accept that most women regard underwear as functional except when they dress up for a special occasion, but for me, each time I dress up is a special occasion. I might, however, think differently if I dressed full time. I don't see that I have a particular fetish about underwear since there are many women who think the same as I do and derive much pleasure out of wearing pretty undies. After all, along with a new hair style, buying a new set of undies is supposed to brighten up a girl's life when she feels down. ...

Accessories: All the little things are important too, like earrings, make-up of course. I love make up. I adore the FEEL of it and the SMELL and the TASTE! Again it is something so alien to the male world. The nearest is aftershave. I love nipping into the ladies and touching up my face and lips. I love having a handbag full of all my bits and pieces for keeping my face in good order, hair, perfume, high heels, a handbag and longer feminine painted nails.

QR180/q11

Cross dressing is something that he just has to do, including going out and being seen. He also really enjoys the limitations that the clothing imposes and its lack of practicality, for example the need to be careful where one puts one's feet and taking care not to snag one's stockings or nails, together with the thinking processes involved in having to co-ordinate colours and outfits. It is enough for him to be out and about in the role of a woman, and he feels quite happy using women's toilets (one of the ever present difficulties of transvestite life.) He just wants to be with women and accepted as an equal – feminine and enjoying the same activities. He has never really enjoyed the company of men and finds the conversations, both the way of speaking ('hard', 'impersonal', 'less caring') and the topics (cars, football, etc.) extremely dull and difficult. He finds it curious that his own mother does not accept his transvestism; he has tried to explain to her but she does not want to recognise it or talk about it – ever, whilst his mother-in-law has no problems with it at all; she is very supportive and even does dress-making for him.

He wishes he had softer skin and shaves his legs because waxing or using an epilator (a type of hair removal which pulls the hairs out by the roots rather than cutting them) causes a rash and he would very much like to have laser treatment to remove the hairs on his arms and shoulders. Like Julia, one of the 'male-femalers' interviewed by Richard Ekins, he was quite 'amazed by how he had been able to pass as a woman once she began to dress like one' (1997: 43) – but unlike Julia, although much of the time he dreams of having been born a woman, he would not consider gender re-assignment, partly because he believes that to have any chance of working, it really needs to be done in one's teens. He is completely heterosexual and realises that if he became a woman, this would be a problem. Surgery removes the maleness, he said, but cannot really make you into a woman – just 'further from being a man'.

He does not feel that he would or could ever change – it is like being born with the ability to sing or draw – it can't simply be removed. He was particularly exposed to his desires because he was surrounded by women but obviously there are many men who have a similar family background and do not experience any wish to cross-dress, so presumably, there needs to be both a trigger (or opportunity) and some inborn urge. Shelly likened it to a concert pianist who is born in the jungle – she or he may have the talent, and that talent would be there no matter what, but since it would be unlikely for the occasion to present itself, no-one would ever know.[7]

Gavin/Gina was 33 when I first met him in 1997 at one of the monthly meetings of the local Oxford group of the Beaumont Society and I then met up with him several more times singly. The first time I met him one to one, one of the first things he told me was how much he enjoyed being a trans-vestite, although this feeling is relatively recent. Until about a year before, it had mainly been associated with guilt and shame, but now he feels none and has decided to celebrate it rather than push it aside. It is also in this last year that he has started to really experiment with make-up and to enjoy it. He doesn't get as much of a sexual high as he used to; 'there is still a buzz but it's more cerebral'.[8] He said that a big fuss is made about whether transvestites are gay or not but although it has been made into a big issue, he cannot understand why – 'some are, some aren't, so what. …

Figure 4 Gina

I really enjoy the gay scene but I just know I'm not attracted to men – why should it matter?' He also believes that gender is not a 'purely binary thing' but there are varying degrees of sex, sexuality and gender.

He thought he probably had less variety in terms of his female wardrobe than many transvestites and he tends to concentrate on clothes that he can wear to go out clubbing. He prefers things which are mildly outrageous and far prefers frocks to separates. He particularly dislikes blouses and would go for a one piece any time. He loves high heels and slinky dresses and although he does sometimes wear tights, will nearly always go for stockings, even with very short dresses (they are more comfortable and convenient, especially for going to the toilet.) He favours fabrics which are very sensual, tactile and smooth or soft to the touch like silks, satins, lace and velvet – and in sultry colours – black, dark reds, maroons and deep purples. He likes shoes so much that he estimated that he had about 50 pairs in his wardrobe – and none of them are flat! On his website, he calls himself 'The Imelda Marcos of Oxfordshire'. Although initially he did buy shoes from specialist TV shops, he discovered very early on that they are badly made and more expensive, so he now buys them from regular shops or catalogues. He described his clothes as being 'very Glam Rock' – in tune with that period of the 1970s when artists like David Bowie wore very slinky, fabulous costumes and their backing singers – male or female – were equally sensuously dressed. He generally dresses at weekends and if there is some reason why it can't happen for a couple of weeks, he does tend to get very stressed. He now far prefers to go out when he is dressed, perhaps as a reaction to all the years of being closet and having to stay in. He is not interested in most 'typically male' activities such as cars and sport.

A year later, when Gavin and I met up for a drink and meal after work, he told me that he had been feeling very low over the last few months. It had been activated by a prospective relationship, mainly because he realised that he found the whole area of sexuality disturbing and, in particular, being the man in the relationship. He described his disgust at the idea of 'all that thrusting' and found the idea deeply unappealing, both physically and mentally. He had been cast into gloom by this and by the increasing realisation that he did not really know what he wanted, not even knowing the right questions to ask to find out. His sleep was suffering from worry and wondering whether he would be happier being a full-time transvestite or even a transsexual. To become a full time transvestite would involve having to go to work dressed and this might cause all kinds of problems. He would, for example, have to tell his superiors at work and he was not at all sure how they would react but suspected it would not be with delight, although his colleagues were very relaxed about it. Secondly, he would have immense problems about which toilet to use at work, especially since his company shares lavatories with other companies in the building and there would no doubt be many who would raise objections and endless consultative discussions. He could envisage having to put a notice on the door saying *'Transvestite using the facilities. Please do not enter if you feel this might upset you'*.[9]

He had been to see his doctor because the depression has been getting so bad and the GP recommended a counsellor – but he was still getting up the courage to talk to her. We discussed various aspects of depression and also of maleness and femaleness. I asked him what was appealing about being a woman – what it is that women do or have or can be which he would want – but he said it wasn't anything he could put his finger on; it is more to do with the dislike of men and being one: 'I mean, men are so naff, aren't they?'. (The OED defines *naff* as 'lacking in taste or style'.)

We talked about a series, then current on television, *Why Men Don't Iron* (based on the book by Anne and Bill Moir, 1998) which explores the differences between men's and women's brains. Gavin said he felt that in many ways, he does have a male brain, but in questionnaires which score one as male or female, he would probably come out as very female. Several times, he said he wished he could 'dump the whole gender thing' and he wished that society would allow for androgynes. He would happily spend most of the time being neither one nor the other and then 'glam up' as Gina the rest of the time (he would definitely lose the Gavin part of him in return for the androgyne, not the Gina part). In my most recent meeting with him, Gavin had come through a further depression and was possibly on the brink of starting a relationship with someone new, although he was very unsure about how she would react to his cross-dressing.

We discussed the androgynous style of the comedian and entertainer Eddie Izzard who, Gavin said, was something of an icon for many transvestites because he has developed a style of wearing clothes which are not significantly different from what a man would or could wear and yet have a feminine touch about them, perhaps through the use of jewellery, scarves or necklines, female accessories, make-up and other details. Gavin still enjoys going clubbing in feminine gear and most of his wardrobe continues to be the glamorous evening wear of satin dresses in deep shades. He also continues to spend a lot of time chatting with other transvestites on the net and visiting their websites.[10]

Simon/Sandra

As a man I feel I am 'me' as I have to be. I feel empty and not fully alive. Life has a quality of burden and duty. As a woman I am 'me' but the outward expression poses problems of relating to others ... (As a woman) I could be openly expressing what inwardly I feel and relating as I feel I am inwardly whereas otherwise I relate to others as who I am supposed to be. ...

(In response to the question, do you think/act/behave differently when dressed?) I used to but now feel much more synchronised. I love the transformation process. When dressing, making up, there is a moment when the image is believable to me and then (sometimes) when I feel it is believable to anyone.

QR26; qs 20–5

I initially spoke to Simon/Sandra (52) on the telephone after receiving her questionnaire and met her in August 2000. She has, in many ways, followed a typical transvestite 'career' in that the desire to dress and amount of time spent dressed have both increased over the years. She was married but now lives on her own and her children have grown up and live in other parts of the UK.

She came to Oxford by train and in female clothing and she described the dilemma she had had to go through on getting dressed that morning as the male part of her fought with the female for acceptance; the male part had argued that since she was visiting an academic, 'he' had better come since he was better at dealing with this than 'she' could be but that at the last minute 'her' sadness had got the better of 'him' and so she had dressed in a white blouse, denim skirt and put her make up on.

Figure 5 Sandra

During the interview, she mentioned that from her experience of having both a male and a female personality, she felt that having a male body made one concentrate on the things which make one alone and selfish, unaware of the needs of others, and part of a society which doesn't really take women seriously because it feels that they don't really know or understand what the world is about ('money, missiles, etc.') and that this attitude, should it be allowed to prevail, will result in an increasingly dehumanised culture. She also felt that most transvestites idealise women's lives (an observation which the rest of this research would certainly seem to bear out) and that if they knew what women really go through would find it most undesirable and would change their ideas. She really appreciates the development of a female persona which increasingly over the years has grown with her 'dressed' self and has considered gender reassignment – to the point of seeking medical advice – but on long reflection, has decided that this is a very male way to attempt to resolve the problem with an 'I'll fix it' attitude; the reality is a second rate woman's life.

After her visit, she wrote to me with some further reflections on the subject and she observed that on the train journey, she noticed that she had forgotten to bring a book to read. She found this interesting since Simon, her male self, always reads on trains whereas Sandra was quite happy to sit and watch the people, be interested in them, how they were dressed and speculate on what took them on the journey. She also noticed how aware she was of herself (Stephen would have been completely unconscious of himself in the world and this is reflected in the way he dresses). She later wrote in a letter, 'The other thing on the train was that the women seemed so *beautiful*. I realise that this is the 'torment of Venus' or something. I sat behind a girl of about 20 or 22; she had on a pair of black trousers and just the way those trousers lay on her leg, the grace, the unconscious elegance and beauty of women. Older women too. There was an old dear who you could just see was living in a world of her grandchildren and thinking 'I hope they're OK', just rejoicing in their existence. I think that is the ultimate feminine experience – you can rejoice in the existence of something or someone other than you'.

She also wondered at times whether she was being 'read', whether she would be perceived as an 'illegal entrant' which also contrasts with her life as Simon who is always sure of himself in the outside world, even though he can't wear 'nice' clothes and continues to represent an aspect of her personality which she is much less sure of in terms of its 'fit' within herself. When dressed as Sandra, she has to reassure herself that it is all right to be dressed in a skirt. This dilemma seems to illustrate very clearly the role that clothing plays in the psychology of transvestism: without the clothes, there is, effectively, no gender. Sandra is Sandra because she is dressed in women's clothing; dressed as a man, she is Simon. This feeling is echoed by many transvestites, both those interviewed by Woodhouse and Ekins and those who replied to my questionnaires.

The Range of Possibilities

It is clear that historically and cross-culturally, transvestism has different implications for the culture by whom it is viewed. Within the UK, however, it is equally difficult to posit a model in which there is some kind of 'ubiquitous' transvestism; in terms of the manner of dressing, the clothes that are most worn and enjoyed, the type of decorations used (jewellery, make-up, wigs, etc.) the degree of effort, intention or compulsivity involved, and the reason for wanting to do it at all; there is an enormous range of possibilities and all of these possibilities are explored in different ways by the individual exploring them. Bornstein gives a slightly tongue in cheek categorisation of the pecking order of transgender possibilities:

Post-operative transsexuals (those transsexuals who've had genital surgery and live fully in the role of another gender) look down on:
Pre-operative transsexuals (those who are living full or part time in another gender, but who haven't yet had their genital surgery) who in turn look down on:
Transgenders (people living in another gender identity, but who have little or no intention of having genital surgery) who can't abide:
She-Males (a she-male friend of mine described herself as 'tits, big hair, lots of make-up and a dick') who snub the:
Drag Queens (gay men who on occasion dress in varying parodies of women) who laugh about the:
Out Transvestites (usually heterosexual men who dress as they think women dress, and who are out in the open about doing that) who pity the:
Closet Cases (transvestites who hide their cross dressing) – who mock the post-op transsexuals. (Bornstein: 1995: 67–8)

(The feedback I received from research is that although the transvestites I interviewed do not 'mock' transsexuals, they do have worries about transsexuality.)

Other researchers in this field (Ekins, 1997, for example) have created categories of transgenderism but although some of the terms are quite helpful, I have not incorporated them partly because their classification did not always accord with my findings and also because their nets had been cast differently in terms of research subjects. Even within the band explored here, which comprises only transvestites and does not include performance, 'drag' cross-dressers and very few pre- and post-operative transsexuals, the reasons for wishing to dress are, nevertheless, so wide-spread as to be frustratingly difficult to categorise, but from the fieldwork done and in particular from the questionnaire answers seven or eight rubrics will be suggested (since the desire to dress forms a crucial part of the use of clothing as a material culture object in this way).

The first and most encompassing of these is that the transvestite is a kind of **'prisoner of gender'**. He may be annoyed by his maleness, by having to be male and one main reason for dressing is to have an outlet for an unusually strong 'feminine side' and the 'female' emotions and attributes which accompany this such as gentleness, softness, vulnerability, caring, etc. (see Appendix D, containing adjectives used by transvestites). Usually, his perception of women is that they are much more appealing in a number of ways, which may be linked to sexuality and sensuality but are as likely to be focussed on women's perceived 'sweeter' natures and temperaments.

Dressing thus allows the transvestite to enter this tractable and ambrosial female world. Comments in the questionnaire such as that given by Christine:

> The gentler side of my nature comes out and I feel that I am able to express myself better. I have a lot of femininity inside me ... I hate my male image as a 'macho' guy in a macho job. (QR53, qs 23/26)

are repeated in many of the questionnaire responses:

> What I find appealing about being a woman is being able to show my feelings, cry when I want, smell lovely flowers, have lovely soft, feminine things around, just be myself. (QR42, q23)

> It is, to me, the appeal of the characteristics that society allows only a woman to display. These would be, for example, the attributes of gentleness, thoughtful-ness, insight, creativity, in fact all the attributes that are classically associated with the role of a woman in society. These are the same attributes that, if displayed openly by a man, would be frowned upon. (QR22, q23)

> Sarah has a definite personality which contrasts with the male persona I feel society expects me to adopt ... she is better at relaxing than I am and I enjoy

being her – I feel more feminine and behave accordingly. I'm also more likely to read women's magazines, do the ironing, etc. (and even enjoy doing it). ... I admire women much more than I admire men and Sarah has qualities which I like more than my own maleness. (QR33, qs 20/21/25/26)

Images of femininity are appealing. Masculinity and 'maleness' are not appealing. Most of my close friends are women and although they (mostly) do not know about me, my dressing makes me feel closer to them. (QR12, q23)

In a word, Fineness. A man can just about tell the difference between a 5-inch and a 6-inch nail. A woman can tell the facets of a diamond. Perception is so much finer, richer: a woman gets so much more out of her experience of the world. (QR165, q23)

Also mentioned as desirable attributes which accompany being dressed, for example, are qualities such as conversational ability, being a better driver and being more tolerant generally.

If there is resentment, it is against a society which, even in a supposedly modern and egalitarian age, does not really allow a full range of emotional expression and in particular, derides men who exhibit passivity, gentleness, softness and so on. Several replies to question 28 (asking why it is important to be able to distinguish a man from a woman) commented on women's ability to wear anything:

We are pigeon-holed. Society must have men and women – but men should have the same freedom as Western women to wear what they like. Nobody bats an eyelid if a woman is wearing a bowler hat or Doc Marten boots (even while wearing a beautiful blouse and skirt). (QR18, q28)

On the other hand, it would seem that TVs are not generally in favour of androgyny, as one perceptive commentator states:

I think men and women have equally important, generally different roles to perform in society, which have evolved over time. It helps the smooth running of society if people are treated appropriately to their gender ... TVs and TSS's would not want a gender-neutral society – they associate with the feminine and accentuate gender differences. (QR103, q28)

In *Why Men Hate Women*, Adam Jukes asserts that it is absurd to suggest that men are afflicted by their gender: 'men might appear to be as much victims of patriarchy (prisoners of gender) as women are and this, no doubt, is how a great many men would present themselves. ... Actually, I believe the notion of men as victims of gender is nonsense. In the final analysis, men have choices which are not available to women. It is true that women, if they are so inclined, can fight against an identifiable oppressor – men – whereas men cannot be described as self-oppressed.' (1993:136) One thread running throughout many of the questionnaire responses suggests, however, that transvestite men do see themselves as oppressed – by a culture which not only requires them to construct and live by a very masculine identity but also humiliates them for a behaviour or activity which is harmless but perceived to be risible and thereby perhaps the more shaming.

However, it does also raise the issue that for the most part, the female they desire to be is very much a male construction and perception of femininity and of women's lives. The woman they desire to be has not only a 'sweet' and 'gentle' life but also a beautiful body (and face?);

> Apart from having a body that really does fit all those beautiful clothes out there, and really being able to flaunt what I've got – come-and-get-me type attitude, this would be all real – no falsies in my bra – I think I'd enjoy the shift in expectations which I perceive society and myself direct at me. More time to enjoy sensitivity and spending time being gentle with myself and others. Less around achieve-task-success type expectations. (QR14, q23).
>
> Girls have more fun. Society treats them better. A woman can just be a woman and doesn't have to project images to suit society. (QR41, q23)

I would very much doubt that most women, if asked, would perceive their own lives as being in any way less full of expectations and are certainly not more gentle with themselves, as borne out by a study of Oxford undergraduates in the mid-1990s, amongst whom it was found that approximately 70 per cent of the females self-reported as having eating disorders; presumably a direct result of judgmental attitudes towards their bodies and the necessity to be thin in order to conform to perceived cultural expectations. The women of my acquaintance to whom I put this notion: that they have much less of a burden than men with respect to not having to project an image to suit society, either stared open-mouthed in shock or laughed out loud. Women may have more of a 'toolkit' available to them in the way of make-up, jewellery, clothing, and so forth, but some regard this itself as a burden of expectation.

The second group are the **transvestites who may become transsexuals,** who have considered or are in the process of considering whether to go 'all the way' and have gender reassignment surgery. For these men, dressing is something which can only partly assuage their need but which is also an essential part of becoming a woman. For them, the experience of living a male life is not only frustrating and unpleasant but does not fit at all with the person they feel themselves to be.[11]

> It's just me (being female) – being male is a bit like a left-handed person trying to write with their right hand – it's possible but difficult and uncomfortable. (QR142, q23)

> When I have to dress in male clothes, I spend all my time wishing I was *en femme*. I try to be philosophical in so far as I have obligations and cannot change over. ... If I couldn't dress at all, I would rather be dead. (QR145, q20)

Some respondents however, have thought deeply about surgery and realised, like most of those I interviewed, that in many ways it does not solve the real problems:

> I have given a great deal of thought to GRS and have concluded that I must be close to being a TSS but not close enough ... or maybe I'm just too much of a coward.

> My main concern is and always has been that TSSs are not regarded as women or men and therefore are not accepted by either sex or society in general. This would not be acceptable to me. I would have to be a woman and be accepted as such by the world but there is no way I can be a true woman even with surgery.

> Personally I do not consider myself to be a man (or a woman). I live my working life as a man and society accepts me as such without question. If I went to work dressed I would not be taken seriously and I would lose everyone's respect. I cannot function as a human being without the respect of the people I work with or care about. Living every working day as a man throughout my life I know how the majority of people react to TVs, TSSs or anything connected and I must say I am not happy with the way we are perceived. I could not take any type of derision.

> As a child, I prayed to God each night to put right the mistake She made when She put my soul into a male body. In my prayers I asked Her to put me into my rightful body during the night so I would wake up I the morning a real girl. For many years I blamed God for my situation but now I don't. I still don't understand Her motives for making me go through life like this but I'm sure She must have a good reason. (QR168, q10)

> Talking to transsexuals, a proportion believe that 'becoming' a woman will work in a magical way and 'solve' the everyday problems that beset us all. As Dana International told Ruby Wax; 'nothing changes'. (QR172, q20)

In *S/He*, Claudine Griggs, a male to female transvestite describes how she felt that she needed to have the gender re-assignment surgery in order to have 'permission' to wear female clothes because these seemed such an essential part of femaleness. Her psychotherapist refused her the operation until she had lived for a while as a woman and she realised in retrospect that this was essential – because although the clothes are vital, so are many other things, such as a handshake, which have to be unlearned and then relearned. After having the operation she says:

> I still engage with the mirror, struggling to see a woman. Self endorsement of an altered body has been as difficult as changing it and on certain days I am reluctant to 'act' feminine, because I don't feel real. If I put on a red shirtwaist dress, beige pantyhose, black high heeled pumps, pale rose lipstick, gold earrings, bracelet and necklace, with gently curled hair, I may responsively feel great, or I may envision an inept drag queen and quickly change into jeans. If duty calls, I'll bear up but cringe all day at the image of Hercules in a gay chorus line. (Griggs; 1998: 6)

Clearly, even after the 'authorial permission' granted by surgery, the clothes are still at the daily sharp end of how to be and feel and act.

The third group are those who might classify themselves as **narcissisistic and auto-erotic**, who are in love with an image which is reflected in a mirror when they are dressed.

> The sexuality of dressing as a woman is essentially a male sexuality. I guess you can call me Narcissus too ... I find I want to make love to my own feminine image; this is why so many transvestite sessions end by the transvestite making love to himself. (QR82, q19)

Hogan-Finlay notes that the term 'auto-gynephilia' has been coined by Blanchard to describe men "who are sexually aroused by the image of themselves as women and in particular, fantasies of the "woman within".' (1996:21)

From their questionnaires, it would seem that this group generally keep their male and female selves very separate and Ekins coins the term 'aparting' for those transvestites who prefer to do this, giving an example of one transvestite he met, Fred/Freda, who will have erotic experiences while masturbating, but would not consider making love to his wife dressed as he would deem this infidelity. (1997: 134)

For men who are shy or lacking in self-confidence, this may also be the simple need for or attraction to a woman who is 'there'; who can be created any time they need her and will not leave them or give them a hard time: 'One thing I find gratifying is about cross-dressing is that I can look in the mirror and see a woman whose behaviour, etc. is under my control', implying a degree of fear or dislike of women because they are not controllable; they may hurt you, leave you or simply not be there when you need them. (QR 211, q29))

It may be a self-conscious choice which seems to contain an element of anger;

> In dressing, I become the girl I want to see. In glamour clothes my wife would not wear, I can see, feel, touch and become the girl I want – no fuss, no bother – it's like a drug – gives full sexual satisfaction, lasts a long time, is always available, always young. I have boyfriends; they find me attractive, arousing. I feel like a real woman, look thirty years younger – I love to flirt and look more female than my ex-wife who is unattractive, zero glamour, past it. (QR52, q.29)

Linked to this is a fourth reason, one of the few well-documented by previous texts, that of simple **sexual excitement**, although this reason tends to be obscured or glossed over by the organisations which represent transvestites for reasons which presumably have to do with being taken seriously. Question 19 which asked which was more important, the *sexuality* of being dressed as a woman or the feeling of *being* a woman, the personality aspect. Although there were many who said that 'being' was far more important, there were a significant number of replies which admitted that the sexuality was currently – or had been when younger – the more important. One respondent said, 'Both, I adore both at different times. But anyway, I think this is a false dichotomy. Surely sexuality and personality are all mixed up. I really don't have much time for the argument I've heard, particularly from the Beaumont Society that it's got absolutely nothing to do with sex. They haven't dug deep enough.' Another: 'I would be a liar not to say the first (sexuality). Dressing has always been a means to sexual relief when I am down or lonely' (QR 143, q19)[12]

Into the fifth category fall those who in some ways see transvestism as having the **'best of both worlds'** in that it enables a man to experience some of what it is like to be a woman:

> My wife once posed me this question (do you ever wish you had been born female?) and I surprised us both by electing, next time around, to be a male to female transvestite once again. I think I would be getting the best of both worlds

... Anything that broadens one's perception of life and adds to one's experience must generally be classed as good. It enhances your knowledge and respect for real women. 'Seeing how the other half lives' may be trite but it is definitely desirable. (QR167, q23)

I like the she side more than the he side of me but in the way I like being on holiday more than being at work – if it went on forever it would get boring too. It's being able to play at moving from one to the other that's the real pleasure. (QR96, q26)

Transvestism can be regarded as an exciting hobby which allows the transvestite to make the best of himself, to explore different styles and fabrics;

I found that cosmetics could knock twenty years off my age. Men's clothes are drab by comparison. I attract more attention as a woman. (QR43, q23)

(In response to 'describe your favourite outfit') Impossible! At the last count I had 116 dresses, 38 skirts and so many different tops, I couldn't count. Also 6 fur coats and dozens of boots and shoes ... As I am a size 12/14 I have a very wide choice.) (QR39, q17)

The main appeal is that I look less ugly and a tad younger. I do however believe that some of us are adrenaline junkies who are getting a buzz from the perceived risks. (QR167, q21)

To me, being a male is what makes cross-dressing enjoyable. I do go out dressed in public, not because I wish I'd been born a woman but just for the sheer thrill of being thought of as a woman when underneath I know different. (QR83, q29)

The last two answers are of particular interest to the central question 'why is there such aversion to transvestism?' on which I reflected throughout the process of considering the questionnaire replies. I suggest that one key reason for the antipathy is that probably everyone dislikes being tricked or deceived – and a skilful transvestite who can 'pass' is inevitably practising a form of deception. The last two responses quoted suggest that, at least for some transvestites, it is also this aspect of dressing which particularly excites them.

For some, it also contains an element of performance, expressed particularly in the kinds of clothes they choose to dress in: 'I love to dress up like a hooker one day, then like a glamour puss the next, sometimes like a nurse or a lady of the manor, a mum to be – six months pregnant, sometimes only in my undies and a pair of long boots on and maybe a rain coat' (QR42, q13). (This respondent also said later in the questionnaire that 'there are a lot of lonely people out there who need help to come to terms with their gender, sexuality and the help isn't there. ... We all need kindness, love, help. There are thousands out there who will never be helped, who live in torment with their gender/identity problems.')

Linked to this is the transvestite who has an **alter ego** which he needs to express and for which a woman's persona seems the best form of expression, possibly coupled with the excitement of simply creating a second self and being able to 'transform' oneself into it. In response to the question 'do you ever wish you had been born female', although many said 'Oh yes', a significant proportion also said 'no'. One wrote: 'Never. It is the ability to change, to express another side of myself. I then change back – the transformation is all.' (QR25, q22) Another commented on the ability to really notice and observe changed behaviours, even whilst in the process of being the created second self (and at the same time reiterating the mental processes which lie behind – the masculine perspective and construction of femininity):

> 'When *en femme* I'm more she than he – I automatically adopt the role. I can act coy, skittish, flirtatious, even – you know – all the things the average male thinks a woman should be – so it's a shame to disappoint and disillusion them!' (Colette, QR26, q25)

For some, the dressed self is a positive advantage: in answer to question 20 (does dressing make you feel you have two possibilities of being you?) there were a number of replies along the lines of: 'Oh Yes! I am a regular Dr Jekyll and Sister Hyde. This presents no problems.' (Mary, QR39, q20) But for others it is not so easy: 'I stay in one room and jump at the slightest noise' (QR30, q25), whilst another stated that his beard – which he had refused to shave off despite another Beaumont Society member suggesting that a hairless chin was rather crucial to the desired effect – was an effective bar to his ever considering going out dressed and also perhaps, kept him rooted in his maleness. (QR217)

There are also a few cases in which the impulse to dress has, for that individual been linked to **personal circumstance**, for example one man explained that after his wife died, leaving him to bring up their three children aged eleven, three and one and a half alone, he had started to dress in his wife's clothes, partly because he missed her so much and partly to strengthen the caring and nurturing side of his personality since he had to be both mother and father to them. (QR27, qs4/18) This aspect is also encountered by Woodhouse, one of whose interviewees stated that his life had altered considerably when he had to 'take over the female gender role', although in this case it was not his wife who died but his mother, when he was 13.' (1989: 39)

Another questionnaire respondent described his dressing as a possible response to the fact that his twin sister had died at birth and 'in many ways apart from cross-dressing, I tend to live – or try to – or maybe am impelled to – live my life for both of us. (I believe it is not unusual for a lone twin to exhibit this tendency.)' (QR48, q29)

It is tricky to categorise and thus limit the reasons for cross-dressing even to several broad groupings like those above. As one respondent commented, 'I think you have chosen a difficult subject that most academics completely fail to understand. They never seem to realise that transvestites don't always feel the same. Sometimes being a TV is the most important thing in the world to me, at other times it sees ridiculous and pointless.' (QR104, q29) What is clear is that clothing is the 'means whereby', the building materials for the architecture of femininity. Clothing can identify, fabricate, conceal or simulate and it is used in all these ways and more. As an agent of mutability and multiplicity it could be argued that it is unparalleled.

Clothing Choices

I love all of it, perhaps especially stockings and tights – but I also love shoes, skirts, dresses, trousers and leggings.

Jean, QR12, q12

… I do get a strong feeling of the sexuality of being female by the way some garments hang or move with my body.

Stephanie, QR19, q19

I like the wider choice of fashion styles. I find the way women present themselves appealing. I like the clothes, make-up, hair, jewellery.

Jo, QR89, q20

Having been born a man and having red-blooded male feelings towards women, I would love to become a glamorous woman, knowing how to have men like putty in my fingers, dressing to tantalise them.

Michelle, QR72, q29

My Mum tells me that when I was three, I cried because I wasn't a girl. When she asked me why I wanted to be a girl, I cried that (as a boy) I would never be able to wear nice shoes. I had started play school and become aware for the first time that boys had to wear boy-uniforms of harsh, non-stretchy, non-colourful, unimaginative fabrics, and I would always have to.

QR30, q22

Someone recently said 'wouldn't life be a lot less complicated if one had never had the urge to dress up as a woman?' We couldn't help but reply, 'Yes, but wouldn't life have been dull?!' I love dressing ... I have a large wardrobe and two delightful dress-makers whose assistance I had the temerity to seek (neither had been asked to make dresses for a man before) and we have had a lot of fun over at least fifteen years creating some very exciting dresses from wonderful mate-rials ... Men's clothing will always, to me, be very boring. I love fine materials and bright colours and wearing pretty shoes.

QR88, accompanying letter

In Part II of the questionnaire, transvestites were asked to describe what kind of clothes they most enjoyed wearing, where they bought them, whether they were chosen for any feature in particular, whether they wore make up and a wig and what their favourite outfit would be, real or imag-inary. Overall, in the same way that there are some 'real women' who prefer very feminine clothing, so do some transvestites, and as some women choose more relaxed, casual wear, so do transvestites. The answers to this section, in particular regarding their choices of clothing, were so diverse as to make any kind of categorisation almost impossible but certain patterns did emerge.

First, it became increasingly clear that transvestites choose clothing in a very similar fashion to the way women – certainly women over thirty-five – choose clothing. They prefer styles which suit them to ones which are this year's fashion but hopelessly unflattering. They enjoy an eclectic range of items and, particularly the ones who go out dressed fairly frequently, have different outfits which are suitable for different occasions, daywear and evening wear, smart clothes and casual clothes. Many commented that they tried to wear clothing appropriate for their age group (although there were a significant number, as described above, who found transvestism a great opportunity to become a much younger looking person.) Rosemary (London) expressed a common viewpoint:

I love to dress as a mature woman, I do like lovely, pretty, pleated skirts and have quite a large wardrobe. I do enjoy silky lingerie in pretty, pastel colours (and for it to match to clothes) ...

I love to wear clothes that are for the more mature woman without being unfashionable – like last Sunday when I went to the Proms. I wore my new pretty blue satin lingerie over which I wore a smart, bright blue two piece outfit with deep blue shoes (courts) and carried a matching handbag. I always wear a wig and light make up during the day … I feel I am like many women of my age and like to buy clothes that are very comfortable but with a lovely style and a good cut. I like soft, pretty colours as I think they go better with my fair skin and hair colour …

My favourite outfit would be like the one I wore for the Proms concert or, like yesterday, just being a woman doing her weekly shopping – a deep red pleated skirt, pink camise top, with black one and a half inch sandals and matching bag. I dress as any mature woman. (QR13, qs12–17)

Rosemary's choice of outfits is echoed by many of the replies – colours may vary and there are variations on skirt length, tailoring details, cut of jacket, type of blouse and shoes, but the preference for clothes similar to or the same as any woman would wear is repeated many times. As one would expect with a similar survey of women's clothing choices, some partiality is also expressed for slightly 'wilder' clothes – mini-skirts, tight leather trousers and bustiers (sometimes accompanied by the wish for the body to go with these) – and some confess a 'fetish' for particular items such as a wedding dress or a particular kind of top or skirt, whilst others favour a Victorian style with corsets, but the majority are for very average (but nice) types of womenswear. Inga, a businessman, summarised this as 'I only wish to look chic. I do not understand the desire by many to look 'tarty'.' (QR43, q13)

This section of the questionnaire was mostly answered with a great deal of care and attention, as indeed it would seem that the clothes themselves are chosen. Several mentioned how much more diversity there is in womenswear:

I like to dress fashionably – for my age – and this has opened up much more than cross-dressing; the variety, especially brighter colours is so infinitely better. Dressed as a man I always wore subdued colours. I also like to be both glamorous and relaxed – but not tarty … I love the variety and colour of feminine clothes, also the style, texture, cut and comfort. It is much cooler and more comfortable to wear dresses or skirts in hot weather. Night-dresses are also so much more comfortable. (QR27, qs 13–15)

Many said that they bought their clothes from the same shops that most women go to – Marks & Spencer (good returns policy), British Home Stores, Littlewoods, Evans (many TVs need larger sizes), department stores, as well as mail order – and also, significantly, from charity shops, which were the most frequently mentioned source of clothing; if there is embarrassment about trying clothes on, charity shops provide an ideal resource since if purchases do not fit or look right, they have cost comparatively little, can be returned to any charity shop and money wasted is at least going to a good cause. Wigs are the only items which tend to be bought from specialist outlets – and several mentioned that although they might have started with shoes from transvestite suppliers, they had soon realised that these tended to be expensive, of poor quality and badly made, so they had resorted to either ordinary mail order firms or high street shoe shops. A significant number remarked that if they went shopping *en femme*, they had usually found shop assistants to be most helpful, even if slightly bemused at first.

Make-up is also bought from main high street suppliers such as Boots (although it presumably requires a degree of confidence to make the first trip to purchase an item such as lipstick.) Some pretend that the article is for their wife or friend whilst others have learned to be completely 'up front' about their purchases and received the same kind of advice that a woman buying such items would with regard to their suitability, colouring and so on. Some said that their wives or girlfriends were happy to accompany them on shopping trips and to give advice on choosing the right cosmetics and clothing.

Many transvestites also answered these questions with a degree of passion about how they had discovered what suited them and which kinds of clothing or accessories they particularly liked – some see it as a work of transformation and would not consider getting dressed without going for the whole effect, achieved through close shaving, bathing, very careful making up and wig. Some described their outfit as they wrote: 'I am wearing: black high heels, nearly black sheer tights, black and white check miniskirt, white knickers and bra, white ribbed top, black necklace (short) and a small amount of make-up (lipstick, blusher, mascara, eyeliner. I look and feel great (in my dreams – like all TVs, I look like a pantomime dame but who cares!)' (QR40, q17)

It seems probable from the answers given in the questionnaires and also from the interviews that much more effort is taken than most women would put in. (In the social meetings that I attended, transvestites happily gave me advice about skin care, nail filing and polishing, hairstyles and suchlike that were new to me.) Many are also very articulate about dress sense – often related to the colour system which divides people up by hair, eye and skin shades into 'seasons', so, for example, an 'autumn' type will look particularly good in certain colours and takes a wallet of coloured fabric samples around when shopping to ensure choice of the right coloured clothing. Many also talk knowledgeably about 'separates', 'co-ordinates', the names of particular styles of skirts, blouses or jackets, the importance of a good 'LBD' (it took me some time to work out that this meant 'Little Black Dress') and are more aware than many women of types of fabric and how they will hang, drape and wash.

Some Conclusions about UK Transvestites

The interviews and questionnaire responses unquestionably show that for many – probably most – transvestites, clothing is much more than a hobby, it is a preoccupation which may border on obsession (as indeed it can for some women) and there are many comments in the questionnaires which state that the respondent simply cannot understand why 'real women' go out wearing dull trousers and baggy jumpers, why they do not exploit their opportunities more since they have such a wonderful world of clothing to choose from.[13] The answers from this section demonstrated a general reaction against both the roughness and the dullness of male apparel and a distinct preference for bright or 'pretty' colours is shown together with silky, satiny or soft fabrics; many would concur with the sentiment expressed by Toni: 'My preference is for silk for blouses and tops with skirts being of the polyester/satin materials as these give the correct flow when walking'. (QR32, q30) Some transvestites may become almost 'fetishistic' about a particular type of fabric or clothing style – Ekins interviews one 'male-femaler' who is particularly fond of taffeta and of 1950s and 1960s glamour wear and says, 'I adore the hats and veils, the earrings and pearls and of course, the seamed stockings and court shoes. Women appeared more fragile and feminine in neat little suits, dramatically simple cocktail dresses and devastating evening gowns.' (1997: 90)

The image conjured is of the desire not only to act as the opposite sex but also for a different era in which women were women ('fragile', in need of protection, 'ladylike' and so forth) – and although my research only post-dates Ekins's by a few years, I would judge from my interviews and the questionnaire responses I received that such preferences are undergoing a change, both in terms of the clothing transvestites choose and the role they expect women to fulfil. I commented earlier that it is difficult to imagine boys of the 1990s and early twenty-first century becoming senti-mental about their mothers' underwear drawer (certainly if their mothers' underwear drawers are anything like mine). This may be a trifling point of itself but it is symptomatic of the shifts which are taking place in women's lives and is, not surprisingly, reflected by the clothing selected both by women and by transvestites.

For those who have the desire to cross-dress, transvestism also seems in most cases to provide a real relief from stress, whatever form the clothing takes and despite most transvestites having been through a phase of loathing themselves when they started to realise that this was not just a hobby or a mild desire but a real need:

> For years I thought I was dirty-minded and thought I would turn into a homo-sexual. I saw a psychologist and was told that if I felt like dressing as a female I should do so as suppressing it would only cause a breakdown. Until I saw a phone number on television, though, I thought I was the only man that felt like I did. I thank the lord that I now know there are thousands of us all over the world. (Ginny. QR37, q30)

The sub-agenda of the hidden and grey areas between the outer edges of this bi-polar world of gender will be explored later, as will the customs of culture relating to the different genders and their approach both to the world and to each other. Sandra's analysis that most men do not realise what real women's lives are like is almost certainly accurate but few are so perceptive, as revealed by comments in the questionnaires in particular. 'Woman-world' remains a sweeter, gentler pasture than the harsher gravel pits of masculinity and thus the attraction of becoming women remains potent. What is clear is that the putting on of clothing deemed culturally appropriate for the opposite sex is a crucial part of the 'becoming' process; in some cases it has almost a ceremonial quality, whilst for others, it is simply a stage or step which has to be gone through in order to reach the desired place (of femaleness).

The clothing itself is also acutely important in terms of the image that the individual wishes to present, transvestites being perhaps even more keenly aware of the subtle differences in colours, fabrics and styles and how these can be used to create the kind of woman that they want to be and what activity she is primarily interested in being engaged in. Both the aesthetic judgement involved and the result strived for are part of the formulation of the female artefactual world, as is the use of such feminine items as make-up, hair adornments and handbags, particularly well described by Shelly.

Transvestism has been (and still is) a mostly hidden activity because there is no social prestige to be gained for a man who does this – quite the reverse – and therefore the desire and commitment to doing it must be extraordinarily strong. For these transvestites, the cultural stereotypes of 'manly' behaviour – strength, aggression, power and so on – are seen with very different eyes, sometimes ranging from mild dislike to actual revulsion, whilst 'womanly' attributes are given a 'pedestal' quality. (Although it would undoubtedly be an interesting topic for study, the 'whys' of this – the psychological, emotional and operative reasons – are not explored within this work, since the aim is to focus on the use of clothing, the cultural responses to transvestism and the domain which transvestites create for themselves from this.)

That response which transvestism continues to evoke, however, is persistently negative – and it is interesting to note that even many 'liberal' and 'open-minded' people, both men and women, usually shudder or giggle, even at the word. If transvestism demonstrates that there are men who wish to emulate women, not only for their clothing choices but also their behavioural and emotional attributes, why are there apparently so few women, feminists particularly, who can welcome the notion of transvestism? As Woodhouse states, 'there are serious contradictions here for feminism. It is simply not enough to state that we must tolerate transvestites, all the while thinking "but I wouldn't want to live with one." The fact of the matter is that a lot of women, feminists and non-feminists alike, want their man *to be* a man, and that most definitely does not include wearing dresses, high heels and make-up.' (1989; xv) I would challenge this on at least two counts; firstly, there are women who do enjoy the fact that their husbands/partners dress in women's clothes – and the 'feminine' emotional behaviours which accompany this such as 'sensitivity', 'gentleness' and 'caring' (all words from the questionnaires or interviews). Secondly, the reality that women – even 'feminists' – have a dislike of, or problem with, transvestites raises a very big question about *why* they should find it so upsetting. I suggest that it demonstrates how deeply and unconsciously the messages run regarding the equation of 'feminine' with 'inferior', 'subordinate' and 'silly'.

The standing of cross-dressing men is, however, not always so perceived; the cross-cultural evidence in the following chapter on the hijras of India and in the final chapters is central to the understanding of cultural diversity in this as in other areas and provides important pointers to some of the explanations.

Notes

1. The stresses of having to conform to male stereotypes may well polarise into very positive or negative experiences for different individuals. *Peace Time*

Conscripts, a series of radio programmes, presented by Charles Wheeler on the experiences of men who had to do national service in the 1950s (broadcast by BBC Radio 4 in 2001), clearly demonstrated that although for some the male-bonding and the discipline of life in the services was character-forming and increased their self-confidence, others were driven to suicide.

2. For example *The Guardian* carried an article in June 1997 headlined 'Genes Say Boys Will Be Boys and Girls Will be Sensitive', which related a study from a research team led by D.H. Skuse, suggested that some male traits might be related to a gene on the X chromosome for social behaviour. Two days later, this was followed by a bitter riposte from Susie Orbach and Joseph Schwartz, which attacked the Skuse material on the grounds that it was based on equivocal inter-pretative factors, but more importantly, for its misleading bias which allowed the reader to understand that a definitive link had been found between biological sex and behaviour, particularly gender-typed behaviour. (Guardian, 12 & 14 June, 1997)

3. I have changed all male names (unless requested not to) but kept the female names.

4. It may be questioned why there are no interviewees younger than thirty-one; the reason is almost certainly that, as other authors have also noted, it seems common for the transvestites not to be sufficiently comfortable with their cross-dressing before their late twenties or early thirties to wish to acknowledge it. Most of the transvestites I met at social evenings were over thirty, and as Gina says later, during her twenties, 'it had mainly been associated with guilt and shame, but now she feels none and has decided to celebrate it rather than push it aside'. See also footnote 8

5. I have experimented with both he, she and s/he in the writing of this and none of these is ideal; s/he is perhaps the most appropriate but is clumsy, so in the end I have used both 'he' and 'she' according to which seems the most appropriate in individual cases. If the interviewee is, for example, dressing full time in female clothing, she seems far more fitting than he.

6. Anthony was by no means the only English research subject to single out Diana Rigg as a role model and object of desire – her name cropped up several times in questionnaires.

7. I heard later from Shelly that he was extremely unhappy; his wife had left him pending a divorce, in part because of his transvestism. Although he generally feels really upbeat about transvestism, the marriage break up has left him feeling dispir-ited and the frequency of his cross-dressing has changed as a result.

8. The progression from transvestism as a primarily erotic activity to one which is more reflective of psychological states is one noted by many transvestites, both in my research and that of others. Hogan-Finlay's research bears this out: 'The identification of developmental phases may turn crucially upon current reasons. For example cross-dressing for erotic expression may occur mainly during the early years of this lifestyle.' (1996: 29) Docter and others have also proposed a typical 'transvestite career path' (1988) which leads from sexual arousal from dressing,

through the development of a female self – and concomitant decrease in erotic associations – to fantasies regarding the 'woman within' and finally, in some cases, fantasising about living full-time as a woman, and possibly, acting on this fantasy. (Hogan-Finlay, 1996: 21)

9. Bornstein also comments on this problem: 'When I first went through my gender change, I was working for an IBM subsidiary in Philadelphia. The biggest quandary there was "which bathroom is it going to use?" To their credit, most of the people in my office didn't really care; it was the building manager who was tearing his hair out over this one. I suppose he felt I would terrorise the women in their bathroom and lie in waiting for the men in *their* bathroom. Finally, a solution was reached: even though I worked on the 11th floor of a large office building, I would use a bathroom on the 7th floor. The 7th floor had been under construction but for lack of funds they simply stopped construction. ... Piles of plaster and wiring ... and pools of water lay everywhere. But there was a working bathroom in the very back of that floor and that's where they sent me. No one ever cleaned it ... it was poorly lit and scary. Isn't it amazing the lengths we'll go to maintain the illusion that there are only two genders, and that these genders must remain separate? (1995: 84)

10. The advent of the world wide web – and internet chat rooms – as a meeting place for transvestites has had, and is increasingly likely to have, even more of an impact for transvestites than for most groups, since transvestism still tends to be a closet activity and is thus ideally suited to the anonymous style of interaction provided by the internet. It will also prove, I suspect, a very useful and interesting medium for further research in this area.

11. Hogan-Finlay notes that some research suggests that there are 'two different types of transvestism that are mutually exclusive and inherently distinct from early childhood. "Nuclear transvestites" are satisfied with cross-gender activities and do not engage in efforts towards feminisation whereas "marginal transvestites" (also called secondary transsexuals) gradually "feel like women" and desire physical changes to live as women on a permanent basis.' (1996: 20)

12. Grosz perspicuously describes the processes (and not-processes) of human desire and how difficult it is to explain or record desire: 'While not entirely involuntary, it lacks the capacity to willingly succumb to conscious intentions or abstract decisions. It upsets plans, intentions, resolutions; it defies a logic of expediency and the regimes of signification. ... Desire's turbulent restlessness defies decoding into signs, significations, meanings; it remains visceral, affective, which is not to say that it is in any way reducible to physiology. (Grosz & Probyn, 1995: 286) Based on Bland's descriptions of the transvestites' paradoxical situation, of pleasure and shame, gratification and deep discomfort, some understanding of the processes of desire and sexuality can hardly fail to be relevant. Clearly for the UK transvestite, the desire is not only sexual but equally – and perhaps more – bound up with the desire for 'femininity'. It is also sufficiently strong for them to jeopardise their relationships/marriages, to upset and defy; and yet is it physiological in the same way that desire for sexual activity is?

13. Some even refer to the beauty and grace of Victorian and Edwardian clothing, as borne out by a journal edited by Peter Farrer, *Men in Petticoats: A Selection of Letters from Victorian Newspapers*, (1987) which caters particularly for those with a taste in corsets. It is interesting to contrast this with Lurie's account of gendered clothing in *The Language of Clothes*. She points out that for most of the last two centuries, required wearing for women has been of a constricting, sometimes crippling nature and that the clothes which seemed so elegant and graceful, particularly those of the mid-nineteenth to the early twentieth centuries were in fact doing significant damage not only to the ability to breathe properly but also to the musculature, particularly of the back and spine, to the extent that they really did render women weak and helpless. Even when the strictures of clothing began to relax a little after the First World War, women participated in sports were still expected to play in clothes which hampered their movement so effectively as to constitute a serious handicap. One wonders whether the transvestites of the twenty-first century would be prepared to compromise their comfort and freedom of movement to achieve the elegance they commend. (1981: 68–9 & 222–3)

4

Disorder within the Pattern – the Hijras of India

Fieldwork in India

When I began research in India, I discovered very quickly that inter-viewing hijras can be a tricky business. I had read as much as I could from the scant material available and discovered a number of notable details – and, not surprisingly, was thus quite unprepared for the interviews them-selves. I chose to concentrate on Jaipur, the capital of Rajasthan in north-west India since it has the reputation of being one of the last places where hijras still have a 'courtly' status and personification – continuing the traditional roles of healer, blesser and performer at weddings and births – unlike the hijra groups in the largest cities, particularly Mumbai and Delhi, where hijras are more likely to be sex-workers even if they still attend ceremonial occasions.

The paths towards interviewing in India were also considerably less clear cut than they had been for the UK fieldwork. It occurred to me a number of times that there are some striking similarities between the hijras' posi-tion both within and outside Indian culture, and that of the gypsies in England. Both groups are a small, but often very visible minority and inspire a degree of wariness and dislike in the resident population which at times quickly converts to contempt and censure. Both are believed to have the power to curse and to bestow luck, both are fiercely protective towards those within their group whilst being antagonistic and on occasion seri-ously insolent to those outside it. Both have their own languages and codes of behaviour which are different from the society within which they live and thus maintain a position of outside-ness, and both appear when you would least welcome them and are immensely difficult to track down – and suspicious – when you do wish to. Whereas the UK transvestites had been communicative, helpful and only too ready to be interviewed, the hijras were difficult to find, awkward, mercenary and churlish – and I realised very fast that my original plan of trying to live in a hijra household for a while would be impossible. (The periods of fieldwork in India were carried out over the course of three winters between 1997 and 2000 – in total, fourteen months.)

My fieldwork with hijras is not intended to be an in-depth study as is, for example, Serena Nanda's (1990). I am handicapped by rudimentary Hindi (no hijra I have met so far speaks English, which meant that in order to penetrate into another language world I needed an interpreter) and by my English-ness and white-ness. It was entirely useless to protest that I was a student who was (a) genuinely interested in learning and understanding more about hijra life and (b) not possessed of vast sums of wealth. When I proved unwilling to or incapable of responding to their demands for outrageous sums of money, they would shrug and walk away, often refusing also to be photographed.

The first problem, then, was with money; hijras are seldom prepared to talk about themselves for nothing and the amount they demand can be in excess of 5,000 rupees (almost £100/$120, or, in context, nearly three months rent for my flat in Jaipur.) The second was that, the hijras became bored very quickly with my questions. Having agreed to pay them some amount of money, they would tell me their life story (it is interesting: both the hijras and the UK transvestites very clearly felt that this was what I wanted and needed to know) and then they would want to be paid and to leave. I learned that in order to achieve some semblance of control over these interviews required considerable stamina and stubborn determination – but even this did not inevitably succeed. The third was that, perhaps because of the poor treatment that they mostly receive at the hands of society, they do not feel a great need to tell the truth, particularly when faced with a question that they do not wish to answer. I had been told by many who discovered that the hijras were to be the subject of my investigations that one could not be sure of their information, but I still naively believed that when faced with an earnest female anthropologist, they would relent and be prepared to part with their innermost truths.

Needless to say, this was not the case, although over the course of several interviews with the main interviewees described here, I did gain some ground and I believe that much of what I have recorded is at least a version of the truth, even if sometimes embellished a little. The question which proved very interesting and to which one mostly suspects that they lie is: 'Did you have an operation to remove your genitalia?', to which the answer almost inevitably comes: 'No, I was born like this'. (And I should note that although the question may sound indelicate, hijras are known for their habitual practice of lifting up their skirts to show their genitalia to passers by – and to me on occasion.) Most hijras know 'other hijras' who have had the operation but are reluctant to admit to it themselves; reasons for this will be suggested in the last chapter.

Empirical research with the hijras would also seem to indicate that their position is currently in a state of transition between a relatively high status and a much lower one. While doing fieldwork, it was evident that the older generation in Jaipur – perhaps about fifty-five plus – still held the hijras in some amount of respect, whereas the younger generation increasingly regarded them with varying degrees of scorn. That I happened to have been doing this research at such an active moment of cross-over suggests to me that there must be a possibility of some evidence which assists in our understanding of these issues. The reasons are unlikely to be simple and single – but it seems clear that they are very bound up with the general move in India towards secularisation, modernisation, urbanisation; in effect, a kind of Westernisation. Sixty years ago, Gandhi famously stated that India's real life was in her villages and approximately eighty per cent of the population at that time lived in rural areas. According to a BBC World Service report in February 2001, that figure has crossed below the fifty per cent mark – over half of Indians now live in urban areas and that figure increases all the time. As M.N Srinivas has commented, India is becoming increasingly Westernised, consumerist and desirous of upward mobility,

> Westernisation is a multifaceted concept … common to all facets, however, is secularisation. Because of Western education, urbanisation and an occupation that requires a journey to work and regular working hours, life-styles have undergone rapid changes, along with the decline of ideas of purity-impurity in extramural contexts and the enclaving of ritual. … India's large and growing middle class is becoming increasingly Westernised. Westernisation is seen as essential to upward mobility. (1997: 17–18)

Half of India's population may still live in the villages, but, through the migration of workers to the cities, through radio and television and films, the process of urbanisation is not limited to the city populations alone. As the 'folkloric' quality of Indian village life changes character, it is hardly surprising that a group like the hijras is one of those most affected and that, in line with their counterparts in the more secular west, this may sometimes carry negative repercussions. Hijras are an unusual group who represent a particular form of adaptation to human diversity – and the effects on them of cultural change are becoming increasingly visible. Amongst this, the predominant view of hijras – themselves largely city-dwellers – has shifted from a quasi-religious or spiritual respect to a secular opinion of them as crooks, liars, trouble-makers and prostitutes.

The nation of over one billion that is modern India is, naturally, very different from the much smaller country of Britain and it might be expected that cultural diversity will be likely to take rather different forms. Although both of the primary research groups face the challenge of a disapproving environment, one cannot fail to be aware that comparing an odd, remarkable community in a distant and 'exotic' part of the world with that of a number of unrelated individuals in a UK context requires different methods of research, different parameters and prospects. Nevertheless, I shall suggest that there are common points of reference, which not only enable a greater awareness of aspects of sex, gender and sexuality in both these societies, but which also contribute towards an improved understanding of the theoretical perspectives in these areas.

Hijras in Context: Who are Hijras?

It has been suggested – by the hijras themselves and by several authors (for example, Nanda, 1990:13) – that hijras have been present in Indian society since Vedic times and they are referred to in the Ramayana, an epic tale and one of the key texts of Indian mythology. In this the hijras appear when the god Ram has to go into the forest to perform *tapasya* (propitiation which may take the form of, for example, solitude or pilgrimage) for ten years. As Ram leaves the city, the inhabitants follow him; he tells them to go back but when he reaches the forest, he realises that a group of people is still following him. He turns to them and asks 'Why are you still with me when I told you to go?', and they answer, 'You told the men and the women to go but we are neither men nor women and so we have stayed with you'. When they eventually leave the forest, Ram gives them a special blessing for having stayed with him and this is why, it is said, the hijras are still respected and were granted the power to heal, to bless and to curse.

The story above is one of many which categorise hijras as a special group; their identity crosses social structures as well as gender boundaries. While they are accepted as a part of Indian culture and society and are even supported in their existence through the deities and associated mythology, hijras hold a position in society which is neither neutral nor, in some cases, safe. Although they are regarded in some areas and by some people with respect, the fieldwork I have done suggests to me that those who offer respect or regard the hijras as in any way benefic are growing fewer, whilst the number who treat them with contempt increase. It seems much more common for them to be viewed negatively and they can be seen as both an exclusive and excluded category. Despite their position in society being one which may often have adverse indications, however, they do at least have an acknowledged position, and one that is accepted as a group in itself, both of which are not found in the UK situation.

Hijras dress as women but shave, smoke and talk like men. Some of the words used to describe them infer that there is something wrong with their genitalia and the society of men-women who fall into this category seem to be simultaneously seen as freaks whilst also being accepted as a part of everyday life by those who pass them on the street. Some hijras have been castrated, whilst others have not – and some, a very small percentage, were born with unsexed genitalia – but their overall signifier is their attire; they dress in the traditional women's wear of the region, most usually, a sari, or sometimes a salwar-kameez (baggy, drawstring trousers with a matching knee- or calf-length top worn by women, particularly in northern India and also known as a 'Punjabi Suit'). They grow their hair long and wear make-up and jewellery. Some are very attractive, others much less so. (Dyanita Singh describes hijras she met from a wide regional area attending a birthday party for the three-year-old daughter of Mona Ahmed, a Delhi hijra, 'there were awkward young eunuchs, sweaty, middle-aged, ox-like eunuchs, and eunuch crones who, when they moved, shook like scarecrows in a gale. A few – like Sonia, a Bombay courtesan – were very alluring'. (1993: 28)) They tend to live in specific areas of cities and may have good relations with their neighbours, as did the ones described by Singh who willingly accommodated a group of 500 visiting hijras in their houses on the occasion of the party, or possibly attitudes of bare toleration or active dislike. During fieldwork, I encountered hijras who described a wide variety of local circumstances.

Economically, many hijras derive their income from occupations traditionally involving performing at weddings and births, some become street performers, singing, dancing, making libidinous jokes and clapping, the latter having become a kind of trademark. The street performer group are generally ostracised, not permitted to mix with society and would encounter great difficulty in finding a regular job. They usually demand money, often with considerable aggression, and if refused, may lift up their sari petticoats to reveal the scar where their sexual organs once were. In these cases, it is very clear that they do not live solely in a private world but demand public recognition. They are also present (and paid) at celebrations, particularly in households where a new baby has been born. On the occasions when I was able to witness their performance in such situations, it was noticeable that although their singing and dancing was good-humoured and often quite ribald, with much joking both in words and play-acting about sexuality, there was an unease which accompanied their arrival – as if they were unwelcome at the beginning but once they started their performance, the assembled crowd really enjoyed the entertainment, clapped and sang and laughed along with them. The hijras used a kind of pantomime to mimic, for example, a pregnant woman, with a roll of material stuffed against their stomach to simulate a pregnant belly. While the other hijras drummed and sang verses along the lines of 'Ah you think sex is so good at the time but there's a price to pay for everything', the acting hijra would then play-act out the labour with a lot of groaning (and accompanying laughter). Afterwards, there would be considerable haggling over how much they were to be paid; hijras have had to become extremely astute and forceful about money and would ascertain from the neighbourhood and material goods around how much they could get away with.

Why the Hijras?

There are a number of reasons for choosing the hijras as a research group. First, they are a very distinct community in the cities and neighbourhoods in India in which they live. Although others like them, men who wish to dress as and to live as women, exist in many parts of the world, hijras are unique to India. As is shown by the interviews recorded in the second half of this chapter, echoed by other hijras I have met, and borne out by those interviewed by Nanda and Jaffrey, there is an undeniable current – even if it is usually an undercurrent – of dissatisfaction and despondency with their lives.

A second reason is that hijras are an extraordinary – and unique – adaptation to the situation in which they find themselves. Historically, it can be difficult to piece together the available information regarding the position of hijras now and how they came by this; the result is by no means always certain and is inevitably subject to regional variations. It would seem that hijras did exist for many hundreds of years before the Muslim invasions and victories between the eighth and eleventh centuries, but that after this, their status as eunuchs led to their developing a role in the royal Mughal households.

Many hijras now live in communities presided over by a type of 'clan mother' or guru hijra, usually elderly and chosen by her predecessor to inherit the position of honour. Perhaps one strong reason for their ability to survive as a group is that historically many hijras received valuable gifts of land, usually from their royal patrons and that this, the houses that they built on the land, and the customs they developed to ensure its transmission from one guru to the next, enabled them to continue to practise in the way that they have for centuries. In addition, from their performance at weddings, which appears to have continued from before the advent of the Mughals to the present day, derives their status as embodiments of reversal, their role being part jester-like, since they are in the position of being able to ridicule and make fun where others are not. Jaffrey even comments that with their 'whimsy and genderless faces', they remind her of Shakespearean fools:

> They were like the shadows and the critics of society. Everything about them suggested paradox; they were not men, nor were they women; they were not invited to perform, but neither were they uninvited; they carried the instruments of song, but made no pretence of being able to sing; they blessed the bride and groom, but through a stream of insults; they were considered a nuisance, even extortionists, and yet they were deemed lucky; they were not paid to perform, but to leave everyone in peace; they partook of the rites of passage that they themselves were incapable of – marriage and birth. They were clearly outcasts, yet were able, through a comedy of manners, to transcend the barriers of rank, caste and class, and reduce everyone to ridiculous equals. (1997: 19)

(Ruth Lor Molloy, a Canadian who produced a small booklet titled *Hijras – Who We Are* designed to increase awareness of hijras and eventually to assist them in educational projects, health and welfare, states that when she heard that they were despised by most Indian people and could not get jobs because they were different, she was 'amazed at the unusual way these hijras had adapted ... (they) have reacted to being rejected with non-social behaviour. But other people have reacted to their non-social behaviour with more rejection.' (1997:3))

Third, if one accepts that clothing is a form of visual code which enables us to understand immediately various salient facts about another person, then the dress of transvestites in any culture demonstrates a particular and unusual kind of communication: a wish to be seen as someone else, someone female. Within Indian society, hijras utilise the non-verbal codes which dress embodies; the most obvious being that the simple act of changing your clothes changes your life. In some contexts, it may arguably be the most important act in taking on the life and associated codes of another human being.

The Need to Categorise: Studies of the Hijras

One of the earliest anthropological studies of the hijras that I could trace was A.P. Sinha's *Procreation among the Eunuchs*. Although written in 1967 it seems to have more of the dominant moral perspective of a late-Victorian or early-twentieth-century work. He describes hijras as either sexual inverts, sexual abusers, or histrionics. 'Sexual inverts', are for Sinha those individuals born with 'tendencies' which could be 'cured' if parents were sufficiently wealthy and sensible to take corrective measures for their susceptible sons. Poor families, by contrast, were often insufficiently sensible, living as they did in a social milieu which 'aggravated' the subject's 'recessive' characteristics. It is hard to avoid the conclusion that Sinha's analysis is less an attempt to explain the hijras than an attempt to explain them away. His arguments pay no attention to the religious and cultural context of the hijra world, preferring instead to apply in a direct fashion the concepts of early sexual psychology with the result that instead of adding to our understanding of the hijras, Sinha's approach rather obscures them in a welter of condemnatory judgements.

Sharma's 1989 study, *Hijras, the Labelled Deviants*, avoids the explicit moralising of Sinha's piece, but as the title indicates, it still takes as axiomatic that to be a hijra is to be a deviant, which inevitably affects the tone of his work. Sharma again constructs three categories of hijra, all of which share dressing as a woman as the dominant and designatory feature. The first consists of castrated males and true hermaphrodites, those who are neither male nor female but an element of both; the second group are intersexed, impotent men who have had all or part of their sexual organs removed; and the third group are normal men born with the usual genitalia who may or may not be castrated but choose to dress as women.

The most recent ethnography,[1] Serena Nanda's, starts to ask important and explorative questions about gender categories and whether 'our own view of sex and gender is as dichotomous, ascribed, permanent and universal as we assume it to be.' (1990:139) Different cultures create many alternative types and notions of gender roles which become accented in a cross-cultural comparison, and this necessitates an enquiry into definitions, for example, 'is gender a permanent and inescapable status?' and 'are the sub-structural ideas which lie at the bottom of gender categories related to wider motifs within society?'.

Nanda notes that, in contrast to Western societies, it is possible within Hinduism not only to accommodate ambiguities such as transvestism and transgenderism but also to view them as meaningful and even powerful. She traces the conceptual existence of a third gender category to ancient

Hindu texts which, for example, 'taught that there was a third sex which was itself divided into four categories' and, in addition, idealised the notion of hermaphroditism since to be neither male nor female allows the transcending of sexuality altogether, thus achieving a major advance on the path to salvation. (21) Importantly, Nanda states that the hijras simply cannot be understood in terms of the gender polarities of Western belief systems but only in the context of Indian and, more specifically, Hindu beliefs and mythologies; 'much of hijra behaviour, which we in the West would be likely to label as pathological and bizarre, becomes understandable when studied from the point of view of the cultural system in which hijras operate' (143) This is very much borne out by this research and we shall come back to the notions of cultural operating systems in later chapters.

Becoming a Hijra

The ceremony which surrounds the operation of castration has been viewed by very few outsiders. This account is drawn primarily from Nanda – who also did not witness an emasculation herself but had it described to her by the hijras she interviewed. The process of having the penis and testicles removed is usually carried out in the early hours of the morning, considered an auspicious time for rituals and ceremonies such as marriage. Many operations may be performed at the same time or it may be done singly, with just the client and the operator present, the latter usually being a hijra known as a *dai ma* or midwife, since the operation is seen as the beginning of a new life. It does not imply any medical training; the process is seen as being in the hands of the Divine Mother. Those wishing to be castrated will usually spend the hours before doing *puja*, Hindu ritual or worship and in this case a kind of vigil. In some cases, black tea with herbs may be given to those about to undergo the operation, but in other cases, a mantra is chanted (*mata, mata, mata*) to achieve a trance-like state.

The penis and scrotum are tied around with a thread and all other clothes and jewellery removed, to symbolise the nakedness of the new born. When the operation is performed, the initiate stands with hands behind head, pelvis slightly forward and at the appropriate moment, two diagonal cuts are made, separating the penis and scrotum completely. The blood is not staunched since it is seen as the essence of masculinity which must be allowed to drain out completely to allow the initiate to be born again without maleness. During the next few hours, the client may live or die, the process and outcome being perceived by some hijras as a struggle between the goddess of life and the goddess of death. The operation itself does not apparently cause much pain but the following weeks of recovery can be extremely painful and the new initiate is treated almost identically to the mother of a newborn baby; for forty days 'she' is brought special food and allowed to rest and recuperate. After the resting period is over, a ritual bearing strong resemblance to the Hindu wedding ceremony is held to celebrate the hijra's entry into a new life. (Nanda: 1990: 26–9)

An alternative version of the castration ceremony was related to Zia Jaffrey by one of her informers who had watched the ceremony. 'A young boy, who must have been about fifteen or so, was wrapped in a sarong, and he had a silk kurta put on him; he was brought and asked whether he wanted to be initiated as a hijra, and he said Yes.' The candidate was definitely male but with underdeveloped sexual organs – and:

> He was taken around the hall … Every hijra present viewed him and then he was brought back. The people present were asked whether they approved of his being brought into the society. Then they said Yes, or this approval was given – whether it was unanimous or not, I couldn't gauge because there was a sizeable crowd there. And then the sardar said, All right, he should be initiated. There was an open space, and they'd brought a wooden platform, on which was fixed a wooden phallus – like a big penis – very thickly oiled. And then the drums started beating and this boy was taken by two strong hijras, and he was made to sit on this thing, and the tempo of the drums increased and he was pressed down on it, and the boy fainted, and the barber came and just removed his testicles! With one sweep of the razor, they were removed. And then that area was cauterised. (1997: 76–7)

Although this boy apparently survived, there is no doubt that all do not – and since the process is difficult and dangerous to life, the motivation to have the operation must be very strong. Nanda asks one of her hijra group the reason why it is so necessary to have the operation and is told a somewhat oblique story about a king who wished to see the hijra's gifts. After demonstrating these in various ways, the hijra crowned these achievements by emasculating himself with a cactus thorn which impressed the king greatly as he understood fully the ritual power of a hijra. (1990: 24)

The Hijras and the Principle of Male and Female Union

Nanda cites a further example in mythology which links hijras with the coming of the rain. A folk tale tells of a drought in Hyderabad. The king is asked by his people to resolve the problem but knows he is powerless, so tells them to make their request to two hijras sitting by the roadside. The people are angered by this since they believe it should be within the king's powers to bring rain but he tells them that if anyone can, it is the hijras. The junior of the two is fearful and wants to run away but the elder takes some cloth from the upper part of her body, dips it in water and gives it to the people. Immediately the rain comes, soon there is too much, but the hijra says 'enough' and it stops. When the people come to pay their respects to the hijras, they have vanished and the king orders that hijras will henceforth be respected in Hyderabad. Nanda comments that:

> Intersexed and impotent, themselves unable to reproduce, hijras can, through emasculation, transform their liability into a source of creative power that enables them to confer blessings of fertility on others. This identification with the powers of generativity is clearly associated with the ritual importance of hijras on occasions when reproduction is manifest – at the birth of a child – or imminent ... and also at a wedding, one of the most important rituals in nearly all cultures for its celebration of male-female union. (1990: 30–1)

Nanda makes a rather different connection between the hijras and the fertilising rains than does Marglin (1985) regarding the Candan Jatra ritual (referred to in the next chapter) – that of creative asceticism, but it is the involvement of the hijras which is significant. Although Marglin's study is primarily concerned with the establishment of sexuality with fertility, both examples serve very well to illustrate three linked points which are crucial to this study; firstly, that the hijras are a well-established group in India, with a cultural and social role supported by mythology and ritual; second, that in contrast to the Bible in Judaeo-Christian cultures, Hinduism is capable of celebrating the issue of sexuality, with the ensuing implications for transvestism; and thirdly, that the female principle has a role in ritual and the wider sacred context which has implications for women's position in society and that this is central to the acceptance of male to female cross dressing.

The notion of hijras as a special group with positive religious and spiritual connotations is portrayed in Michael Yorke's documentary, *Eunuchs: India's Third Gender* (1991), one part of which portrays the lives of several hijras in Rajasthan. Those he met lived in one of the few remaining thriving eunuch communities of provincial India, presided over by their guru, Shardabai, in a mansion, seen by those who live there as a kind of cloistered community and carefully veiled from the outside world. Shardabai's family of eight disciples is in addition to her being 'in charge' of 105 eunuchs in the surrounding countryside. She has the power to appoint to the territories in her control and there are strong ties of duty and respect between guru and disciples. Implicit obedience is expected to the guru or head of the family in this closed society where castration guarantees permanent loyalty, security and nurturing in the transition and ways of the third gender.

Shardabai rules rather in the way of an aristocrat, with firmness and affection; neighbours bring her their sick children, relying on her to cure them: 'these people respect me, they all love me, they like my prayers and their children get better. I heal them in the Lord's name; I heal with a true heart and give them hope. When they grow up they'll give me a living'. The old Rajas of Rajasthan gave them land and property in return for blessings and even paid them regular salaries. This way is coming to an end for the hijras, even in the courtly world of Rajasthan – there are fewer all the time who can still earn their living through performing blessings, particularly for wealthy patrons and thus many turn to prostitution (although arguably, sex has always been part of hijra life.) Mumbai hijra prostitutes interviewed by Yorke said that although some clients realise what they are, some don't. Most are castrated and make popular hookers because they have no inhibitions. They told the camera that many of their customers found women insipid after a hijra.

This is not to suggest, however, that becoming a hijra is not without serious drawbacks. They may be treated well by some but they are also the subject of bullying, ridicule and even violence. Many appear to perceive themselves as vulnerable and thus fall prey to an unscrupulous lover who 'protects' them but also lives off the earnings that the hijra brings in, equivalent to a prostitute's 'pimp' in the West. Many also die or suffer considerable ill-health as a result of the operation.

Hijras and Religion

Many hijras, in common with most Hindus, pay their respects and address daily prayers to 'Mata-ji' ('the mother', a name applied to many forms of female deity and also implying the wider, empyrean mother- principle) but the other deity of consummate importance to the hijras is the god Siva. This almost certainly derives from Siva's dual aspect as both the ascetic who refrains from sexual activity whilst being the primary creative force in human union and fertility.

Hijras may worship at Siva temples, and in particular, identify with and supplicate to the form, well known throughout India, of Siva

शिवा आधानारीस्वारा

Figure 6 Siva Arddhanesvara

Arddhanesvara, ('arddha' meaning half) the 'hermaphrodite' depicted with a left female half and right male half and the most auspicious aspect for ensuring fertility through union. 'The half male, half female god, Arddhanesvara does not simply combine the masculine power of aggression and the feminine power of devotion but triumphs over these two opposites to be a super-god. Likewise the eunuch is not just a neutered male but has renounced sexuality and risen above the conflicts of being neither male nor female: they are granted power to curse and bless beyond the ordinary mortal.' (Yorke: 1991) Elgood further comments that the *lingam*, or phallus, which is found in all Siva temples (and many others besides) is usually set beside or within a *yoni*, the symbol of the female genitals, portraying the union of the masculine and feminine, and that the *linga* 'can also be seen as symbolising the axis mundi – the bridge between the earthly and heavenly energies.' (1999:46) A *vatsana* or devotional poem by Basavanna (1106–1167) refers to Siva as 'the lord of the meeting rivers' and explicitly to his dual sex potentiality:

> Look here dear fellow:
> I wear these men's clothes only for you
> Sometimes I am man,
> sometimes I am woman.
> O lord of the meeting rivers, I'll make war for you
> but I'll be your devotees' bride.
> (Tr. Ramanujan: 1973: 29)

India (as has been remarked by many visitors and scholars) contains many juxtapositions and apparent paradoxes. Hinduism, arguably something of a Western construct itself in many ways, is known for its diversity and breadth of belief, whilst Indian society and culture is renowned for its contrasts. Underneath the apparent openness and welcome to believers and deities from many faiths and the freedom to worship as one chooses, however, is the extraordinarily rigid structure of the caste system, inherited at birth and from which one is only released through death.[2] Within this paradoxical system, hijras are given a solid place in society whilst simultaneously being reviled by many. It is interesting, then, that some of the hijras whom I met and talked with, and those interviewed by others including Nanda and Jaffrey, were Muslim. Some had converted – at least in some respects – from Hinduism to Islam despite the fact that Islam is positively against castration,[3] whilst Hinduism does not speak against it and furthermore, is the religion which offers them a solid foothold in a complex and hierarchically bound society.

Perhaps because hijras are a group partially legitimised by Mughal/Muslim experience and incursion, historically, as a group, they have become nominally aligned to Islam and – as Nanda notes – although 'the collapsing of the role of the hijra and that of the Muslim eunuchs leads to certain contradictions ... these seem easily incorporated into the hijra culture by hijras themselves; only the Western observer seems to feel the need to separate them conceptually.' (1990: 22–3) Jaffrey acknowledges that, almost certainly, a clear reason why hijras become Muslim and are found mainly in northern India is because of a connection to the Islamic Mughal rulers, where eunuchs were useful both in the traditional occupation of guarding harems and in their administrative systems. (1997: 29)

However, although this is an inherited custom which may shape some outward functions such as names, it is not the single defining identity of the group as it has developed. When a new hijra joins the community, taking a new name is a small – and quite individual – part of this process which brings a range of cultural and religious beliefs and customs to the transition. The Muslim part is probably a historical accretion because it stemmed from the way the group developed and, arguably, the hijra phenomenon is not primarily a religious phenomenon – it just uses what is available. Because in India, all of life tends to be much more lived within a religious framework, hijras thus inevitably invoke religious elements to that change. It is more difficult in religious terms not to do or be that – to be a transvestite or transsexual within a secular frame – as the transvestites in Britain are. Most importantly, the religious history of the hijra group may explain some of their own religious customs and rituals but society's view of that group may stem from the structuring of society and social views, primarily from the structures of Hinduism.

This remains a paradox, however, which I questioned throughout my research and I do not feel I ever reached a completely satisfactory answer, only some insights (sometimes into entirely other matters.) It should also be said at this point that hijras come from both Hindu and Muslim backgrounds and although many of those who have 'converted' from Hinduism to Islam have, for example, inscriptions from the Koran in their houses and worship at the tombs of Muslim saints,[4] they may also wear *malas* and *mangal sutras* (Hindu necklaces with special significance), they continue to do *puja* (the Hindu form of prayer and worship, usually involving candles, flowers, images of the deities, sprinkling with water and oil) and many wear *bindi*s (the red dot in the centre of the forehead, very definitely associated with Hinduism and no other religion.)[5] Some of their names are Muslim (Razia, Ruksana, Sultana), some are Hindu (Tara, Priya) and some are used by people from both faiths (Chand, Shabana, Chameli, Gauri and Jaitun.).[6]

Part II: Fieldwork with hijras

A new hijra is born

YES!

A sari without a woman

YES!

A coach without wheels

YES!

A stone without a fruit

YES!

A man without a penis

YES!

A woman without a vagina

YES!

(A traditional chant recited when a new hijra joins a group, collected in Udaipur from a hijra named Gulshan by Katya Antonopoulos, a journalist whom I met whilst researching hijras and intended for an article called 'Gulshan, the Eunuch of Udaipur' which she was in the process of writing.)

Some of the comments and discussions I gathered in the course of interviews are interspersed among the description of hijra life which follows, but the four below, with Shabana, Tara, Jaitun and Chand, together with Leila's information, I have included in their entirety. They are condensed from several interviews – usually four or five with each hijra – into the versions below, and are followed by a very different account of transvestism from Ramdhan, a boy in a remote Rajasthani village.

Jaipur – Shabana

'Main ne kya kiya isse paane ke liye ...?' – 'What did I do to deserve this ...?'

Shabana is a thirty-year-old hijra and lives in a house in the Sanganeri Gate area of Jaipur with other hijras. The house is crammed into an alley behind a busy commercial street and is a warren of small rooms, mostly overflowing with items of clothing, food, pots and pans, washing equipment and religious items.

Shabana first knew that she wasn't like other children when she was in 5th class at school (i.e. around nine or ten years old) because she realised that she didn't feel entirely right playing with either the groups of boys or the groups of girls. She preferred the girls and most people thought she was one but later, in eighth class, when the boys started to grow facial hair and their voices to break, she also started to develop facial hair and everyone began to stare at her, to dislike her, and they stopped talking to her.

At home, her family started to be worried by the fact that she was developing some male characteristics whilst still displaying some female ones, and they mostly kept her at home. They had thought that she must be a girl because she had no real penis and they had not realised that her genitals were seriously different – she explained this by saying that she had grown up in a village, where considerable modesty is observed, and that her mother had tried to hide her abnormality. When her moustache began to be apparent, she felt deeply ashamed and abnormal and she cut it in secret. She was horrified at the maleness as she felt sure that she ought to be a woman. Her father started to behave very coldly towards her and then one day he took her aside and said: 'My daughter, I cannot keep you any more; my prestige will go down, so you must leave.'

One day, soon after this, her father went into Jaipur and found a group of hijras and told them to take her away and a few days later they came, a group of about five hijras, to fetch her. She was about fifteen or sixteen. Her mother cried a lot when they came and ran away so that she didn't have to watch her daughter leave. For several days and nights before, she had cried day and night and said things like 'Oh – now I shall never be able to go to my daughter's marriage and help her with her children'. Shabana herself thought: 'Why has God deceived me?, What did I do to deserve this?'

Nanda describes the case of Salima in *Neither Man nor Woman,* who encountered similar prejudice. In Salima's case, the doctor would seem to have been the most philosophical about the situation, saying 'No, [your penis] won't grow, your child is not a man and not a woman, this is God's gift'. Salima also mentions that after her father realised she would never be a proper male and, like Shabana's father, he was raging, he then calmed down enough to go on pilgrimages to pray for her to be normal – although these came to nothing. By the time she was at school, however, when Salima was beaten and intimidated by the other children, her parents would protect her and tell the bullies off for attacking a child whom God had made in this way so that eventually Salima herself learned to understand: 'I was sent to my mother's womb by God. That is the gift my mother got. Like any child, I am a gift for her.' She joined the hijras when she was about ten or eleven and says that although she was scared of them to begin with, 'they used to talk to me so kindly and gently ... my heart opened to them and after that ... the pain in my heart was lessened (1990: 99–100)

Shabana told me that she still feels upset by the shame she brought on her family – and her father's rejection of her – but she now realises it was inevitable. She said goodbye to her family and house and she felt miserable, but also relieved as she felt she couldn't live in a place where everyone except her mother seemed to hate her. She still thinks about her mother and wonders how she is and worries; she has not seen her since she left.

The hijras took her to their house in Jaipur where an old hijra called Fatima is the guru of the house (although each time I was there, I was told that Fatima was away). Most of the hijras are Muslims, so Shabana became a Muslim also, although the shrines in their house are both to Hinduism and Islam. She continues to wear Hindu items of jewellery and to use Hindu devotional items, such as flower *malas* (garlands) and incense. When she arrived, Fatima, the guru, recited some mantras (prayers), sprinkled water on her and she entered into the house. For several days, she just cried and cried. The guru told her not to worry and that if society cannot accept people like them then they have to create their own world, to make their living as best they can and if necessary, to fight, but mainly they have to live separately and to keep away from society. Later, Fatima gave her a ring as a token that she was part of that hijra family.

She was looked after and told not to worry by all the hijras. They assured her that they would all take care of her and she would be happy. After about a week, she began to settle in and make friends and she felt more comfortable. The atmosphere and the relief of being with other people who understood her was considerable, although there was often fighting between hijras in the household. They taught her the traditional repertoire of hijra songs and she also learned to play the *dholak* (drum). After about a month, she started to go out with them when they went to play and sing at weddings and births.

There are about 25 or 30 hijras living in the house; some are now very old and don't go out any longer. These are taken care of by the younger ones, in much the same way that they would be in an extended family household. The groups who go out to perform at functions are usually of five or six hijras, though they can be as few as three or as many as ten. One of them plays the drum while the others sing and dance and clap. They also go on visits to shops and stalls to take money. The shopkeepers usually give them 10 or 20 rupees and if they refuse to give, one of the hijras pretends to start undressing – or in some cases actually does – and once they pull up their skirts, the shopkeeper usually hands over the money. But the big money comes from weddings and births, where they can earn as much as 10,000 rupees (approximately £150 or $240) if the family is rich. In the daytime they go out to earn money and in the evening, they cook and eat together. The household chores are divided up between them with some being responsible for cooking, others for cleaning and so on.

I asked Shabana about her clothing (when I met her, she was wearing a green sari of nylon chiffon with a red and pink flower pattern and border) and she said that there was no difference at all between what she wears and what any normal woman would wear; she does not, for example, combine female garments with any items of male clothing. She mostly wears a sari with a *choli* (blouse) and petticoat, especially if she is going out, although she doesn't usually wear the *pallu* (the end part of the sari which goes over the shoulder and down the back) over her head as a woman might. She also sometimes wears a salwar kameez (long top over drawstring trouser bottoms) but not so much now she is getting older, and usually only inside the house. She usually prefers to wear bright colours, although she does have one or two outfits which are in browns and golds.

The saris are sometimes from performing at weddings – they form part of the payment – and they are given by the hijras doing the performance to their guru. The guru will keep some and divide others amongst those who need or deserve them and this sometimes causes some fighting, but mostly everyone ends up with something that they like. If the saris are disliked by everyone, they will either be given away or sold. Usually, their salwar kameez suits are made by tailors from material they have bought in the market, but sometimes they will buy them ready-made. Shopkeepers are not generally very nice to them, however, so buying material from the bazaar is easier.

She makes a clean shave everyday and wears a *bindi* (the red dot on the forehead, worn by Hindu women.) She wears make-up most of the time, but especially when going out – blusher, lipstick and kajal round her eyes, foundation if she is going somewhere special, and sometimes *sindoor* (red powder worn down the parting of the hair to denote a married woman – again, a Hindu rather than Muslim custom). She wears quite a lot of jewellery – rings, *malas* (prayer beads worn round the neck), a *tabiz* (a silver box on a cord round the neck, more Muslim than Hindu), and several bangles on her wrists. (She – and most of the others I talked to – desperately wanted my wrist watch, rather to my surprise since it was a rather dull and plain Swatch, but their interest in it seemed to be because it was foreign).

She thought that the main differences between a hijra and an ordinary

Figure 7 Shabana & Tara

woman were not in the dress but in their behaviour, in that hijras smoke, which few Indian women do, and they swear and talk like men, whilst at the same time acting like women in many other ways, for example, the way that women habitually and almost constantly re-arrange their *pallu* or *dupatta* (the long scarf which drapes across a salwar kameez). There is also a great difference in both the way they have relationships and with whom they have those relationships, although she would not say more than this. Some hijras behave in a much more feminine way than others. For example, many hijras far prefer 'feminine' chores – domestic work around the house such as cooking and cleaning, sewing and polishing – but there are some who are more masculine and these, she said, are often the most aggressive ones.

She explained that some hijras do develop breasts but others use cloth to pretend – they use a bra and usually a half-blouse – one which stops above the waist. They shave the hair on their chests and arms and legs. In the evenings, after 9 or 10 p.m., some of them may go out to earn more money from sex. Sometimes the men don't realise, because it is dark, that it is a hijra, not a woman, but if they try to complain or refuse, the hijra will say 'Why did you catch me if you don't want?'

I asked her whether she is happy to be a hijra and if there are any problems, and she replied that now it is OK and a reasonable kind of life, but that it took some years to get used to it and that it is not a life, she would have chosen for herself. She is very grateful for the fact that she has a 'family', particularly since hers rejected her, and that she knows that there will be someone to take care of her in her old age. She also thought that she was better off in Jaipur than a hijra would be in a bigger city like Mumbai, where almost all the hijras are prostitutes and there is a lot more social difficulty. She said that she had met hijras from Mumbai who have no real houses, just pavement sheds and these are under constant threat of attack by local thugs who personify the hatred and ridicule with which the Mumbai hijra community is mostly regarded.

I tried to explain a bit about transvestites and transsexuals in the UK and to ask her whether she thought that being a hijra was preferable (rather a tricky question, given that she has no real idea of life in England), and she replied that she would much rather be in a hijra's situation, with a proper position in society and acceptance, albeit with all the difficulties. Sometimes, but not often, she is proud of being a hijra, usually on the rare occasions that some person who still believes in the old ways shows her respect. She also said that she was not proud of a hijra's power to curse and bless and very seldom used it. She does not see herself as having a very nice life and often feels cursed by god, but she feels that given the circumstances, this is about as good as it can be.

Jaipur – Tara – age 25/26

Tara lives in the same hijra house as Shabana and came to join the hijras when she was about eighteen or nineteen.

She was born a boy, with the full male genitalia, but from childhood wanted to be a woman. She has always used female words for herself when speaking (in Hindi/Urdu, the word for 'his' and 'her', 'she' and 'he', and so on are the same but the gender is given in the masculine or feminine ending of the verb stem in the sentence).

She grew up in Jaipur and her boy's name was Tarachand. Her family was 'very nice', quite well off, 'middle rich', and she went to a Hindi-medium school for boys, where she was given a very rough time by the other boys and constantly wished to escape (she never got into physical fights, despite much provocation). She had two sisters, one older, one younger and she played mostly with her older sister and started to dress in her clothes from mid-childhood, nearly always in secret (though her sister knew) because she knew it would cause major family anger and upset. Her story is in many ways echoed by one of Nanda's interviewees, who describes the way that she hated wearing trousers and used her pocket money to buy *lungis* (wraparound cloth like a skirt) and make up. (1990:57)

Because Tara's desire to wear women's clothes and to live as a woman was so strong, she eventually decided herself that she had no option but to leave her family and join the hijras. One day, while out shopping, she met a group of hijras and simply asked them if she could come to live with them. They agreed, but she had to fight with her family for months before they would allow her to go. She could have just run away, but she wanted to have their blessing and she thought it would hurt them too much if they woke up one day and she wasn't there. Eventually, her father said OK because he could see that he was more of a she and he was quite embarrassed by her. Also, she had a younger brother which meant first, that her father had another son, a 'real' son, and second that her brother could be the heir without any argument. She misses her mother and her older sister very much, but her sister is married now and therefore lives in the house of her husband's family, so she cannot meet her, even in secret. She wishes deeply that she had been born a real woman and could have continued her relationships with her family like a normal person. She does have mutilated genitals but they are cut, rather than cut off. She did this partly by herself, before she joined the hijras (she would not have cared if she had died in the process, she was so miserable and desperate about being a half-man) and partly after she joined, but she did not want to talk about this at all.

Tara said that she enjoyed very much being pretty and attracting the attention of men, but that she realised this would happen less and less as she got older and she wasn't very happy about it, but the older hijras know tricks to keep your looks and attracting power as long as possible. She loves playing with her hair and make-up with the other hijras, plaiting flowers or ornaments into their hair, experimenting with different looks and lipsticks. Her hair is now down almost to her waist and she wears kajal, nail polish, earrings and a thread from her guru hijra round her neck. She is particularly proud of her hair, which is long and wavy – and Nanda comments that growing one's hair long is essential for hijras, and that serious offences are commonly dealt with by cutting hair short since this is humiliating to the offender. Tara confirmed this, saying that she would do anything to prevent this happening. (Hair is also crucially important to British transvestites – most of those I interviewed, or who responded to the questionnaire, mentioned that a wig was an essential part of their 'kit' – and wigs are given a prominent position in the catalogues and websites which supply transvestite items.)

She usually wears a salwar kameez and prefers *churidar* (trousers which are tight from the knee to the ankle) to salwar (the baggy style) because she thinks they are more eye catching and flattering, as well as bright-ish colours and quite bold patterns. She looks forward to getting more jewellery in time, preferably gold and expensive. Sometimes she wears a sari, mostly at functions, but although she thinks that it makes her look more special, she prefers the salwar kameez because it makes her feel freer and more like a young college girl. She shaves every day, including her chest, but her legs are naturally unhairy and always have been.

She loves shopping in the bazaars and looking at fabrics and fashions, but this can be a problem as the shopkeepers have no respect and make fun of them, so they have to learn to live without modesty or shame. Often, the shopkeepers ask them to dance or sing and sometimes they are abusive.

She would not describe herself as happy, exactly, but she appreciates the advantages of this life – a lot of freedom and not much responsibility, no marriage or children, it is quite easy to earn money and there are few restrictions. She absolutely had not wanted to get married and this had been a major source of conflict with her parents. I tried to ask her about converting to Islam when becoming a hijra, but she just said that the Hindu religion does not allow for hijras – and when I pointed out that hijras are in the *Ramayana* and *Mahabharata*, she just looked confused. (Whilst many of the hijras interviewed by Nanda seemed very aware of the mytho-logical and religious heritage of the position of hijras within Hinduism, I met few who were at all interested in or concerned with this.)

Jaipur – Jaitun – 46 years old

Although I met Jaitun a few times in the company of other hijras at their house, she was always very quiet – almost mute by comparison with some of the others. I saw her only once on her own for a fairly brief interview – about three-quarters of a hour – because she was not keen to talk for very long. Some of the information she gave was rather confusing and contra-dictory and this narrative is pieced together from the things she said both in the interview and at other times. Like most of the hijras I met, she was adamant that she had not required an operation because she was 'born like this', but she did say that there were many hijras who had had the opera-tion. She even insisted that I took a photograph while she held up her skirts (as a kind of tunnel) and although I did this, there is very little except a dark patch visible on the photograph.

She grew up in a family with a mother, father, brothers and sisters and when young, was treated as a girl by everyone because she had been born with indeterminate genitalia. She went to a mixed school for two years, from the age of six or seven till eight or nine – in Kota (a town in

Rajasthan, about five hours from Jaipur) and was not teased because no-one knew that she was any different from a normal girl, although later, when people locally came to know, they did start to call her 'hopeless' and 'worthless'. She went through some very miserable years, but now she is happy and feels pleased with her life. She is still completely accepted by her family – they recognised that she had little option but to become a hijra – and she goes quite often to visit them in Kota.

She came to Jaipur when she was fifteen (although later, she said sixteen and also twenty) having worked for some years as a servant in a bungalow in Kota, cleaning and washing. A group of hijras used to come past the house periodically and they would call to her to come and join them because they recognised her as one of them. I asked how, but she just said they knew – for example by the way she talked and walked. So one day she decided to leave Kota and join a hijra community in Jaipur. She said that she had known she was unlike others from the time that she could first think – although later, she said that before she was sixteen, she did not necessarily realise she was different because life was much simpler. (I would suggest that this apparent contradiction is simply that she perhaps was aware of some degree of difference at an early age, but it was not until she was fifteen or sixteen that she realised how life-changing this difference was.)

I attempted to describe transvestism and transgenderism in the UK and to ask Jaitun about the position of hijras in India – and whether there were different possibilities in India. In reply, she gave the following, somewhat confusing answer: 'sometimes there are men who just wear the clothes – and some of them do this full-time – and if they do this, then they are hijras – and some also choose to have the operation' (and some do die in the process, but she had not known anyone to whom this had happened because it is kept secret.)

I queried whether she thought that hijras were treated well – with respect – and she replied that probably the only place where they have a good reputation is in Mumbai, because there, they can be employed sometimes in the film industry, not just as actors, but also as, for example, make-up artists. But when I prompted her about the place of hijras in Hindu religion and mythology, in particular whether the form of Siva as Arddhanesvara was important, she said that yes, this does matter and it does lend hijras a degree of respect. She also mentioned the story of Arjuna, saying that most Hindus in Rajasthan know about Arjun's time as a hijra, particularly because this happened in Beratnagar, about 70 kilometres from Jaipur; she thought that this provided 'a strong connection between the spiritual life and the position of a hijra'. (Arjuna, a principal hero of the *Mahabharata*, became a hijra for a year; he refused a goddess and was condemned to be neither man nor woman, but the goddess was persuaded to commute his sentence to one year.) I asked whether she had been asked as a hijra to apply her attributed powers of blessing and healing and she said that certainly, people do call her for this – and that true 'born' hijras have a special power – they have (are born with) 'something on their tongue' so that whatever they say will come true. She added that only hijras who have been 'born like that' were part of her community, but then, when I tried to clarify this, she said that her group did include men who had become hijras because they felt they were born into the wrong sex.

Towards the end of our meeting, I asked her to tell me about the apparently unusual position of hijras in that many are both Hindu and Muslim – and why many hijras convert from Hinduism to Islam on joining a community. I tried to do this without directing the conversation too much, although this was difficult, particularly since the interview was conducted through an interpreter. Jaitun said that she believed in 'both' – both Ram (the Hindu god), and Allah – but also very much in 'devi' (the goddess), and 'Mata' (the Mother) – and she went on to say that there are still some people who believe that hijras are a form of deity, but only those 'born like this'. She said that hijras go to both Hindu and Muslim houses to perform – and that she believes there to be more Hindu than Muslim hijras. She was brought up as a Hindu but converted to Islam because she felt Muslims to be more broad-minded – or at least, more broad-minded than people think. She thought, however, that the 'special' position of hijras – in particular that by being both male and female, they achieved a kind of 'one-ness' to which their powers could be attributed – was declining and that they are less respected. Before, even if people did not see them as holy, they at least treated them with the kind of consideration that they would a disabled person (an interesting echo of Shelly's comment regarding UK transvestites out shopping) and now even this is disappearing.

Jaipur – Chand – 60 years old

I have two versions of Chand's life: one from Chand herself and one from Leila Beghum, a Muslim woman who lives in a house very nearby and who accompanied Chand when she came to visit me and then afterwards, came again and told a lot more, not only about Chand's life, but also many of the other hijras whom she has got to know. Her information follows on from Chand's narrative.

Chand was the first hijra I ever interviewed and it was not long before she was bored with my questions and wanted her money. She said that she always refers to herself as 'she' (as indeed all the hijras I met do.) She earns most of her money from dancing and singing at weddings and birth celebrations. Unusually, she does not live with other hijras, but just with her two adopted children (one girl and one boy). She used to live in a house with ten or twelve hijras, with others from different parts of India staying very frequently, but now she lives alone. She does have a *chela* (disciple), but this *chela* wants to move to live with a different guru, so she does not talk to her. She also stressed that she had been 'born like this' and had needed no operation to remove her genitals.

She comes to know about celebrations from a network of informants including cleaners, *dhobis* (launderers, who are to be found on the corners

Figure 8 Chand

of most Indian residential districts), midwives and hospital workers. The latter inspect the baby when they have a chance and if it is a boy, check to see if he has a fully formed penis. If he doesn't, and there is just skin and a hole, they will remember him and come back for him when he is older. Sometimes, the parents say 'Yes – take it – he is one of you' straightaway, although this has only happened once to her personally. In her own case, the hijra who came to be her guru had to battle for seven years in the Jaipur courts with her parents for custody. When her guru finally won, she never saw her parents again, although she does see her sister sometimes. She is a Muslim but said that there are also hijras that are Hindu and that they all believe in all religions.

I asked her about her clothes (she was wearing a sari when I met her) and she was fairly dismissive of this line of questioning, asserting that her clothes are exactly the same as any woman's. She does wear make-up but she doesn't try as hard to look pretty as she did when she was younger. She doesn't ever a wear salwar kameez (but then very few Indian women of her age do either.)

She said that she had had a very happy life as a hijra and would not change it if she could; she has much more freedom than an ordinary woman but can still enjoy the life of a woman, in particular, less responsibility and the ability to look after children. I asked her whether she would prefer to have more freedom of expression, as transvestites in England do, or whether she would prefer to be in India, where hijras have a defined place in society and she (not surprisingly) said that she would definitely rather be in India. (She did want my wrist watch though.)

Supplementary Information, supplied by Leila

Leila Beghum, my informant, has lived in the hijra quarter for a long time and knows many of the hijras very well. To the story which Chand had told me when she was there, Leila added that the reason why she, although Leila called him 'he', lives alone is because she is so bad-tempered that no-one is prepared to share a house with him anymore. She fights more than any other hijra Leila has come across and will make a drama out of even the most trivial things. Once, she beat the hijra who was her *chela* so badly that she ended up in hospital and it turned out to have been because the *chela* had borrowed her hairbrush. She has, however, also been known to be very kind, particularly to those who come to her because they believe that she has special powers, and if people give her respect, she will bless them (and, Leila said, her blessings really work.)[7] Chand had said that she earns most of her money from singing and dancing, but Leila added that

101

now she is getting a bit old to do this very often, so sometimes she has to resort to begging fruit and vegetables from market stallholders. She also said that Chand had once had a wife and that she was certain that he had not been 'born like this' and had had an operation. She then told me a number of stories about the hijras she knows.

One day, in Koth, where she comes from, she was sitting next to a hijra who was six feet tall and very handsome and she asked him, 'Why are you a hijra?' He replied that he had felt very womanly for a long time and used to enjoy dancing at weddings and parties and one day, the hijras asked him to join them. He told them that he didn't mind joining them for the weddings and dancing, but he certainly wasn't interested in having any operation. They left him then, but a few days later, kidnapped him and took him to Bikaner, where he was drugged and they cut everything off then put him in a pit of cow-dung for three days, as is the custom. (Cow-dung is both holy and believed to be antiseptic.) After this, he felt helpless and he had no choice but to go with them.[8] He wanted to leave but they told him he would have no life without belonging to their group and if he tried to leave, they would not have him back, so he reconciled himself to it and decided that this life would be all right – and it is: he is quite happy.

In general, life in a hijra household can be both very supportive and also extremely volatile. If a hijra wants to leave her guru, the guru will become very angry and shows it by cutting off the *chela*'s braid and taking back the ring or other piece of jewellery they were given at their initiation, which effectively makes them an outcast. They also levy a fine of several thousand rupees. If, on the other hand, a guru decides that one of her *chelas* is too cunning, they will try to sell her onto another guru and these transactions can be very profitable, perhaps paying the guru between one and five lakh rupees (one lakh equals one hundred thousand rupees – about £1,500).

She thought that nearly all the hijras in Jaipur have at least one lover, sometimes many more, for whom they are more like mistresses than prostitutes, and the hijras in turn have amorous relationships with boys for their own amusement. Because homosexual relationships are still considered beyond the pale in India, there is a big market for this. The hijras stand on the street looking for customers and (she said), if they cannot find a paying customer, they will often offer themselves for free. She knows all this because when they fight, she can hear their arguments very clearly, and they do not have sex because they need the money but because of their desires. Some of the boys that they sleep with become hijras themselves; there was one boy called Anil who used to come to Chand for sex and he eventually decided that he wanted to live there and become a hijra. His family ('good, kind, gentle Punjabis') begged him not to; they locked him up for three months but one day he broke a window and escaped – and went off to have the operation. He still goes to visit his parents sometimes but they dislike him now and want nothing to do with him. He mainly lives out of Jaipur and when he comes to visit, there is always a group of five or six boys hanging around.

After ten o'clock in the evening, the hijras mainly stand around on the main roads of Jaipur and demand money with menaces. Sometimes, they even carry weapons – usually knives – though this is a recent development and, once they have bagged a customer, will allow him to take them away and then produce the knife and demand more money, threatening them either with disturbance (and possible disclosure) or physical violence.

One hijra, Shami, who converted to Islam, has done the *haj* (the pilgrimage to Mecca) twice, despite the fact that her father was a Brahmin priest in the main Hanuman temple on Johari Bazaar until his death a year ago; Shami became a hijra twenty years ago. Her guru gave her the money to do the *haj* on condition that she did not sleep with any other man ever again – and Shami has kept to this.

Leila thought that most hijras had unusually bad tempers and a tendency to be sharp-tongued and bitter, although there are also some very sweet-natured ones. Nearly all of them have chosen this way of life (but perhaps because they felt it was the only option open to them, the only place for them in society.) Despite the fact that they say that they prefer domestic chores, her experience is that their houses are usually very messy, with clothes and other items strewn everywhere. This was mainly my impression too, from the times I entered a hijra household.

Samred Kalaen – Ramdhan – A Young Transvestite from a Village

Whilst Ramdhan does not fall into the hijra category, I have included this narrative because he is an interesting example of someone growing up in a village with strong female leanings who, in the city, would almost certainly be a candidate for becoming a hijra. His narrative also has some very clear comparisons with the stories from UK transvestites which appear in the previous chapter. In the remote village in which he lives, however, the option of joining a hijra community has not arisen, but he demonstrates, through his behaviour and story, similarities to UK transvestites. His preferred dress for some time has been as much of a version of women's dress as he could get away with without receiving hard beatings from his father. When I interviewed him, in 1999, he was seventeen.

When I talked to him, as with all the interviews, it had to be via an inter-preter, especially since his first language is the local Rajasthani dialect, and

Figure 9 Ramdhan from Samred Kalaen

in this case the person doing the interpreting was related to him. I found out about him through a family in Anopura, a village outside Jaipur, whom I have got to know very well. Ramdhan is their distant cousin and lives in a village in which they used to live but from which they moved in their great-grandfather's time because it had no road to it and was therefore rather cut off. Ramdhan's village is quite difficult to reach and involved a bus journey of about 10 km further on than Anopura, already 37 km from Jaipur, followed by a twenty-minute jeep journey over sand dunes, and finally a half-hour walk.

Ramdhan told us that his marriage took place when he was seven years old (a very common marriage age for both boys and girls in this area). He did not really have much idea at that age, either about marriage or about what would happen to him in the future. He does not live with his wife yet (the girls generally come to live in their husbands' homes at the age of about sixteen) but she knows about his cross-dressing and desire for a woman's lifestyle and does not mind.

He started to adopt women's dress from as far back as he can remember. He did this by copying the women's style of wearing a shawl as a head covering, together with wearing necklaces and kajal round his eyes. When he started to wear full women's clothing (borrowed from his sisters and cousins) – the *gagra* (long skirt), *cabja* (blouse) and *lughri*, (semi-transparent cloth, usually brightly coloured and worn like a half-sari, tucked into the waist of the skirt and then over the head and face) – his father beat him very much, so he stopped, but he still continues to wear his shawl over his head, together with the kajal and women's jewellery. He has now reached a kind of compromise with his father, who has been forced to accept that beating does not stop Ramdhan from having a deep need to dress and act as a woman, so he no longer beats him and Ramdhan wears a *gagra* inside the house, but with a T-shirt instead of a *cabja*.

He also found women's way of behaving came to him very naturally and when he is shy, covers the lower half of his face with his shawl like a woman and giggles. He almost always sits inside with the women, not outside with the men, and by choice, he does women's work. I noticed that he had quite a high-pitched voice, like a woman, although I don't know whether he had consciously chosen to adopt this. He has a full male anatomy and no desire for relationships with men. He simply feels himself to have a much stronger feminine side and wants to take care of children and do the domestic work that women do.

He seldom talks to anyone and, at first, told me that he has a very happy life, apart from the censure he sometimes receives (particularly from his father, the only person in his life who gives him real problems). Everyone else loves him for his sweet nature. He never went to school because, in his generation, the girls seldom did and he wanted to be with them and be like them. He does wish he could grow his hair long, but he insisted that he didn't want to *be* a woman, just to wear the clothes. Later, however, he said that if there was an operation that could make him a woman, he would definitely have it. (His confusion perhaps reflects that of many UK transvestites.)

I asked him to describe the kind of clothes that he would like to wear if he was completely unrestricted and he said that it would just be the same as any village woman wore, but when I asked him if there was any item that I could give him as a gift, he chose a plain black *gagra* (skirt) – something which village women have not chosen to wear for two generations – the textile style currently in fashion is for vivid floral patterns on a brightly coloured background.

He has never met anyone else like himself but he does not consider himself a freak and continues to wear women's clothes as much as he can. I was not allowed to ask him whether he would consider joining the hijras, because, my interpreters said, he didn't know they existed. (This is quite interesting in itself and I felt at the time that they would not question him about hijras because it might put ideas into his head.) The interpreters seemed sure that if the hijras knew he existed, they would come for him.

I had had the opportunity to speak to Ramdhan's sister a few days before I met him, when she was visiting the village where I was staying, and their two versions of events bore each other out in every detail except one; she said that he had never had any idea of leaving the village and that he was completely happy with his life. Towards the end of my talk with him, he admitted that he thought often of running away and had sometimes contemplated taking his own life. Not surprisingly, Ramdhan's story does not have any parallels with Nanda's or Jaffrey's research since he has not become a hijra – although it does have some more obvious ones with UK transvestites – but it is precisely because of this that his situation is uniquely interesting.

The Position of Hijras within the Indian Cultural Framework

It seems likely that the hijras of India have been regarded in a rather different light than their Western counterparts not only because they have some thousand or more years of mythological and religious role-models which act as a supportive conceptual paradigm but also because they reside in a culture in which the prevailing attitude towards the principles and precepts of life itself is – or at least has been – significantly different. These include the laws of *dharma* and *moksha*, an intrinsic part of the philosophy of reincarnation, which, in its entirety, provides an indigenous and pertinent frame of reference in which all beings are seen to have been incarnated into life with a particular path which they must follow and this will be discussed in more depth later.

The hijras, like the untouchables or those born disabled or impaired, are part of an overall schemata and the doctrines of Western religions can never apply to life or the human condition in quite the same way. In addition, they could be considered less psychologically disadvantaged than Western males who wish to dress as or become women, since hijras do not live in a culture in which all reference to deities or the divine is almost entirely male; as Michael Allen points out with reference to the Indian ideal of womanhood,

> This symbol of self effacing love has revealed to the Hindu mind the presence of a divine reality within, over and above the personality of the visible mother. To the Hindu, God is the mother of all creation. A nation that has educated itself to look upon God as mother has learnt to invest its view of woman with the utmost

tenderness and reverence ... to look upon the female of all species as forms of the one Divine Mother.' (1982:10)

There are many reasons why this apparent considerable respect for female autonomy and power is not exactly evident in practice but the existence of a potent female deity (in her several manifestations) is nevertheless a significant symbol in the patterning of ideas on the internal and external planes of thought and understanding and provides a strong contrast to the transvestites in Western society. The cultural context of hijras may be rooted in the mythological past but, as more recent developments demonstrate, their future is evolving in a number of different directions, some more positive than others.

The Changing Position of Hijras in Indian Public Life and Media

The traditional role of hijras is indubitably a site of change and transition – as has been discussed, their position as members of the community who attract some regard as well as reluctance is declining – but there are also signs that they are continuing to be a presence, even if their traditional role is shifting. As far as I have been able to discover, there are no texts as yet regarding the position of hijras in the worlds of, for example, politics and films but a source which has provided much of the information discussed below is the world wide web.

One location for hijras has appeared in the Hindi movie industry (known as *Bollywood*) and based in Mumbai. A website called 'Screen India'[9] discusses the rise and fall of the hijras, declaring that they are – and have usually been – crudely portrayed in Hindi films. Hijras have formed a suitable brunt for coarse or mocking jokes whilst simultaneously being treated with fear and disfavour by the Mumbai public at large (although, as is clear from the extract below, there is a limit to the mockery and the public seem to have made it clear that the worst excesses are too distasteful):

Earlier, new mothers would call them to sing bawdy songs but with the rising decibels of MTV they've lost this only respectable means of earning. Today aerobics to trim the extra-cellulite is more important than having hijras doing a dance number on the street in front of their apartment blocks. Even at weddings they are forgotten in the cacophony of stereophonic CDs ... In mainstream cinema the hijras have so far existed more as clown than humans with a heart. Actors, mainly comedians, would cross-dress with deliberate crudity so as not to be mistaken for a woman but taken for a hijra in an attempt to evoke laughter. Fortunately, this brand of gross humour did not go down well even with the front benchers and therefore, the mimicking of a hijra died a slow death.

There have been a number of films which have featured hijras, for example *Sadak,* directed by Mahesh Bhatt, which featured a hijra named Maharani and which won a *Filmfare* award for the actor – but the hijra is portrayed as a cruel, obdurate creature and the film did little to paint hijras in a kinder light or improve their position within the Indian community. Hijras have also been used in the song and dance routines for which Hindi movies are famed, for example their number in *Kunwara Baap* which became immensely popular in the Indian charts. 'Perhaps, for the first time ever, hijras were happy to be a part of mainstream cinema, never mind if it was just one loud song in a lengthy film. The song became a hit and it was sung at college picnics and children's birthdays to mimic the hijra community. And the hijras were back to watching films that made fun of them.' (screen india website)

The portrayal of hijras in Hindi movies may have been predominantly unkind, but there are exceptions; for example there is one film which has given hijras a different kind of representation. *Tamanna*, released in 1997, was directed by Pooja Bhatt, the daughter of a movie mogul who was given a production company by her family on her twenty-first birthday. Her father had once written an article about a hijra named Tiku, a hijra with a large heart he had met in one of the meaner parts of Mumbai. Pooja was so taken with this story that she decided to make Tiku the hero of her first film and, as an (anonymous) website writer discusses:

> *Tamanna* comes across like a whiplash on our faces. Tiku, the hijra picked out of real life and performed brilliantly by Paresh Rawal, repeatedly underscores the fact that often, people born genetically as men, may be physical embodiments of manhood but in their hearts and their souls, they are sexless, they are the real hermaphrodites. Tiku is more of a man than all the men put together in the film. The hijras in the film make fun of him because he avoids them, thinking that by living with ordinary people he can forget the gender-deviation of his existence. Later, as he finds his income as a make-up man in films dwindling, he is forced to put in his lot with the singing-dancing hijras to pay for the education of his 'daughter'. Once they accept him into their fold, the whole community of hijras build up a solid wall of resistance and rebellion, of violent protest when Tamanna is kidnapped and is likely to be killed by her biological father. Films like Tamanna which celebrate the solidarity and the loving hearts of the hijras symbolised in the character of Tiku, can bring the community greater respect than any organisation or book. (www.expressindia.com/screen/aug08/films2.htm)

The writer suggests that the hijra community, secretive and marginalised, caring little for social acceptance, but sensitive to derision, is ripe for further exploration by the Bollywood industry:

> Many of them have turned to crime and prostitution. But none of these facets have been explored by our film-makers ... Once employed by sultans to guard their harems, these eunuchs or castrated males live today on the fringes of society, ostracised but occasionally venerated for their supposedly magical powers. No director has explored the possibility of making a feature film focusing on this collective and cloistered community till the Bhatts came on the scene.

A hijra does also feature, however, as the hero of *Square Circle*, released a year earlier (Amoi Palekar, 1996) and described by cinema programme notes as a 'landmark film of popular Bollywood cinema dealing with hostile social conventions of gender and sexuality'. In this film, a young woman who was about to be married is abducted, having been mistaken for another woman who wanted to run away from their village and go to work in the city. Despite her protests that she is the wrong girl, she is taken against her will, and eventually, when she does manage to escape, is far from home and easy prey for a gang of boys who find her wandering by a river, rape her and leave her bruised and bleeding. She meets the hijra, who, initially reluctantly, looks after her and helps her to find her way home – although when they reach it, her parents reject her as a slut and want no more to do with her. The upbeat notes of a rather dark – and potentially tragic – film are almost entirely provided by the hijra, who gives her wise words, practical care and eventually, a reason to find her way in life.

In Mani Ratnam's film, *Bombay* (1995), a hijra also plays a cameo role as a rescuer and bestower of wise words. At one level, *Bombay* is a classic Bollywood-style tale (although the film was made in Tamil) of the difficulties posed by a Hindu-Muslim love affair, but it then uses this as a vehicle to engage the observer's emotions when set against the Hindu-Muslim riots in Bombay in 1992–3. The Hindu-Muslim couple escape from their restrictive families in Tamil Nadu, are married in Bombay and have twin boys. They live very happily, albeit with some surprised reactions at their joining of the two religions but with no opposition – and one of the boys is given a Hindu first-name and Muslim surname, whilst the other has a Muslim first-name and Hindu surname. Even the couple's parents start to become reconciled. But during the unrest, by which time the boys are about 6, they become separated from their parents. One boy is saved from being trampled by the hijra, who then takes him home, feeds him and looks after him.

Although the hijra does not appear for more than perhaps 5 minutes of the film, her unqualified kindness and the words she says, which are some of the most penetrating with regard to the violence, give her a strong voice. The boy, traumatised by his experiences, asks 'What does it mean to be a Hindu? What does it mean to be a Muslim?' And the hijra replies 'I don't know and why do you ask me, the *bichwala,* (the middle sex)?' And she tells him that religion is only a medium to reach god – the Hindus have one religion and the Muslims another, but both go to god, the implication being that her position as an in-between is analogous to the religious situation; both should be respected.

Whilst three films, which portray hijras in a different light from the mockery with which they are usually treated, clearly do not make a case for a whole new perception of the hijra life, they do perhaps mark a state of mind which is not entirely hostile to their way of life and which is prepared to view them with compassion as well as distaste. Hijras have also featured (albeit to a very limited extent) in high profile activities such as modelling for designer collections; they recently featured presenting the designs of Kum Kum Chowdhury in Lucknow (2001). One hijra model, interviewed on the television programme *Bombay Blush* was clearly thrilled by this opportunity, saying, 'It's fabulous – and what it really does is help us to get recognised by the whole world. We may have had a hard life but we can still be beautiful.' (BBC [Scotland], 2001)

Hijras are also appearing in the media in the sphere of politics as reported, for example, by *The Times of India* (17.2.00), which stated that hijras, 'who have faced centuries of oppression and derision, are looking to the ballot box to provide an escape from a life spent as sexual outcasts on the margins of society.' Through fighting local and national elections hijras are creating and consolidating a role for themselves as community workers – far beyond their attendance at weddings and births. In some cases, they have particularly set themselves up as anti-corruption candidates – a popular platform in India – as one is quoted, 'I am not a *hijra* in a Mughal court who watches courtiers indulge in pleasures in gay abundance. I intend to clean up the system. I have done.' (N. Vittal interviewed by Onkar Singh, http://www.rediff.com/news/1999/dec/21inter.htm)

The victory of Shabnam Mausi, another hijra, elected to the post of MLA (Member of the Legislative Assembly) in Madhya Pradesh, is reported (12.3.00) on the 'netguruindia' website:

The victory of a Eunuch is something unique in the history of Indian politics and as such is significant index of change ... the message is loud and clear, as the metaphor of impotency and non-deliverance, so typical a trait for our politics,

has so rarely hit the nail on the head. ... Shahdol (the election district) is dominated by Rajputs and Sohagpur has been the home turf for the Congress for
three decades. But this time, even upper castes claim to have voted for Shabnam,
furious at the lack of development and some say, at the downsizing measures ...
The lower castes, especially Dalits, hail her victory as their own. The common
refrain being 'we have defeated the Thakurs with a Eunuch'. ...

Therefore, the victory of a Eunuch, should not only be viewed as a cynical
reproach for mainstream politicians but also as an expression of good-humoured
revenge by the backward classes against their oppressors. (http://www.netgu-
ruindia.com/news/12Mar00.html)

It is wise, though, to set these positive developments in context. Jaffrey
finishes *The Invisibles* with a kind of postscript, written three years after
most of her travels and study were completed. Returning to the hijra
household where she had previously spent time and talked at length to the
occupants, she discovered from a new group that most of those she met
had died (several together, of carbon monoxide poisoning). The new hijras
were considerably less hospitable and Jaffrey comments that 'there was a
sense of chaos among the new order; I could see that the new leadership,
under the new guru, would be a crude and defiant one. Gone was that
gentle grace and politeness to outsiders who came with respect ... the hijras
were defensive and fearful of the outside world'. (1997: 280–1)

My own fieldwork echoes Jaffrey's encounter, in that I found most of the
hijras I met difficult to talk to, uncivil in their manner and considerably more
interested in financial reward than in any notions of hospitality or friendship
– an unusual situation in India, where there is a culture of welcome and willingness to engage in conversation. Certainly the hijras have more than most
to protect and keep private but I was sometimes surprised by the degree of
their unpleasantness and their grudging behaviour. In addition, hijras have
also started to receive attention in their capacity as sex workers as India
wakes up to the problems of HIV and AIDS. One newspaper report states
that 'in the span of an hour a eunuch sex worker may service up to seven or
eight men. They most often do not insist on the client using protection, for
the myth that a eunuch, not being a complete woman physiologically, cannot
receive or transmit HIV, is only one of the many myths they harbour.' (*The
Metropolis on Saturday*, 1.3.97) This article further suggests that hijras have
received little effort to integrate them into the mainstream and, because of
their ambiguous status, receive poor treatment from the Indian legal, social
and political establishment – although perhaps this will change if hijras
themselves become involved in these arenas.

It may be that some hijras are now recreating themselves to make the transition into new spaces of possibility. It would appear, even in the context of modern means of communication, that there is sufficient cultural resonance to enable the survival of the hijras in a modified form. Potential reasons for this are explored in later chapters. What is clear, though, is that the old ways are being eroded.

Notes

1. Jaffrey's book, *The Invisibles*, is more recent (1997) than Nanda's but is not strictly an ethnography, being a wonderful fusion of the anthropological, the historical and a travelogue.

2. As Quigley notes, the word 'caste' itself can be seen as a European fabrication: 'an extremely unhappy translation of two quite different indigenous concepts, *varna* and *jati*, which are generally believed, both by Hindus and by outside observers, to correspond in some way. In a sense, the history of the debate about the nature of caste can be viewed as the attempt to discover exactly what the correspondence between varna and jati is.' (1993: 4)

3. Mohammed is recorded in Hadiths as saying, 'the one who castrates himself does not belong to my religion. In Islam, chastity takes the place of castration.' (Jaffrey, 1997:28)

4. Hijras I met were particularly interested in a shrine near Ajmer (in Rajasthan) to the Sufi saint Baba Darga, sometimes also known as Nawaz Kharib.

5. The question of religion for hijras would, I believe, make an interesting research topic in itself, but would require an immense amount of investigation and cannot therefore be explored in any depth here.

6. Regarding names, Jaffrey quotes from Preston (1981) – the letters of R. D. Luard, a sub-collector in Pune (near Mumbai) who describes in 1836 his seven hijra case histories, noting that all came from rural India, 'three were shepherds and one was a Muslim. All assumed fanciful Hindu names, followed by common names, like surnames, given as a sort of family name, to distinguish them from other hijra groups, and possibly revealing the line of succession from guru to disciple.' By contrast, another Englishman – Mr Goldsmid of Indapur, noted that although hijras could have come from any caste, they 'upon emasculation take the names of Mussalmani women, and as such, live and are buried.' (Jaffrey:1997, 204)

7. I can also bear this out. On the Evans-Pritchard principle from his fieldwork among the Zande, of doing what the locals do, I asked Chand for a blessing for my mother, because I had had a phone call from England saying that she had had a heart attack and was very ill. Chand said that she would, and when I phoned home the following day, my mother had surprised the doctors with the degree of her improvement and was out of danger.

8. Like Nanda, (1990:xxiv) I never met a hijra who had not joined the commu-

nity voluntarily, although newspaper articles and popular notions of hijra life continue to support the belief that kidnapping and abduction happens. Leila's story is the only personally related information I encountered of a kidnapping and I remain slightly dubious as to its veracity, although she was very confident that this had happened.

9. http://www.screenindia.com//aug08/films2.htm

5

Crossing Gender Boundaries in Cultural Context: Fieldwork Comparisons and Cultural Influences

The transvestites of the UK and the hijras unquestionably present very different models of cross-dressing. The hijras most certainly form a coherent group whilst the UK transvestites are individuals who may or may not meet up from time to time. It is not surprising then, that they required a rather poly-methodological approach. Whereas UK transvestites were only too willing and ready to talk, for hours and about everything – and were very happy to spend their own money coming to visit me to be interviewed – the hijras would seldom talk unless given money, usually demanding quite large sums. Almost without exception, the most important thing they wanted to have on record was their life story. The UK transvestites were, however, usually willing to discuss other issues in great depth such as clothing fabrics, styles, frequency of dressing and so on and it was therefore possible to write a much more richly detailed section on the material culture aspect of clothing for the English than the Indian context. The hijras were at most prepared to talk for half an hour to an hour; after this they wanted to take the money and go. Although the interviews which appear in Chapter 4 were the result of several meetings, the constraints of financial resources, time and language all contribute to there being comparatively less material in the Indian fieldwork.

The empirical research and the ethnographic examples in the previous chapters both show that transvestism changes meanings in different contexts. In particular, gender-crossing may either be a role which is chosen and for life, as exemplified by the hijras, or it may be a part time activity which is lived in sharp contrast to the everyday world, as it is for many transvestites in the UK. For some amongst the hijra community, the idea that it is 'for life' is emphasised by the physical changes which they are prepared to undergo. Some UK transvestites, like Janett Scott, may choose to live permanently as a woman but not have surgical changes. (And, as mentioned in the introduction, although transsexuals might appear in some ways to be the more obvious comparative group with the hijras, this work has focussed on transvestites, because the fascination here is with the material culture aspect of gendered clothing reversal they embody.)

The hijras' more fixed gender change is in contrast to many of the transvestites studied in the UK, who cross-dress for varying occasions but have no intention of 'becoming' the opposite sex permanently. This is also the case for groups where transvestism is used in a ritual context, such as the 'Naven' ritual described by Bateson (1958) and discussed in Chapter 6; in this context cross-dressing may well be of a different form again, an activity performed by nearly all members of the group for a short period of time. In addition, for the hijras (and, to a more limited extent, the Brazilian travestis, also discussed later), transvestism creates 'difference' but, because it has an essential element of a cultural, ceremonial context, it also constitutes a form of 'belonging'. UK transvestites, unlike hijras, have little history, no 'tribe' to join with associated ceremonies of belonging, but they do have a much greater range of personal freedom of expression, even though it may be restricted by cultural antipathy.[1]

There are some similarities between hijras and UK transvestites, the first and most obvious being that they both dress in clothing designated by their culture as belonging to the opposite sex. This transgression of such a strong social norm also inevitably leads to both groups (insofar as the transvestites can be perceived as 'a group') being regarded by others and themselves as marginalised and existing on the periphery of society. In common with many marginal groups, they tend to fare better in cities, since urban environments function as centres of possibility, large enough to encompass and support sub-groups. The differences between the communities are, understandably, much more striking and I have attempted to arrange these differences into categories, although the features mentioned may inevitably overlap and be applicable in more than one category.

Cross-Dressing and Clothing Choices

Although there is no ubiquitous costume for transvestites in Britain or in India, many factors render a different situation regarding clothes. In India options are fewer and there is less individual choice regarding clothing. Both UK transvestites and hijras wear what can loosely be designated as 'women's clothes', but there are differences which mainly stem from their different position in each society. Hijras wear either a sari or salwar kameez and occasionally, a form of Rajasthani women's dress consisting of a *ghagra* (long skirt), *choli* (short, tailored, tight-fitting blouse) and *odhni* (a kind of half-sari which is tucked into the waistband of the skirt and taken over the shoulders and head), although this latter is much less common. Many of the hijras' clothes are given to them in return for performing and, when choosing over the lengths of silk and woollen shawls, the items most prone to be fought over are those in attractive and (usually) bright colours. They are less defined by concepts of 'fashion' or trendiness but more interested in items which display wealth – and they particularly dislike 'traditional' (old-fashioned, rural), 'villager-like' items, since the move to the city is still seen as a move up the social ladder.

Rajput women in Rajasthan may also wear a version of a *ghagra* with a longer, tunic top and slits in the sides (*janpar*) to enable the *odhni* to be tucked in – but I have never encountered a hijra dressed in this costume. In Rajasthan these more or less form the entirety of female clothing choices, although clearly, throughout India, there are many regional variations in dress and therefore options. There are now some girls who wear jeans and T-shirts, but they are still fairly rare, expecially outside the large cities and they seldom continue in this dress after marriage.

Men in India, on the other hand, have a greater range of clothing choices, since they have the possibility of either Western dress – adopted by most men in cities, especially in the middle class, educated sector – or of the traditional *kurta* (long shirt) and *lungi* or *dhoti* (cloth wrapped around the torso and legs), usually accompanied by a turban. In practice, traditional dress still tends to be worn by low income or low caste men, or those from a village, but it is also often the choice of middle and upper class men for formal or religious occasions, or conversely for relaxing at home.

In Britain, the question 'what are the gender-based dress codes?' is clearly a troublesome and complex one. So many styles and forms are possible that an outline can only cover the basics. For most men, dress still tends to be some variation of trousers, shirt, pullover, possibly a tie, fitted jacket and/or coat, almost always in dark or muted colours, possibly a cardigan (although these might still be shunned by the most fashion-conscious) and, mainly in an informal situation, a T-shirt or sweatshirt. For women, the answer could be 'just about anything'; any of the above range of mens' wear, although possibly styled slightly differently, and an enormous range of other items, primarily including skirts and dresses, from very short to very long and in widely divergent styles; jackets and cardigans, which may be skimpy, tight, or very loose and unstructured, and many more, including a huge range of accessories – bags, hair adornments, jewellery, belts, and so on.[2]

Miller states that he has 'a rather uneasy feeling that we live in a world that has gone beyond our capacities of ordering' and certainly the women's fashion arena seems to substantiate this. (1994; 396) The choices for a transvestite in the UK are therefore correspondingly abundant. In addition to the choices of normal, everyday wear, they may have a particular predilection for wedding dresses, ball-gowns or formal but feminine suits, often in pastel shades (the kind of thing described as 'mother-of-the-bride' wear) – or for very slinky, sensuous dresses such as the ones Gavin/Gina prefers which are generally worn to a club or party. These are all forms of women's wear but do not generally form the staple of most women's wardrobes, especially the wedding dress/ball-gown items. On the other hand, the transvestites who prefer such items seem to be in a minority. For most, their choices revolve around the type of clothing which most women would wear, most days, even to John/Joy's preference for women's jogging bottoms and a T-shirt top; there are sufficient subtle differences to make it worthwhile and meaningful for him.

Broadly, although there are inevitably exceptions to this, UK transvestites do appear to adopt the kind of clothing that, had they been born female, they would prefer, given their social circumstances, lifestyle and income, occupation and background. One of these exceptions which does demonstrate another clear difference between the British situation and the Indian, however, is that some UK transvestites hanker after a particular type of clothing which is redolent of another era. One example is the 'male-femaler' interviewed by Ekins and quoted in Chapter 3, who idolises 1950s and 1960s 'glamour wear' and says that 'Women appeared more fragile and feminine in neat little suits, dramatically simple cocktail dresses and devastating evening gowns.' (1997: 90) This sentiment is echoed by some (though not many) of my questionnaire respondents who have become entranced by a particular type of clothing style – especially one which reflects a period in which 'men were men and women were women'. This also suggests a nostalgia for and idealisation of, not only that period, but also what it represents – the security of sex and gender roles which were considerably more defined and where each sex understood its place in the cultural world. Such yearning after a time which has gone is unlikely to have a parallel for the hijras.

It is also worth noting that whereas women in Britain have free access to almost any item of male clothing, this could not be said to be true of India. Casual, Western style clothing is still shunned by most girls, though less so every year. Also, in India, in common with many post-colonial countries, there has developed a convention where most urban men wear a form of Western male clothing but the women have remained in traditional dress of one form or another. Established traditional dress for women in Rajasthan is usually the sari or *ghagra* and *odhni* but the fashion for the salwar kameez, imported from Northern and primarily Muslim areas, has now been embraced by a large proportion of women. One hijra commented to me when we were chatting, 'Oh, she is old, so she can only wear sari' – referring to a hijra of about fifty – because even the salwar kameez was seen as belonging to a different age and educational group. The salwar kameez was adopted mainly by college girls, but has now become much more widespread. I have only once seen a woman in Jaipur wearing Western female clothing (a summer dress) and I discovered that she had spent several years living in Britain. Even female shop assistants in places where Western style women's wear is sold do not choose to wear it.

For me, the preference for a salwar kameez is entirely understandable. I generally adopt this form of dress on arrival in India since it has many advantages – it is stylish, becoming, comfortable, works for a wide range of temperatures and one never has to worry about which top to wear with which bottom. It is noticeable, however, that it has not become popular in Britain amongst non-Asian women – despite high-profile fashion designers such as Jemima Khan trying to introduce it at the highest levels of fashionable UK society. I have no decisive answer to this, although there are aspects which suggest a possible parallel with transvestism. (For example, one possible reason is that it is more common to find any group 'upgrading' to the clothing of a group perceived as higher up the social hierarchy than 'downgrading' to copy the 'lower' group.)

Differences in Lifestyle

The hijras are different again from Western transvestites in terms of the many avenues available in Western cultures, perhaps precisely because there are so many possibilities. In general, the most obvious of these is that whilst a hijra makes a decision for life – both in terms of no going back and in terms of it forming the mode of living throughout the day – the UK transvestite may, allowing for other forms of external constraint such as work and family, dress for any amount of time in a month, for as long as they choose. In a secular context, the penalties for being a transvestite, particularly a 'regular', heterosexual transvestite, can be heavy, in particular, the fear of discovery – as Woodhouse observes:

> The younger transvestite may spend the week working as a man, using his leisure time for cross-dressing ... (rendering) the development of female features much more of a problem. While beard growth or bushy eyebrows will counteract a contrived feminine appearance ... plucked eyebrows, traces of make-up or nail varnish can act as dangerous betrayals contradicting both physical and social masculinity. (1989: 38)

On the plus side, the scale of options open to a British transvestite are infinitely greater, from the man who cross dresses for a few hours a month in the privacy of his own home, right through to the full-time transvestite who lives entirely as a woman, even if he has no modification or surgery. (See Appendix C regarding frequency.) The interviews with UK transvestites Suzanne, Joy, Shelly, Gina and Sandra demonstrate that even within this small number, there are significant differences between them, not only in terms of their clothing choices (Gina goes for glamour while Joy prefers casual tops and bottoms) but also in terms of when, where and how they dress. Because there has been no institutionalisation of the role, the potential for individual agency and alternatives are countless, as is the context. The hijras, on the other hand, have an established role – they make a choice once and must live with it; reasons for these widely differing constraints on personal individuality and freedom of self-expression will be discussed in the last chapter.

The compensation for not 'belonging' is greater freedom of movement between the possibilities, particularly in the charged sphere of gender and sexuality. The penalty is an absence of place, belonging or role. The Western transvestite who guiltily borrows his girlfriend's clothes may well experience emotions such as those described by Bland in the introduction: anxiety, shame and tension. It has been noted that in a secular context, 'drag queens' are far more likely to perceive cross-dressing as a 'fun' activity and I would suggest that the performance aspect, which involves a sturdy component of 'belonging' is a powerful part of that. In addition, a further difference between the two cultures is that the image of a 'transvestite' conjures, for most people in Western society, that of a very clearly cross-dressed male and this is reinforced by theatre, films and most forms of media reporting.[3] In Britain, this is something transvestites struggle against. In India, it is something which has few parallels, although the film *Mrs Doubtfire*, starring a cross-dressed Robin Williams as the father who wished to continue to see his children after separating from his wife and had to resort to dressing as a female nanny/housekeeper, was remade as a Bollywood movie – *Chachi Char Soh Bis* (Auntie 420) – at the end of the 1990s.

It might be suggested that hijras have more in common with transsexuals than with transvestites and certainly the surgery aspect of both groups would seem to indicate this. I would propose, however, that in the different stories of Shabana, Tara, Jaitun, Chand and Ramdhan, experiences and events emerge which suggest that in an English context, at least two – Tara and Ramdhan – would identify much more with Western transvestites and Tara would probably not have opted for a full hijra life if other choices had been available. Although she begged her parents to allow her to join the hijras, Tara wanted to be a woman mainly because she wished to express her feminine qualities and wanted to play with clothes and hair and so on. She might well have opted for transvestism rather than transsexuality.

Similarly, in the supplementary information given by Leila, the man who was kidnapped and felt 'quite womanly' but was clear that he did not want any operation, would almost certainly have stayed a transvestite (although this story is related by a third person and may therefore have received some variation in the telling.) With Ramdhan, the village transvestite, it is rather difficult to know, since I was prohibited from asking about whether he would consider becoming a hijra, but since he is heterosexual and seems very content to live his life as it is, provided he can dress in female attire and do women's work, it seems improbable that in a Western context he would opt for surgery.

Jaitun and Chand, because they are older, accept hijra life quite happily, but may partly be due to their age and the fact that hijras commanded considerably more respect and status when they joined the community. Shabana is in a different category again because she was born with certain indeterminate/intersexed features. In childhood, she looked sufficiently female, including genitally, to be brought up as a girl but her problems started as a teenager when facial hair began to make an appearance. During my meetings with her, it did strike me that in the UK she may well have been a candidate for medical intervention – and she seemed to me to be the most distressed about having to become a hijra – partly because, as she says, joining them was not her choice but her father's; he decided to ask the hijras to take her (primarily because he was worried that his prestige would be affected by having such an effeminate son).

It could be suggested that hijras share common features with drag artistes – and certainly they do earn money from performance which relates to their male-to-female status and, to a certain extent, they share some of the rather crude and outré mannerisms and vocabulary which professedly accompany this life, although the hijras' is still different in several ways. Drag artistes play much more on the 'camp' aspects of their lives; they emphasise their homosexuality and dramatised 'glamour' to give distinctiveness and colour to their performance – and very well known artistes, Lily Savage for example, seem to have a predilection for heavy sexual innuendo. The hijras' version of this is much more concerned with the humour around sex within marriage which produces children.[4] Both hijras and drag queens are also usually associated with male-to-male sexuality – and both behave like men in many ways, in strong contrast to the UK transvestites, who act and dress as men when in their male role but modulate their voice, change their walk, cease swearing and acting in any kind of manly manner when in female mode in their attempt to become as distinctly feminine as possible. There are, however, some significant differences between hijras and drag artistes and the most obvious is that at the end of the day, drag queens take off their make-up and wigs and their feminine clothing when they go home. For them it is a performance, whilst for the hijras, it is their full-time life.

The hijras, although they do 'perform', for example at births and weddings, are not only performers; they retain their make-up and female clothing for all activities. But, because of the niche created for them in Indian society, they do belong. The lone transvestite, on the other hand, is not performing for someone else but from his own preference (although the compulsive element described by Bland and also several of my interviewees and questionnaire respondents suggests that the motivation is not simple enjoyment). By doing so, he places himself both as an outsider and as a trickster and these, I suggest, provide potential clues as to why the spectacle of transvestism arouses such anger and hatred in Western cultures. They are breaking the rule which states that one must be identifiable; as Barnes and Eicher state: 'What is crucial is that the message communicated is understood by both the wearer and viewer.' The hijras communicate their difference from men or women by belonging to a separate and readily identifiable group – they take care that this is so and thus have no 'secret' – whereas for those English transvestites who choose to go out dressed, the aim is to 'pass', i.e. to deceive as convincingly as possible, through mannerisms and behaviour, which are more difficult to enact convincingly, and also through clothing which is the crucial appearance clue to the onlooker.

Some transvestites I met in the UK at social evenings spoke wistfully about transvestites in other cultures being able to dress without social censure – but when I returned from the Indian fieldwork, I did discuss the reality of hijras' lives with some of my UK interviewees and, not surprisingly, none could imagine wishing to join a hijra community. The 'operation' in particular filled them with horror; the rough manner of the incision itself (with no anaesthetic), followed by the bleakness of a castrated life appalled them. Most also commented on the restrictiveness of a hijra's world, the renunciation of lives they had known, not just the break with friends and family – which some UK transvestites who decide to go 'full-time' also experience – but the break with regular working life, the loss of friends one has made, albeit that they are replaced with a ready-made 'family-community', and the general abandonment of all that seems normal in life. The commitment to hijra life is undoubtedly a significant and life-changing one in ways that transvestism in the UK, whatever the distress it causes, need never be.

We might also still question why these two very different situations obtain within the two cultures. Nanda's comment that 'the widespread association of the powers of asceticism with self-castration in Hindu mythology, particularly associated with Siva' (1990: 31) seems clearly related to the fact that such a life does not, arguably could not, exist in a Western context. Most studies of transvestism in the west are from a medico-psychological base – as studies of individual deviancy – doubtless because we live in a culture framed by Western, modernist ideologies with a predominant creed of individualism. When viewed from the cultural perspective, transvestism offers a somewhat different contrast of the position of the hijras with that of the transvestites in Britain.

The fieldwork here suggests that in India, traditional understanding in the area of cross-gendering is heavily influenced by Hinduism and the cultural understanding associated with it which pervades Indian life. Hijras have an understanding of what it is to be a hijra and can account in this way for their own internal history. This may be increasingly divergent from the way that broader Indian society views them because the space which has traditionally existed is being eroded as Indian society becomes more Western, 'modern' and secular but this in turn lends weight to my earlier observation that belief systems are a crucial part of the underlying structures which shape the sex, gender and sexuality discourses in each society. British transvestites, by contrast, exist within a society where the locus is more individualistic, which has developed a profound belief in the concept of a single, integrated persona, which perceives sex and gender in binary terms, and which has few female or gender-exchange religious archetypes. Unsurprisingly, then, there are no real third gender possibilities and thus it is very difficult for a transvestite or transgender 'group' to exist in any substantive way. What is also interesting and valuable here is what we are about to explore: the symbolic and social structuring of gender.

Transvestism within Contrasting Cosmological Contexts

There is an enormous contrast between the ways that Western and non-Western societies view matters of sex and gender and sexuality. One of the reasons *why* sex and gender are so powerful as systems of control is that they are considered so normal and natural that they are rarely opened up to be questioned in a radical fashion. They are also ideas which have become reified over centuries. Academic discourses on sex and gender have tended to concentrate on the economic, political and social worlds of cultures leading (with some exceptions) to a rather underdeveloped area of study and analysis of the imaginative and spiritual worlds – the religious, mythological and cultural roots – which underlie the more obvious struc-tures of the societies being studied.

Attitudes to transvestism cannot be divorced from attitudes towards sexuality in general. Cross-cultural and comparative understanding of this factor in the study of opinions on transvestism might usefully be seen from the perspective of the question: 'Within this culture, is sexuality pleasing to God/the Gods?' The answer is naturally not a straightforward one; whilst there are areas and cultures within the Judaeo-Christian tradition in which sexuality is not regarded with divine disfavour, the Protestant and Calvinist traditions of Europe and the migration of this dogma to the Americas have generated a view of sexuality which mostly ranges from ambiguity through to contempt.

Whatever the religious context of a culture, or the restrictions imposed, sexuality is not one of the components of life which can be swept under a doctrinal carpet, which will 'go away' if ignored for long enough. Transvestism has often been viewed as one of a group of deviant behav-iours; something which gives even greater grounds for societal consterna-tion than irregular sexuality. Its association with homosexuality, even if inaccurate, also raises fears and taboos. As social roles change in late twen-tieth century Britain, male transvestism is perhaps more extensively talked about, but it is still mostly regarded with ridicule or distaste.

The strength of feeling on these matters mirrors a culture in which the binary division of sex is seen as entirely natural and reflects a view which can be traced back to the Bible, in which views of gender are binary in nature from the outset. As Genesis 1:27 states, 'male and female he created them'. The Bible also emphasises the need to maintain clear gender boundaries, one of the most obvious being that of the animals going two by two into the ark. In addition there has been the key influence on Western cultures of the classical philosophical tradition, which for so many centuries formed the centrepiece and frame of reference of thought and culture for the educated and powerful ranks of society.

Plato wrote much on the significant differences between male and female. His concept was in many ways unusually broad-minded regarding sex and gender, but he could still only conceptualise two-ness. Since Greek and Roman thought has been particularly influential in the development of Western thought, it is hardly surprising that we have inherited very strictly delineated notions of binarism with regard to gender, sex and sexuality. The brain may be limitless in its scope but our concepts made manifest in language do not permit much outward transgression from the binary rule. However, Plato's writings on the superiority of the soul over the body offer insights which can also be seen as challenging this binary divide. At first this may seem surprising, as he primarily identified men as having more developed souls and caring less for the life of the body; most women were categorised as inferior to men because of their foolish preoccupation with the body. He did not insist, though, on women having female and therefore inferior souls since he allowed for the possibility of an 'atypical philoso-pher-ruler' type of female with a female body but a male soul, and for an opposite which he typified as a cowardly soldier – a male with a man's body but a female soul. Ambiguity is neither ruled out nor ignored but the possibility is acknowledged of individuals whose bodies do not match with their souls. Halperin's study of Plato's *Symposium* (1990), for example, provides important insights not only into the ways in which the masculine and feminine have been subject to separation and division in Western soci-eties but also into the devaluation of the feminine so clearly reflected in the discrepancy between tolerance for women adopting male clothing and behaviours and men adopting women's.

Women's lack of control in Western societies arguably connects directly to their lack of presence – and is echoed by a notable absence of female symbolism in cosmology, particularly within the protestant tradi-tions of northern Europe and North America. Robert Graves stated this most clearly – albeit rather dogmatically – in his argument that the early Christians adopted notions from Judaism, 'hitherto unknown in the West, which have become the prime causes of our unrest: that of a patri-archal God, who refuses to have any truck with Goddesses and claims to be self-sufficient and all-wise.' (Graves, 1961: 475) Perhaps a significant part of the underlying difficulties of Western societies to allow for and accept transvestism, the crossing of the binary divide, and the resulting lack of a range of possibilities, derives from the deficit of potent female figures.

There are miserly few examples of gender-abrogating possibilities in Biblical texts, mythology or folklore. God is a very rigidly defined masculine, patriarchal figure – He is part of a Trinity which contains a male Holy Ghost and a Son. His prophets, teachers and priests are almost entirely men; even the angels are male.[5] In Roman Catholic regions, the Blessed Virgin Mary and some female saints have retained a position of influence and potency, but in Protestant terrain even these are largely absent. This has a double effect for transvestism. First, men are considered deviant for wishing to 'downgrade' themselves by dressing in the clothes of women – as Woodhouse states, 'why should a man want to appear as a woman? Why should he wish to masquerade as a member of the second sex, a group dominated and oppressed by men?' (1989:xi) And indeed, Kate Bornstein, author of *Gender Outlaw* and recipient of gender re-assignment surgery says in one interview: 'After surgery I found out what being a woman meant and I thought "*Uh*, I don't want to be one of those".' (Bornstein, 1999)

Second, I would suggest, transvestites are deprecated because there are no core female figures in cosmology, little or no female conceptualisation of divinity, no remaining tradition of priests dressing as women (unless one considers that, as Leach suggests, and particularly in the higher echelons of Roman Catholicism, Christian priests do dress in garments generally viewed as the preserve of women),[6] there is therefore no divine or mythologically accepted context for men to cross-dress. The Judaeo-Christian tradition certainly seems either never to have had any iconographic or mythological structure referring to the position of the transvestite, or to have lost it completely. Although Judaism and Christianity are both clearly male-dominated, they are also both relatively asexual and consequently the use or power of gendered symbolism is largely absent. This contrasts sharply with a religion like Hinduism in which sexuality is clearly present and generally positive.

Within the classical tradition in Western societies, transvestism certainly has long roots being clearly traceable to the Graeco-Roman era, where there are well documented examples from mythology, art and sculpture. In mythology, however, there are very few references to broken or disconnected gender boundaries, one of the only examples being Tiresias, the male seer who became a woman for part of his life.[7] Indeed, of the pantheon of Greek and Roman gods, although there are female deities, they are generally of reduced power and it would be difficult to find an equivalent of Siva Aardhanerisvara. Zeus/Jove can turn himself into a swan, a boar, a horse – but not a woman – and Poseidon/Neptune, Pluto/Hades, Saturn/Chronos do not choose to do this either.[8] Nor do they include any kind of third gender; Mercury/Hermes can be linked to images of androgyny – and to Hermaphroditus – but the implications here would seem to be asexual and androgynous rather than an image of conjoining, of wholeness or divine sexual union as found in India and also in a number of other cultures.

In contrast to the absence of the feminine at the Classical roots of western cultures, and the lack of sustenance for transvestites in the Judaeo-Christian tradition, Indian mythology and folk tales are rich with stories of gods who become goddesses (or women) narrating tales of, amongst others, effeminate male gods (Arjuna), powerful, aggressive female goddesses (Kali), half male-half female (Siva/Parvati) and folk tales of the hijras themselves. Siva is acknowledged to be the lord of antithetical qualities:

> Siva is the reconciliation of all opposites: therefore he is both creator and destroyer, terrible and mild, evil and good, male and female, eternal rest and ceaseless activity. His consort really only part of himself – his sakti, the 'power' by which he creates, sustains and destroys. In the so-called Sakta cults which worship the female Sakti rather than the male Siva who, being ever immersed in a Yogic trance, is deaf to the prayers of men, Siva's consort is worshipped to the exclusion of Siva himself. Usually she is represented not as the mild Uma or Parvati but as the dreadful Durga or Kali who, with lolling tongue, drinks blood out of a human skull and who, to this day rejoices in the bloody sacrifices of goats at her great temple in Calcutta. In the full figure of Siva, however, the male and female principles are united and he himself is said to be half man and half woman. (Zaehner; 1962: 85)

The important religious role of transvestism in Hindu mythology, and the union of the male with the female (to ensure harmony and fertility) is also illustrated by Marglin's study of rituals in Puri, Orissa (eastern India). Marglin points out that the images of Indian women as impure and subordinated which generally prevail do not exhaust the cultural landscape. Female potence is allied to *Sakti*, the principle of the female power of life, and is primarily control over food, household and thus life maintenance. These are reflected in the ritual, *Candan Jatra*, which she describes and which revolves around 'the auspicious nature of female sexuality, its power to ensure the fertility of the land (which) is imitated by certain males who offer their masculinity to a goddess and identify with her and with her powers of renewal'. (1985: 53) The ritual clearly illustrates the significance of the precepts of Hindu belief and mythology. It clarifies, for example, how it is that in Hindu belief, hijras are linked with the quality of auspicious eroticism which does not stem from women or men but from the sacrifice of masculinity; further, it illuminates the connection between female sexuality versus male asceticism and the fertilising nourishment of the monsoon rains contrasted with the preceding aridity of the land. It also includes, as part of the ceremony, boys dressed as women.

The implications for hijras as bringers of divine union to human situations are various and, whether born with unusual genitalia or self-castrated, are part of a tradition which symbolises divine union through being both male and female and through the act of parting with whatever genitalia they have in order to achieve another level of both maleness and femaleness. In the Vedas and other Hindu texts and tales, there are multi-layered stories of the transfer of male to female and female to male, each enhancing the powers of the other. As O'Flaherty observes, 'many of the transformations in these myths [in the *Devibhagavata Purana*] involve the transfer of power from one sex to the other.' (1980: 129)

It is partly because of this union of male and female, the 'divine union', aspect of their being, which obtains in many forms throughout India, that hijras have traditionally been granted a place which attracted respect as well as ridicule. In addition, Hinduism recognises that dual-sex-ism is clearly not a condition which one could have chosen – and it is one which has religious connotations, being of the aspects of Siva. Thus, by being out of the ordinary in terms of anatomy, hijras may claim a clear association with the divine ordering of the world – and a legitimacy, particularly with regard to ritual, which is derived from Hindu cosmology. The implications of sacred status for those men who willingly sacrifice their masculinity are clear – and a significant contributory factor to the position of respect and acknowledgement of divine gifts which the hijras traditionally receive. The presence of culturally supportive symbols such as those found in Hindu texts, folk tales and also rituals such as Candan Jatra enhance the 'mythic' quality of the sexually impotent but empowered group which is the hijras. In addition, hijras (together with, for example, the cross-dressed shamans of Siberia and Native America) are found within societies which have a cosmological system in which the major deity(ies) are conceptualised as either female and male – or neither male nor female – or having components of both. And by being neither-man-nor-woman (or both man and woman), it is possible for hijras to be perceived and categorised as having a special place which is closer to the 'Creator' or 'God', who is, in essence both and neither. The next chapter will discuss concepts of duality and of crossing the sex and gender binary divide around a wider cultural compass.

Notes

1. As mentioned in Chapter 4, the advent of the web is likely to provide some interesting developments since, arguably, it functions as a type of 'virtual community' thus enabling the creation of a group or tribe, together with facilities of support, communication and a sense of shared history and (possibly appropriated) mythology.

2. While I was living in India, I had access through cable television to the Western fashion channels and was stunned by the range of items available – from bits of macramé tied up with leather thongs to something that looked like a bin-bag with a colossal unwieldy belt; tops that revealed more than they concealed in slinky, see-through, gossamer fabrics to tops that looked as if part of their construction might be cardboard; skirts of absolutely any length and impossibly tight or ballooningly huge. It is accepted that most of these would not actually be worn by most women, especially not for their everyday tasks, but it is, nevertheless indicative of the tremendous range available – and that there are very few items which would really be hopelessly beyond the pale.

3. Probably the most memorable transvestite performances are now those on film. Tony Curtis and Jack Lemmon struggling down a station platform in high heels for the first time in *Some Like It Hot* remains a classic amongst humorous portraits of transvestites, and more recently, Dustin Hoffman in *Tootsie* is described by Garber as 'of all the cross-dressing films of the eighties, (the one) that most captured the popular imagination.' (1992: 5) Both are part of the visual image of transvestites of many people, not only in America but Britain and Europe; and both have leading role transvestites whose heterosexuality is made very plain.

4. For example Nanda describes a routine which I have also witnessed, in which a hijra, performing at the home of a new-born baby, parodies the process the new mother has just been through with a cushion under her sari to represent the pregnant belly. She acts out the progress of the pregnancy from conception to birth, evoking the activities with considerable humour and a great deal of waddling – and causing much mirth from the onlookers as she mimes and sings about the process. (1990: 2–3)

5. Theological orthodoxy may suggest that angels are sexless, but certainly the words in Greek (*angelos*) and Latin (*angelus*) from which the English word is derived are both male-gendered and in art, angels are usually depicted as male.

6. Briffault, like Frazer, gives numerous examples of the tradition of priests dressing in female attire and comments that 'it is the general custom of the Roman clergy to be clean-shaven and they are commonly referred to on the continent as 'the third sex'.' (Vol. II, 532)

7. There are other examples – indeed Ramet contends that there are many – and gives examples (in a footnote) of Kaineus, apparently 'transformed from male to female' and of Atalanta, 'reincarnated as a male athlete'. (1996; 16; fn.3) I would take issue with Ramet, however, that Kaineus is scarcely known and certainly cannot claim to be a central figure of classical mythology (I searched for any

acknowledgement of him in some dozen classical mythology reference texts and could find nothing about him at all), whilst Atalanta, although better known, has a reputation mainly as a huntress and an athlete. Ovid variously praises her as surpassing all men for her fleetness of foot and her beauty (1955; 240) and as 'the girl warrior from Tegea, the pride of the Lycaean grove' (187) but I could find no mention in Ovid or any other text of her reincarnation as a male athlete.

8. Ramet again states that many examples of gender reversal are to be found on Olympus, but then, as her examples, can only uncover two – and these hardly of gender reversal; the first is of Zeus becoming a bull on at least one occasion, and the second, the occasional designation of Artemis as 'bear goddess'. (1996; 4)

6

Dressing Up/Dressing Down: Reconsidering Sex and Gender Culture

Is transvestism a sex move or a gender move? – while I was doing fieldwork both in Britain and in India, I kept returning to this question. In the case of both the hijras and the British transvestites, it became very apparent that when they dress as women they feel like women. One could say that most transvestites in Britain are men who wish to explore what it is to be a woman, whilst hijras are men who live as women. But what are the wider implications for current thinking on sex and gender?

Some organisations, like the Evangelical Alliance (a British Christian organisation), have a very clear perspective on these matters. Their recent booklet, *Transsexuality*, states that 'transvestites have a compulsion to dress and act like members of the opposite sex, often to obtain sexual arousal'. (2000: 6) Their perspective, that transvestism is an 'erotic compulsion' (ibid.), echoes the common perception in Western societies that transvestism is mainly about sexuality whether carried out by those of homosexual or heterosexual orientation. But in the West over the last century by far the most common approach found in written material on transvestism is from a medical and psychological/psychiatric perspective which sees cross-dressing as a form of deviance. Woodhouse observes that the treatment of children for 'cross-gender identification' shows up very clearly Western cultural notions of how important it is for men to achieve masculinity, since cross-gender identification is determined to be of much greater concern (and thus in need of medical/psychological intervention) for boys than for girls.

The development of psychological models have typically focused on particular attitudes and behaviours of the transvestite's family, for example distant/unemotional fathers and envious mothers, and the creation of patterns for which cross-dressing is one end result. (See, for example, Hogan-Finlay, 1996:14) My own research, based on transvestites' interviews and questionnaire responses cannot really be said to verify this. For example, whilst it may be true of some transvestites that their mother was a much stronger figure in their lives than their father, it is certainly not true of all, nor even enough to base a theory on, although since this was not the primary focus of my research I shall not be proposing any theories of my own along these lines.

George Rekers, Professor of Neuropsychiatry & Behavioral Science, Research Director for Child & Adolescent Psychiatry, Chairman of Faculty in Psychology at the University of South Carolina School of Medicine in Columbia, and author of several books and journal articles on this subject, presented numerous papers on Gender Disorders through the 1980s and 1990s, including one to the North American Social Science Network in 1995.[1] Although it is not possible to quote at length from this here, it does make interesting reading, firstly because it is both typical of the work in this field (which does not appear to have changed significantly in the intervening decades) and, secondly, because it is a clear account of medical thinking in the area of transvestism and gender mimicry – in particular, the desire of boys to dress as and behave as girls. This would seem to be considerably more worrying to the medical establishment than the desire of girls to act as or dress as boys – something echoed by the general responses in Western society to transvestism.

Rekers suggests that one major factor contributing to juvenile gender behaviour disorders is the rise of families and other 'alternative' types of households 'of various combinations of unmarried adults' where the father is largely absent – and the subsequent attempts of society in the Uunited States to normalise this (through, for example, changes in television programmes and the revision of books which deal with such subjects). In the meantime, he asserts, research material has been growing which suggests that an absence of father has detrimental effects on the socialisation of children and that 'clinical and research data accumulated to a sufficient degree to enable the mental health professions to officially identify a newly recognised form of psychopathology – Gender Identity Disorder of Childhood.' (American Psychiatric Association, 1986). (The quotes which follow are also taken from this paper.) Rekers seems unaware of material (from ethnography, for example) which would suggest that cross-gender behaviour has existed throughout history and culture, but rather identifies the problem as one of modern society, clearly believing that the pendulum has swung too far in 'eliminating all distinctions based on sex', and advocating a return to 'normal' families.

He illustrates his point with a case history which bears a considerable resemblance to the stories of transvestites from my fieldwork in the UK which appear in Chapter 3. This is perhaps not surprising since the men I interviewed or who responded with a questionnaire have grown up in a culture comparable to that of America. It also, however, bears a striking similarity to the story of Ramdhan, in Chapter 4, a sixteen-year-old boy from a remote Indian village where culturally, socially, psychologically, very little is similar to an American childhood. His research subject, an eight-year-old boy named Carl, chose to imitate girlish behaviour to a very great extent both in his voice and his appearance, and showed a pronounced preference for female items of clothing, cosmetics, hairstyle and games. He encountered problems at school from various forms of ridicule, being labelled a 'sissy fag' by his classmates, and these resulted in considerable isolation and depression. He had been assessed as 'normal prepubertal male with a normal 46XY male karyotype', leading Rekers to identify his behaviour as psychological and the 'potentially more serious disorder of Cross Gender Identification' (as opposed to 'Gender Role Behaviour Disturbance' which a boy might well grow out of). Rekers's case history conveys a number of important points. First, of course, it is a clear demonstration that (outside the context of performances such as in the stereotypical rugby club dinner) men who model themselves on women in any way are perceived as adverse and unacceptable. But through its discussion of the 'process of normal sex role socialisation', it also reveals some of both the process of socialisation and its purpose, uncovering as it goes some of the formulae of gender formation. More than that, it demonstrates how, in practice if not in theory, some parts of the medical professions acknowledge the gender as opposed to sexual components of transvestism.

The description of Carl, a boy who has rejected masculinity, both reveals and conceals – it describes his behaviour patterns but says little about his motivations and emotions, an absence echoed in much anthropological work on sex and gender issues. Transvestism also shows up the oddity of gender reversal in the context of the knowing male, choosing to be female. If men's activities are accorded higher status while female spheres of activity are devalued (as they appear to be, to varying extents, in all societies we know of) why would some men choose to devalue themselves by dressing as women? It seems clear that the *feelings* of transvestites, particularly about issues of masculinity and femininity, are of paramount importance in understanding a transvestism, and that this has important consequences for an anthropological treatment of this subject. By exploring the passion of a proportion of individuals to dress as (and sometimes live as) the sex opposite to their own biological gender, we enter the debate over the universality of human emotions and desires and their place in propelling human agency and action. These are interestingly illustrated by the concepts of two very commonplace words in the English language, 'hard' and 'soft'.

Woman = Soft, Man = Hard: Concepts of Language made Material

My interest in this was aroused because the words 'soft' and 'softness' cropped up so often in the questionnaires and in interviews that I realised they warranted some deeper exploration and thought. What I began to recognise was that the contrast between these two words shows up very clearly the conceptualisations which take place behind the words themselves and their accepted meanings. The UK transvestites make it very plain that for them, cross dressing is, to varying degrees, about expressing their desire to explore the (perceived) gender attributes of women. For them, the female behaviours they would express may well include 'softness', 'gentleness', 'vulnerability', 'passivity', 'elegance', 'sensitivity', 'tenderness', 'intimacy' and a whole host more – all adjectives cited from the responses in questionnaires. (See Appendix D.) As stated in one of my questionnaire replies:

> 'It is, to me, the appeal of the characteristics that society allows only a woman to display. There would be, for example, the attributes of gentleness, thoughtfulness, insight and creativity, in fact all the attributes that are classically associated with the role of a woman in society. These are the same attributes that, if displayed openly by a man, would be frowned upon.'
>
> QR22, q23

These adjectives and their implications in terms of the differences between men and women suggest an image of woman as a being with greater sensitivity, awareness (particularly of herself as a physical being) and 'mystique', and are held particularly by people from societies with a cultural view that ornamentation and desire for physical and inner beauty are the especial domain of women. Men in these societies, including most Western societies, would appear to have inherited and absorbed the perception that preoccupation with adornment is not for them and that analysis, reason, the life of the mind, physical labour and technological domination are where they fit into the world.

The example of *softness* is particularly revealing. Concepts of 'hard' or 'rough' and 'soft' or 'yielding' run through the English language and most native English speakers would have no trouble in identifying situations, individuals or objects to which each was applicable or appropriate. To be, for a moment, methodically stereotypical, a 'hard' man conjures an image of a 'bloke', probably in leathers or jeans with a short and possibly spiky haircut (or a 'hard' helmet) and heavy, unyielding boots; his speech is rough rather than gentle and if he does much more than utter monosyllables, his conversation is likely to contain plenty of 'hard' talking.

In another context, the 'hard' man of the business world is fairly ruthless and 'hard'-hitting, tough and uncompromising, 'hard'-working, 'hard'-headed and intractable, possibly 'hard'-fisted and ungenerous. He may have become rather 'hard'-boiled and inflexible from his background of a 'hard' childhood. The *OED* defines 'hard' as 'firm, unyielding to pressure, solid, not easily cut, reliable, highly penetrating', and goes on to give 67 further idiomatic uses and phrasal verbs, most of which imply toughness and severity, such as 'hard-sell (aggressive salesmanship)', and 'hard nut to crack (difficult problem, person or thing not easily understood or overcome or influenced)'.

Most of these would be easily identified culturally (in a Western context at least) as typically male traits – or at least more desirable or easily forgivable in a man. A woman incurring the 'hard' label might perhaps be described as 'hard'-bitten – an attribute which very few would aspire to and having none of the prowess implied by a male who is, like cinema hero Bruce Willis, a 'die-hard'. *Soft*, by contrast, with all its implications of mutability and yieldingness, is most definitely a trait most desirable in a stereotypical woman in this culture, despite our now being a century on from the end of the Victorian era. (In *The Fine Art of Gentling*, W. Chadwick draws a parallel between desirable qualities in women and horses in Victorian England:

> The scientific language that in the nineteenth century positioned the horse in a new relationship to man's control bears an uncanny similarity to the language which constructed gender around the ideology of 'separate spheres' ... Thus Thomas Pennant in *British Zoology* (1812) explains that the horse 'is endowed with every quality that can make it subservient to the uses of mankind, including courage, docility, patience, perseverance, strength, benevolent disposition and a certain consciousness of the services we can render them'. The ideal middle class woman, we are assured over and over again, should be docile, patient, persevering, benevolent, etc.) (in: Adler and Pointon: 1993: 96–7)

Interestingly, 'soft' is defined by the *OED* first of all by what it is not: '1. Comparatively lacking in hardness, yielding to pressure, malleable, plastic, easily cut' (or penetrated) 2. Having smooth surface or fine texture, not rough or coarse (soft skin, hair, raiment) 3. Mellow, mild, balmy ...' and goes on to give 38 further definitions, only about half of which have a second word added, such as 'soft-drink' (non-alcoholic and by implication, not a 'real' drink), 'soft-headed' ('idiotic') and 'soft-spot' ('sentimental affection for'). The others are further meanings simply derived from the word 'soft' such as 'flabby, feeble, effeminate, silly, sympathetic, compassionate, not sharply defined or strident, gentle, quiet or amorous.' (After I had conceived and written this section, I discovered, perhaps unsurprisingly, that this, too, had first been thought of by the Greeks – and is probably from where our notions derive. Winkler notes that Aristotle equates softness with femaleness and hardness with maleness, in particular with reference to the masculinity of the Hoplite (heavily armed foot soldier); *malakos* (softness) was equated with weakness and cowardice.) (Halperin et al, 1990: 182–3) And even more than in daily life, the necessity for hardness and softness in different – and sexed – bodies is crudely obvious when referring to sexual intercourse.

It is interesting, then, that of all the adjectives used by transvestites to define both the qualities of femaleness to which they aspire *and* the clothing which they most like to wear, 'soft' or 'softness' recur by far the most often. The soft and silky blouses or stockings which they want to feel against their skin are the material embodiment of the cultural values they would appropriate and the tractable female world they desire to belong to. The clothing becomes the personality and is reflected back in it. The example of *softness* thus demonstrates how transvestites' feelings about masculinity and femininity are translated into their actions and embodied into items of material culture. Given the significance of clothing as the artefact closest to our bodies, transvestism thus informs our understanding of the social construction of the body. Theories of body and dress have tended to consist of two different strands of explanation. Firstly, the body can be seen as representing something beyond itself, in the sense that cultural values are imposed on it – it is socially formed (and deformed). Secondly, each individual body can represent coded social meanings, so that the body is an object of formation. Transvestism however links ideas of social constructionism to perceivable reality through clothing and embodiment – transvestites are the embodiment both of the material culture items they wear and of the cultural values which obsess them and yet are forbidden.

For many transvestites, the process of dressing in clothes which signify and embody the outer qualities which they wish to manifest (soft, yielding, silky, smooth, elegant, tasteful, and so on) is a fundamental part of the act of becoming these things. This may, as is clear from the interviews with

Dan/Shelly and Gina/Gavin, make them feel as if they have an entirely separate female personality – or it may make them feel 'whole'. As Pauline states in her questionnaire, 'dressing allows me to experience those things that I cannot allow into my male self. I am now a whole person, not a half one ... there are two of me but they make a harmonious whole'. (QR63, q18/20) In addition, because they have 'become women' they feel they are able to be valued for these qualities rather than despised.

Gendered Emotions and the Ceremony of Naven

Gregory Bateson's work on the Naven ceremony, performed by the Iatmul and the Kwoma, living in the Sepik River Area of Papua people of New Guinea (1958) furnishes a valuable insight into the importance of the gendering of emotional responses though a specific and ritualised form of cross-dressing practice. The primary purpose of the ceremony is, in his view, to conjure a fit between the expression of inner emotion and outward appearance. The ritual involves ceremonial use of transvestism; both men and women dress in clothing worn by the opposite sex on occasions which demand emotions generally attributed to the other sex. Bateson describes the full ceremony as follows:

> The outstanding feature of the ceremonies is the dressing of men in women's clothes and of women in the clothes of men. The classificatory wau[2] dresses himself in the most filthy of widow's weeds, and when so arrayed he is referred to as nyame ('mother') ... Considerable ingenuity went into this costuming and all of it was directed towards creating an effect of utter decrepitude ... bellies ... bound with string like pregnant women. In their noses, they wore, suspended in place of the little triangles of mother of pearl shell which women wear on festive occasions, large triangular lumps of old sago pancakes.(1958: 12)

When the cross-dressing is female to male, the scenario is very different as the participants clothe themselves in the most resplendent apparel they can find rather than the most unkempt. In a ceremony witnessed by Bateson which celebrated children working their first sago,

> only female relatives performed and their costume was in sharp contrast to that of the *waus* described above ... The majority of women, when they put on the garments of men, wear the very smartest of male attire ... borrowing the very best of feather head-dresses and homicidal ornaments from their menfolk ... Their faces were painted white with sulphur, as is the privilege of homicides ... Their costume was very becoming to the women and was admired by the men.

In it, the women were very proud of themselves. They walked about flaunting their feathers and grating their limesticks in the boxes, producing the loud sound which men use to express anger, pride assertiveness. Indeed, so great was their pleasure in this particular detail of male behaviour that the husband of one of them, when I met him on the day following the performance, complained sorrowfully that his wife had worn away all the serrations on his lime stick so that it would no longer make a sound. (14–15)

In the case of a major Naven, great preparations will be involved, but a Naven may also be much simpler and include simple gender-reversed gestures or actions. Gender differences are also expressed and expected in other ways than clothes and actions, in particular, behaviour, described by Bateson as the *ethos* and *eidos* of Iatmul culture. Men are expected to be proud, dramatic, noisy, arrogant and ostentatious, whilst women are expected to be quiet, shy, retiring, co-operative and nurturing;

The most important generalisation which can be drawn from the study of Iatmul ethos is that in this society each sex has its own *consistent* ethos which contrasts with that of the opposite sex. Among the men … there is the same emphasis and value set upon pride, self-assertion, harshness and spectacular display. This … tendency to histrionic behaviour continually diverts the harshness into irony, which in its turn degenerates into buffooning. But although the behaviour may vary, the underlying emotional pattern is uniform. Among the women … attitudes are informed, not by pride, but rather by a sense of 'reality'. They are readily co-operative, and their emotional reactions are not jerky and spectacular, but easy and 'natural'. (198).

From these gender-specific behaviour patterns, Bateson deduces that the transvestism which is such a feature of the Naven ceremony can be attributed to the emotional requirements of the situation: women, usually shy and inconspicuous, show their pride in a public demonstration, and because this type of behaviour is unfamiliar to them they take on male dress attributes and cultural ornamentation. Men, on the other hand, are 'not accustomed to the free expression of vicarious personal emotion. Anger and scorn they can express with a good deal of over-compensation, and joy and sorrow they can express when it is their own pride which is enhanced or abased; but to express joy in the achievements of another is outside the norms of their behaviour.' (201) Both sexes are taking on a role which is unusual for their gender and the adoption of the opposite sex clothing aids them in the performance of the Naven ceremony. Their embarrassment, Bateson sees as a 'dynamic force … which in course of time has become a cultural norm.' (202)

For the Iatmul, the transvestism in the Naven ceremony is a custom or technique which allows men and women to function in a role which is anomalous for their gender by taking on the opposite gender personal characteristics through their clothing and decorations (and simultaneously stating through their appearance that they are carrying out a role which is strange to them.)[3] The point is that it supports the premise – if one agrees with Bateson's analysis – that what is happening is not only the reversal of gender-coded clothing but of gender-coded emotions and behaviours. Again, as with the *softness* example cited earlier in relation to British transvestites, it is clear that clothes serve as an external symbol of emotions. There is also the issue of transvestites' *perceptions* of masculinity and femininity. If transvestites are seeking to explore the (perceived) gender attributes of women, are they seeking to act like women, or to give expression to their own 'feminine' feelings? How does this differ from the masculine construction of femininity which appears, for example, on the Western stage?

Masculine Representation of the Feminine

The male construction of 'woman' has a long cultural history. In Shakespearian comedies, many parts require the transition of gender for a leading character for part or most of the play, while the 'principal boy' in the English pantomime tradition is traditionally played by a young woman. The crossing or blurring of boundaries is provocative and titillating, which may account for its exerting continuing fascination for the media. The ancient Greeks used transvestism in drama through the construction of a female character, used to impersonate a concept of 'woman' and – largely a male projection of attributes which are non-male as opposed to female and often opprobrious and unrealistic for this reason. As Halperin says, men required the silence of women so that they might imitate them better. (Halperin et al: 1990: 212–17)

In 'Why is Diotima a Woman?', his study of Plato's *Symposium*, Halperin also suggests that the function of the character Diotima is not to 'speak for women but to silence them', since she exists not a female character in her own right but as one who 'stands for' women, being 'constructed as a lack of male presence, as the universal alter ego of the masculine subject or its complement or its supplement – she is constructed as the 'other' or, as Julia Kristeva (1970) puts it, a 'pseudo-other' and to study her is simply to study men's projection onto her'. (1990: 289) For Halperin, Plato does not so much represent women as re-present them, as not the woman's perspective but the man's: an invented and characterised 'woman' who epitomises the values which the Ancient Greek culture chose to give her whilst denying the actual experiences of 'real women'. In addition, he acknowledges that 'the point of all these rites after all, is to turn boys into men, not into women; for the cultural construction of masculinity to succeed it is necessary that the process intended to turn boys into men may be genuinely efficacious.' (ibid. 291–2)[4]

Perhaps also, then as now, drama in general allows men to empathise with women, partly by permitting them to express a particular emotional range – denied to them in the formulaic masculine gender stereotypes of strong and powerful – which includes pity, compassion, fear, warmth and irrationality.[5] Halperin's point about turning boys into men, not women, does however throw a complementary light on this subject. Winkler noted that

> 'masculinity (for the Greeks) is a duty and a hard won achievement and the temptation to desert one's side is very great. This odd belief in the reversibility of the male person, always in peril of slipping into the servile or the feminine has been noted by Greenblatt (1986) who observes that for the ancient world the two sexes are not simply opposite but stand at poles of a continuum which can be traversed. Thus "woman" is not only the opposite of man, she is also a potentially threatening "internal émigré" of masculine identity.' (Halperin et al, 1990:182)

This echoes aspects of the medical perspective discussed earlier. There is a strong suggestion here that, in becoming a man, it is necessary to adopt those emotions defined as masculine – and avoid those defined as feminine. What might lead a man to contradict such strong cultural conditioning; to incur almost certain ridicule because the wish to express his 'feminine side' is so strong? One major role of transvestism would seem to be the pursuit and discovery of an outlet for dimensions of masculine identity which are culturally ascribed as feminine (and vice versa). This strikingly reflects concepts developed by Jung which seem to me to be very directly relevant to the notions under discussion of maleness/femaleness, gender and sex.

Jung and the Inner World of Opposites

Jung's studies of *The Anima and Animus,* and *The Shadow and the Syzygy* (first published in 1953 and 1959) are of particular interest to this research, since they concern the projection of unrealised qualities thought to pertain primarily to the opposite sex and resulting in the creation of a shadow anima or animus. The idealised qualities are then projected through 'transference' onto a real member of the opposite sex. At its most simplistic, the anima is the female soul image of a man, the animus the male soul image of a woman (although Jung has been criticised for invariably defining a person's soul image as the opposite gender). (*Aspects of the Feminine*, 1982)[6]

Jung questioned what happens to these internalised and opposite-sex parts of ourselves, particularly in societies where demonstration of opposite sex qualities are inhibited or discouraged. In relationships, he proposed, we project the inner 'shadow' figure of the opposite sex part of ourselves onto another person. A man, for example, might have difficulty in expressing traits such as those feminine ones listed above and will therefore 'project' these onto his female partner thus, almost always, causing difficulties in his relationships with her – since she has to 'carry' these projections, a burden of which she is seldom consciously aware but subconsciously only too aware.

In Western culture, the business world in particular can be seen as earnestly masculine and, Jung argued, it is masculine values which have produced a culture which neglects 'the soul' and the balancing influence of the feminine psyche. This has inevitably produced an asymmetry in Western society – in favour of logic, reason, external activity, analysis – and Jung inquired what had happened to the rest of the qualities of which humans are not only capable but in serious need. One perspective of transvestites could be that rather than creating gender dissensus, they are in fact seeking a form of sexual unity – in itself a sense of meaning and holism.

Some feminists, such as Raymond (1979) and Steinem (1983) have perceived transsexuals and transvestites as interlopers in the female domain, as men using their male status to try to get behind the portal of women's experience – and further, that he can be seen as giving birth to himself in a female identity, thus entering and appropriating women's envied ability to give birth. Transvestites in the UK to whom I have put this have argued that although there may be envy involved, they are not trying to 'muscle in' but to demonstrate their respect for women through their emulation – a form of 'imitation being the sincerest kind of flattery', as some put it. Another possible interpretation and result of this desire to act as women is that transvestites are giving expression to the qualities of the opposite sex within their own personalities – and, unlike some other men, achieving this without needing to use another person for this purpose.

This echoes both Bateson's explanation of Naven and Eliade's interpretation of ritual transvestism, where it is suggested that the need to 'return to wholeness' is experienced by mankind in general and that ceremonies which involve cross-dressing – playing the part of the opposite sex – are partly in fulfilment of this desire for wholeness:

> The myth of the hermaphroditic god and bisexual ancestor is the paradigm for a whole series of ceremonies which are directed towards a periodic returning to this original condition which is thought to be the perfect expression of humanity ... in which the sexes exist side by side as they co-exist with other qualities, and all other attributes, in the Divinity. (Eliade, 1958: 424)

Transvestite roles in other societies may represent, for example, magical qualities, gender ambivalence, social category, power relationships or supplication to a deity. Alternatively, they may refer to an individual's choice of symbolic ambiguity, a desire to kick against cultural norms in a very visible and obvious way (changing appearance on the outward side of the skin may be the first step in signifying that change is taking place at an inward level, or marking the self as something other than the expected norm). Gell deliberates on the connections between the inner and outer of a person:

> The contrast between 'inner' and 'outer' is always only a relative rather than an absolute difference. The contrast between 'mind' (the internal person) and the external person, though real, is only relative. If we seek to delve inside the person all we seem to find are other persons ... and if, as sociologists rather than cognitive psychologists, we try to give an account of the external aspects of persons, (we find that) ... our inner personhood seems to consist of replications of what we are externally ... so ... it may not be so aberrant to suggest that what persons are externally (and collectively) is a kind of enlarged replication of what they are internally. (1998; 222)

Gell's proposition – that people become who they are through the events and replications which happen in their lives, and that there is a constant negotiation and re-negotiation between inner and outer selves to create a fit between the inside, the outside and the world beyond – is of particular assistance in understanding transvestites, perhaps UK transvestites in particular. To me, it suggests that they seek to create through their outer appearance the fit with the inner self they consider to be very real and significant, certain and undeniable. There is a clear relationship between dress and the men who use it to construct an image – perhaps iconic – which locates them mentally in a different world, for example one in which they relax quietly or converse with others (preferably women). But, I would suggest, the female image they see of themselves in the mirror reflects back their 'other self' which, they often note, complements their idea of themselves as a totality. As Butler comments, when discussing Lacanian notions of the self in the mirror, 'One might say that it (the image in the mirror) confers an ideality and integrity on (the) body, but it is perhaps more accurate to claim that the very sense of the body is generated through this projection of ideality and integrity. Indeed, this mirroring transforms a lived sense of disunity and loss of control into an ideal of integrity and control'. (1993:75)

Sex, Gender or Sexuality?

The primary motivation behind transvestism – at least that practised by the UK transvestites with whom I carried out research – would seem to be clear. Rather than being an erotic compulsion (although this element may be present), transvestism is primarily a gender phenomenon – but one which cannot be satisfactorily separated out from issues of sex and sexuality. The evidence from Western transsexuals throws more light on this; it suggests that sexuality seems to be of considerably less importance to the sex-changer than gender or sex. For the transsexual who decides to choose full gender re-assignment, the surgery, as well as pre- and post-operative treatment, can be appallingly painful and difficult but the reason many still continue to go through with it is because the other option – continuing to live as a misfit male – worse.

Although this fieldwork (in the UK) focuses on transvestites, I did meet one man who was in the early stages of planning to go ahead with gender re-assignment surgery. For several years, he had had a close and loving relationship with his girlfriend up to the point where he started to talk about changing sex. Not surprisingly, his decision radically altered the course of the relationship (they had been talking of marriage) since the woman wanted her partner to be a heterosexual male. When one follows through the implications of this – that many men who have the operation are heterosexual males beforehand and mentally continue to be so after surgery – it comes as something of a shock to realise that they have to choose, in a very real way, between gender and sexuality. By having surgery, they are excluding the very group with whom they would most like to have a relationship – heterosexual women – since those women want a male partner. Who is left for them to have a relationship with? Lesbian women (whom they say are not their first preference), straight or gay men, both of whom they find unappealing, others who have had the operation (who at least have the advantage of understanding what they have been through), or celibacy. Griggs describes this process as she encountered it in the years following gender re-assignment surgery:

> It was a rare and distressing predicament to find general society criticising me for not dating men and also discouraging sexual attachments to women, which was my own proscription as well, yet to find family members urging or demanding that I form a relationship with a woman and being unhappy about even the suggestion of intimate relationships with men ... my parents cannot hide the fact that they consider my relationships with men to be homosexual (bad) and my relationships with women to be heterosexual (good). The rest of the world works in reverse. And there was an encounter in 1977 with a man I knew from high school. ... I was wearing a tight-fitting red turtle-neck sweater with dress slacks ... he stared wide-eyed at my upper torso and said: 'Claudine, wow! You look so gooood!' He appeared to be speaking to my breasts, which was disconcerting, and then gestured with an easy, locker-room manner. 'You must really enjoy playing with those.' As nearly as I could figure, he thought I was a man who had gained a female body so I could have a heterosexual relationship with myself. (1998:73)

This raises the interesting point that in having the operation, a transsexual may well be choosing gender over sexuality – and yet in our society, there seem very few things that one needs to be gendered *for* except sexuality; sexual relationships are one of the only places where gender is the key defining object – clothing being one of the few others. That this decision is a very difficult one is well documented (Morris 1972, Bornstein, 1994, Griggs, 1995, etc.), and it is the more acute when combined with a personal history of feeling misunderstood and profoundly out of place (which can hardly have failed to have occurred, given the mass misunderstanding which prevails towards gender dysfunction in this culture). Some transsexuals are so completely certain that they cannot continue to live in a 'wrong sex' body that they make the decision with a degree of conviction they feel in few other areas of their lives. Nevertheless, a certain proportion of transsexuals commit suicide after surgery and yet others choose to change back – insofar as this is possible.

Transvestism is still in many ways a different category from transsexuality and yet there are threads which predominate in both, as well as the areas of overlap in between the two. One of the most obvious would appear to be gender which, much more than sex, seems to be crucial both to the transvestite and the transsexual. My interviews with British transvestites have suggested that, contrary to popular belief, transvestism may well contain elements of sexual excitement but its much more important function is to enable these men to express a strong feminine side – one which, for them, refuses to be suppressed. Although both the UK transvestites and the hijras are biologically male, they wish to enter the 'gender-world' of the female – and it is an interesting concatenation of ideas that the male who has female leanings or tendencies must somehow be not-all-man; not a proper, manly man. Hence, presumably, the common assumption that most transvestites are homosexual.

Crossing Gender as an 'Institutionalised' Role

Whitehead's work on the Native American two-spirit people is invaluable in understanding this. Two-spirit people (or berdaches) have been the subject of much research in the last twenty years with particular interest and direction coming from the growing Lesbian, Gay, Transgender and Bisexual movements in the USA. Although many of the early accounts of the two-spirit people described them with considerable antipathy, the more recent research (for example Williams, 1986) has commonly portrayed them as representing a 'best of both worlds' lifestyle, in which sexual choice was not only allowed but also supported and, in some cases, rendered sacred; and, more importantly, that they demonstrated a society in which there was a form of 'institutionalised homosexuality'.

Certainly the culture which created a space for two-spirit people can be seen to illustrate the possibility of alternative forms of the construction of sex, gender and sexuality, but does it do so in the way these accounts seem to propose? Whitehead (1981) suggests not and I would agree with her. She challenges these arguments by suggesting that berdachism is considerably more of a gender role than a sex role, since it is particularly indicated through the use of women's clothing and tools – and thus occupation – and is not necessarily indicative of sexual orientation: 'assessed against the data … the "niche-for-homosexuals" argument begins to unravel at the edges. First there is no evidence that homosexual behaviour as such was used as a reason for promoting reclassification of an individual to the gender-crossed status. In contradistinction to occupational and clothing choices, cross-sex erotic choice is never mentioned as one of the indicators of the budding berdache'. (1981: 95) It is also interesting to note that, although there are folk tales of male genitalia supernaturally disappearing and being replaced with female genitalia, unlike the hijras, no surgical changes took place among the berdaches.

Whitehead further questions the logic of sexual object choice to the role of the berdache:

If sexual object choice should conform to public gender, then why should not public gender conform to sexual object choice? The American Indians seem to have followed only one step of this logic, and even that not consistently ... Sexual object choice was indeed gender-linked ... but that is because the berdache had a foot in both camps, being by anatomy one thing, by occupation the other, he had a claim on the favours of either sex. (1981: 96)

However, this still does not explain why homosexual partnerships had no 'gender transformative effects', and she suggests that if the position of the berdache is linked to current research on transsexualism, which states that the wish to assume the opposite gender is not affected by sexual orientation, this does make much more sense:

In the American Indian mind, the salient fact about the gender-crosser was his/her preference for the external social identity of the opposite sex. If all a person wanted to do was engage in homosexual activity, there were opportunities for doing so without all the ballyhoo of a special identity.' (ibid: 97)

Whitehead proposes that, although it clearly does not add up, it is perhaps not surprising that the role of the berdaches has become conflated with 'institutionalised homosexuality', because in the last 200 years 'the homosexual has come to be the nearest thing to a cross-sex or dual gender category in Western society' – and indeed, given the 'centre of gravity' in the two cultures (Western and Native American), 'the Western homosexual *is* the logical counterpart of the of the berdache'. (ibid: 97) The crucial point, however, is that this centre of gravity in the two cultures is radically different: for the Native American Indian, the emphasis is on clothing and occupation – gender – whilst for the West, and contemporary America in particular, it is sexuality. As she states, 'the only solution to this paradox is to conclude that sexuality, hetero-sexuality typed though it may have been in the native mind, fell outside the realm of what was publicly and officially important about the two sexes. *Sexual object choice was very much the trailing rather than the leading edge of gender definition.*' (ibid: 96, my italics)

Whitehead's emphasis on the primacy of gender, with sexual object choice as a secondary factor, certainly resonates with my British fieldwork. UK transvestites, particularly under the umbrella of their main organisation, the Beaumont Society, are resolute in their assertion of their heterosexuality – and yet cross-dressing is clearly used by the homosexual community, particularly in its performance aspect as 'drag'.

Fieldwork with hijras also supports this argument. There is no doubt that they have sexual relationships – I heard and read of hijras who were married to (or cohabiting with) men, but also of others who were married to women. According to Leila (whose information appears in Chapter 4) Chand, one of the hijras I interviewed, had definitely been a husband before he was a hijra. In one hijra's narrative (in Nanda), Kamladevi states that, 'There are two types among us. One type has relationships with men, the other type has relationships with men and women' (1990: 57), and later, Kumari says, 'here in Bastipore ... even men can come into the group. You know that Meera, at Gasworks Street, she is a real man. She had a wife and daughter and she has a boyfriend and got that boyfriend married to her own daughter. In Bombay the hijras will not allow a man to come into the group. They will not let a man leave his family and join them. To be a hijra, you should not have any relations with a woman.' (ibid: 63) Kumari's assertion that this should not happen only belies the fact that it does – and although it may not be common, is sufficiently widespread to be accepted practice, at least among some hijra communities. I would surmise that the reason hijras have relations with men *and* women, rather than men *or* women is that for many, one of their primary sources of income derives from relationships with men.

Sexual components to transvestism certainly do exist. Whitehead's argument does not eliminate references to sexuality: it locates them as a secondary issue. This too has been borne out by my fieldwork and by the findings of others – despite the frequent denials of groups such as the Beaumont Society –for instance by one of my questionnaire respondents who, as I have cited earlier, says that he wants 'to make love to my own feminine image; this is why so many transvestite sessions end by the transvestite making love to himself.' (QR82, q19)

The Brazilian Travestis

Sexuality does play a key role in the lives of some transvestite groups. Andrea Cornwall's research into the *travestis* of Salvador, Brazil, is a study of cross-dressed men in a context where 'ambiguity of gender is part of the prostitutional world' (1994: 111) and is most useful when trying to understand and describe the range of possibilities in this area. Like the West (but unlike India for the most part), Salvador accommodates more than one form of cross-dressing and context in which it takes place. As well as travestis, two other kinds of cross-gender behaviour have been identified by Cornwall: *transformistas*, who appear in a particular spatial and temporal setting, such as a night club, perform for the allotted time as transvestites and correspond to the groups known as drag artistes in the English-speaking world; and *Carnaval* which attracts many cross-dressed men who do little to hide their masculinity, their beards, genitalia and hirsuteness being clearly visible.

For travestis, dressing as women is a significant marker, but is clearly related to the nature of the travesti existence – in a world where sexual transactions are a signifying feature. As Cornwall describes them:

> Their depilated bodies are clenched at the waist to produce curves, their breasts accentuated ... While they present the codes of femininity, it is the presentation to excess that render them identifiable as travestis. As one remarked ... she could see no merit in being a mulher (woman) as, 'when a *mulher* passes no-one bothers to look but when a travesti passes everyone wants to look, to have ... to be a travesti'. (118) ... On the *trottoir*[7] and the terreiro (traditional 'cult' houses), travestis adorn themselves in feminine trappings. They shape their bodies to exaggerate the curves identified with the female body, with a 'hidden extra': bodies with breasts and a penis. They do not self-identify as *homens* (men) or *mulheres* (women) but as travestis. (1994: 111)

Travestis would seem to most resemble the category that in the West would be classified as transsexuals but unlike Western transsexuals or hijras, although they often alter their bodies through surgery, this is more likely to take the form of silicone implant breasts than removal of the penis and testicles. Unlike the hijras, many travestis are committed to keeping their penises, considering that it is their unusual anatomy juxtaposed with dress which makes them of particular interest.

However Cornwall suggests that although travestis symbolise the penetrated, appearances can be deceptive – it is not only that they wish to be in possession of a penis for its interest value, since they openly state that emasculation will render them 'useless' in sexual transactions and one may therefore presume that they are not just the 'passive' partner or fellator. The Brazilian travestis are a strong example of expectation of homosexuality associated with cross-dressing, and yet, as Cornwall's fieldwork makes clear, some are still expected to function as the penetrator – and thus in Latin American terms, the male – by their customers. This is an important factor in the light of the arguments put forward by Whitehead about the berdaches. There are also interesting similarities and differences between hijras and travestis: travestis, like hijras, retain both male and female attributes in terms of anatomy and gender-ascribed cultural behaviours but they differ in significant ways. Travestis commonly take hormones or have implants to improve their breast potential, which hijras do not seem to do; whilst travestis seldom have an operation to remove their penis and testicles, which hijras commonly do.

Anatomically, it might therefore be more accurate to describe travesti and hijra characteristics as male and non-male rather than male and female – or perhaps *both/and* and *neither/nor*. they adopt female mannerisms (though, like the hijras, they are capable of throwing their 'femininity' to the wind when they want to – they have a reputation for mugging and for becoming become aggressive, threatening and violent if a client is difficult) and travestis are usually addressed by female pronouns but, as Cornwall notes, on the whole, they 'do not think that they are, nor are they taken to be, "really" women or men ... as one travesti pointed out, "real women" can give birth, transsexuals can never achieve 'true' femaleness'. (1994: 113) Like many UK transvestites, they are clearly aware that no amount of surgery can really affect a transformation: as Shelly pointed out in Chapter 3, 'surgery removes the maleness but it can't really make you into a woman – just further from being a man.'

In assessing the travestis, Cornwall argues against the concept of a 'third gender' category, commenting that the ideology of gender, and of trans-vestism as a branch of that, has attracted theories which posit equally fixed models. She suggests that what is needed is a set of criteria which acknowl-edge not only the situational and contextual associations of transvestism and gender, but also the multiplicity of possibilities. This rejection of the 'third gender category' is also sustained by research on the berdaches. There is evidence that the concept of gender duality remained in Native American societies. Even the name 'two-spirit person' chosen by Native American Indians themselves to supplant 'berdache' suggests a combina-tion of the customary dyad; a further term, which implies 'third spirit' for example, has not been coined. ('Berdache' was imported by the conquista-dors, and etymologically derived from the Persian, for 'kept boy' and there-fore has seriously negative connotations.)

Epple's work with the Navaho provides further evidence that a third category is not a consideration. She observes that, because their cosmology inclines them to see things in gradations between pairs (for example day and night) rather than batches of separately defined pluralities, they speak of all things, including humans, as an 'inseparable' and 'cyclical' dynamic process. (1997:176) Epple's work is primarily focused on the conceptual constructions of the Navaho however it is enlightening regarding the concept of a third gender category – and it does seem clear that the defining feature of berdache life was the desire to cross gender, particularly demon-strated by clothing and work.

Jaffrey also argues against the concept of a third sex, in contrast to Nanda who would locate the hijras within this. I would maintain, however, that in both cases, the hijras and the Western transsexuals are forced to choose gender over sex, since they must give up many of the things which really define gender. In the case of the hijras, they are eunuchs, but, unlike eunuchs they self-define as women – and in the case of Western transsexuals, the societal expectation is still very strong that one must be one sex or the other.

Binary Categorisation as 'Common Sense'

These considerations suggest that notions of a third gender category – as an analytical tool rather than a societal perspective – elude rather than contribute to an explanation of transvestism. But they also show that it is not just views of gender and sexuality which vary widely across cultures but views of sex itself. In Unni Wikan's study of the Xanith of Oman, she notes that 'it is the sexual act, not the sexual organs, which is fundamentally constitutive of gender. A man who acts as a woman sexually, *is* a woman, socially.' (1977: 309).

The question must arise, though, as to what extent such men are seen as men by the society in which they live. In Western societies, such men would still be seen as men because of their biological sex (and under current British law, as at autumn 2001, a post-operative transsexual is still defined by their sex at birth for a matter such as marriage, although this may be set to change). It can, however, be argued that this view is not universal but that it rather reflects the fixed, binary (and medico-biological) view of sex which is so dominant in the West.

One of the difficulties in exploring these issues is that, of all the ideological systems of control which dictate our behaviours and thoughts, sex and gender are arguably among the most powerful – probably the most powerful – and have the added force of being considered so normal and natural that the thinking process which might be activated to question these convictions seldom arises. Critically, though, such 'common sense' notions are culturally bound, and potential reasons for this will be uncovered in the next chapter; what is seen as 'natural' in Britain may be very different to what is 'natural' in Salvador, Rajasthan or elsewhere. 'Common sense', culturally constructed, is almost certainly responsible – more than any specific contemporary dictates from religious or institutional life – for a prevailing social view that there is something deeply suspect about men who wear women's clothes, that there are some characteristics and personality traits which rightly belong to men and others which are the domain of women. From this we derive a sense of the concreteness of the 'other' as a concept. Arguably, the mindset of the 1970s which perceived two distinct categories, in both senses – male/female and sex/gender – is still axiomatic. Few, if questioned, would have any trouble in identifying male and female as a bipolarity, as things which are in opposition to each other conceptually – and often in reality: they would state the apparently obvious – that we are all born into a sexed body which is either male or female. 'Anatomy is destiny', as Freud is reported to have said. But even biology is not always as straightforward as one might expect, as genetic research increasingly reveals.

Masculinity, Femininity; Genetics and Mosaics

The male/female categories can seem such a manifest division that it is difficult to steer a course very far away from them. Some commentators, however, have questioned not just the culturally attributed traits believed to be associated with either male or female, but the biology itself. Academic thought may have developed far beyond the 1970s acceptance of sex as biology and gender as culture, but is still grappling with the implications of this. Fausto-Sterling begins her first chapter in *Sexing the Body* with an example which serves to demonstrate that such assumptions are not so straightforward, even biologically. In 1988, a Spanish hurdler, Maria Patino, competing in the Olympic Games, forgot to take the doctor's certificate stating that she was female. She therefore had to be tested by the IOC doctor, and she failed the test, since it was found that she had a Y chromosome and testes within her labia. To all outward appearances, she was female but 'inside', it seemed she was (part) male. She did later successfully challenge this, on the grounds that chromosome testing is unjust and only one of many features in the human make-up, but the IOC still routinely carry out the testing. After 1968, 'the IOC decided to make use of the modern "scientific" chromosome test. The problem, though, is that this test and the more sophisticated polymerase chain reaction to detect small regions of DNA associated with testes development that the IOC uses today, cannot do the work the IOC wants it to do. There is no either/or. Rather, there are shades of difference.' (Fausto-Sterling, 2000: 1–3)

This is just one example, and in one specific category, which demonstrate that maleness and femaleness are not as surely categorised as has been – and probably still is – generally believed in Western societies. Even in the world of anatomy, genetics and chromosomes, there are shades and indistinct boundaries. In addition, there are many ethnographic examples which describe divergent ways of attributing maleness and femaleness and, as

Moore points out, even in the binary-divided west, 'this is the era of Michael Jackson, Boy George, Prince and Madonna.' (1999:154) It is a question which holds such fascination that it continues to be explored through biological models. So little is understood as yet regarding the genetic development of masculine and feminine properties within the human body that so far, much of this material is speculative. Hogan-Finlay states that:

A recent paper by Witelson (1991, in *Psychoendocrinology* 16, 131–53) spoke of 'neural sexual mosaicism'. She suggested that it is highly unlikely that a single biological cause will be found to accommodate for those behaviours that are currently labelled as 'masculine' or 'feminine'. She noted that prenatal development is affected by many factors, including atypical hormone levels resulting from dysfunctional foetal glands or dysfunctional maternal hormone activity, foetal receptors and maternal stress. Such prenatal antecedents may ... set the stage for sexual orientation and, it may be added, for transvestism. However these factors, in and of themselves, should not be seen as sufficient conditions for the development of sexual orientation or cross-gendered behaviour in general. (1996: 9)

Although sex and gender have been hotly debated topics for such a long time, there is still a long way to go in terms of research, especially in the field of biology and genetics. Popular findings which have been latched onto by the press are generally in the area of, for example, the human genome project, producing headlines such as 'Scientists have found the gene for ...' and fuelling the idea that our genes are somehow like buttons, which can be pressed to obtain a particular result. John Gray's *Men are from Mars, Women are from Venus* is part of this much broader, popular language of genetics and has become a best-seller since its publication in 1993. It uses the analogy of different planets (Mars and Venus) to explain that men and women really are different and should acknowledge and negotiate these differences. 'By continuing to recognise and explore our differences we have discovered new ways to improve all our relationships'.(1993: 3) Arguably, this new-wave essentialism is simply further pressure to conform to the binary divide through its stress on absolute and inevitable difference between male and female, with little allowance for female behaviours within a male or male within a female.[8]

In terms of the reflections of transvestites in Britain on their own childhoods, many explained in their questionnaire answers that they felt there were particular circumstances or events which had contributed to their desire to cross-dress. Others felt that it was something which had been in their biological make-up since they were in the womb. Still others thought that it might be a combination of the two – that a foetal abnormality had occurred which still had to be 'triggered' during their upbringing. Much confusion exists around sexed and gendered identities and the necessity for categories which go beyond the binary divide. In relation to the sexual behaviour choices of transsexuals, for example, Ramet points out that:

> Sexual behaviour, however, is not directly relevant to the subject of gender reversal. Not only is same-sex sexuality a separate topic not to be confused with gender reversal, but in two-gender systems, in particular, it becomes semantically treacherous to speak of 'same-sex' and 'heterosexual' liaison on the part of a cross-gendered individual. The confusion which can arise from these terms and be discerned in the disagreement among those therapists attempting to describe male-to-female transsexuals who are attracted to women; for some therapists, such transsexuals are 'heterosexual', for others, 'homosexual'. When antonyms can be understood to mean the same thing, it is time to look for an alternative vocabulary.' (1996: 3)

This need for a new vocabulary echoes much of what has been covered in this chapter. It also supports the notion that transvestism, to a large extent, is primarily a gender phenomenon which relates to the need for transvestite men to realise their own emotions – those emotions perceived by them as being 'feminine' and which have been suppressed, either by others or by themselves, in the process of their changing from boys into men. Within a cross-cultural context, it becomes increasingly apparent that notions of sexuality and gender are far from uniform across societies.

These issues raise the question of how far it is sensible to separate issues of sex, gender and sexuality when examining a phenomenon such as transvestism. I would suggest that traditional arguments about behaviours and biologies, nature and culture, which attempt such separation are flawed, particularly those put forward in the 1970s, such as those by sexologists Money and Ehrhardt (e.g. 1972) or by feminists such as Ortner (1974). Transvestism furnishes an example which offers insight into the discourses of sex in divergent societies and shows not only that the definitions implicit in such theories would have to be seriously distorted to make them work, but also that it is necessary to understand how the discourses on sex are constructed in different societies. Rather than separate categories, I would argue that sex, gender and sexuality might more fruitfully be understood, as Griggs states, as 'part of a "gestalt".' (1998: 20)

I have found Errington's ideas eminently helpful when working with these ideas (although the English language, usually so rich in its multiplicities, shows up its impoverishment in this field; I wish there were a third word that could be brought into use). She suggests we need not two, but three designations – which she terms Sex (upper case), gender and sex (lower case) in order to distinguish between the sex which infers biologically sexed bodies and Sex, the cultural construction of biology particular to the west. (Moore, 1999: 153). This study of UK transvestites would make an obvious case for the notion that we cannot separate sex and gender because we only see Sex *through* gender. This is, however, inevitably underpinned by Western cultural concepts of personhood and the conflation of self and role which prevails, particularly in Britain and America, whilst for the hijras, a different construction is evident. The need to contextualise is as strong here – perhaps stronger – as in any anthropological and social research because of the tendency to assume that Western ideas in this field are general, normal, universal and this too will be discussed more fully in the next chapter.

Gender has been called 'the culturally established correlates of sex' (Goffman, 1979: 1) and I would agree with Moore and Errington that we can only see biological sex through the ways in which our own society perceives sex. Since these discourses contain all our inherited assumptions, including language and clothing, we have no way of seeing them without our cultural baggage. In the West, steps have been taken to separate out sex and gender, almost like the lenses of the viewfinder through which they are surveyed. But this too is only one view of sex – and a rather ethnocentric one – since the separation itself is part of the West's own cultural tradition. It is therefore not surprising that the Western perspective, based as it is on a fusion of ideologies which include Graeco-Roman, Norse and Christian, should be perceptibly different from the Indian. It is also to be expected that within a Western context, the possibilities of different gender attributes and acceptable behaviours has so far remained largely a one-way traffic: for females to wish to become like males is relatively socially acceptable, even if it is sometimes proscribed, but for males to espouse female traits is somehow not only pointless but deeply ridiculous – unacceptable in a way that homosexuality is not (perhaps because homosexual men are at least expressing a preference for other men?).

The Correlates of Gender Culture – Transvestism as Material Objectification

Both the British transvestites and the hijras are crossing boundaries not only of sex but also of gender – and the variety of their behaviours and use of sex/gender crossing could be plotted at many points of a theoretical sex/gender/sexuality graph. Both demonstrate that sex and gender must be viewed as a conjoined totality within any one human and within society. The value of transvestism, as a social-anthropological tool, is that it anchors abstract concepts to a visible phenomenon, to objectifiable material culture. Other anthropologists have noted that textiles can form elaborate documents, but transvestism does something else. The role of gendered clothing externalises the categories of sex, Sex and gender. Politics is often about perception rather than reality, and the (much hauled over) politics of sex and gender is particularly about perceptions which alter, mutate and possibly dissolve completely, whilst material culture, in this case clothing, is by its very nature, objectified and rooted in the item, the 'thing'.

There is a separate question, however, relating to issues of sex and gender, and it is one that is of great importance when undertaking a cross-cultural study of transvestism. This is the issue of why there is such disparate treatment of transvestites in different societies. I shall come back to this in the next chapter, but it is clear that 'gender culture' is all important. Conceptual frameworks of gender culture are set by a society, inevitably based on a number of 'certitudes' which form a 'common sense' model as suggested earlier in this chapter. Many of these 'certitudes' are informed by belief systems, even if these are not predominantly those of the majority of the members of a society. Prevailing frameworks of ideologies and notions of what is 'natural' and 'normal' are reflected in and reinforced by, for example, literature, art, ceremonies and rituals (whether at a secular or religious level) through to newspaper articles and pub conversations.

It is clear that, within these gender cultures, the spaces of possibility for transvestites vary widely from one society to another. Transvestism illustrates rather well the current inferences of the cultural discourses, in terms of whether space has been allowed for it or not. In some cultures, such as India and the Native American Indians, space has been allowed. With the hijras there is a clear message: no confusion because space has been allocated. In the UK there is confusion because there is no place and therefore, to a British sensibility, transvestism makes no sense. The question arises as to why these spaces are or are not possible.

And to understand this, we must go beyond contemporary social facts. Although there has been considerable change in societal structures in the areas of work, power and economics, this has not really been matched with changes in terms of religious or cosmological systems, beliefs and practices. In part, the predominance of Marxist-style ideologies, especially during the

1970s, within fields such as anthropology has led to a rather underdeveloped view of the importance of symbolic structures and their effects on the social. As Moore suggests, it has not always been helpful that issues have been viewed as an ideological question; 'the social and the symbolic, while never completely divergent, resisted any easy theory of reflection and could certainly not be said to determine each other. Some of the best anthropological work during this period was concerned with investigating the refracted relationship of these different aspects of gender, but the continuing influence of Marxist and neo-Marxist frames of reference meant that the issue was most treated as a problem about ideology rather than one about how to theorise the intractable relation between the social and the symbolic.' (1999; 152)[9] I cannot argue too strongly how vital it is that anthropology, which has a long history of interest in cosmology and belief systems, starts to consider these in relation to gender structures. I suggest some reflections below, but this area is wide open for further research.

Cross-Cultural Evidence and the Conceptualisation of Gender Crossing

Variable perspectives of sex, gender and sexuality across cultures are very evident. Belief systems clearly play a part in this and it seems evident that the position of the hijras (and the North American berdaches) are supported in their role by a cosmological view of the world in which there is a broader concept of divinity than one in which God is conceived of as entirely male. Wikan's study of the Xanith (1977) might seem to contradict the conjecture that gender-crossing is best supported in cultures which have a dual-gender belief system, since the Xanith are men who live as women – either permanently or temporarily – within the structures of a strongly Islamic society and Islam would seem to be largely free from cosmological female figures. But I would contend that this particular space of possibility has been created and allowed because it provides for other, more dominant sex and gender aspects to be maintained, in particular the purity of women. Omani society, in recognising the male need for sex, and rather than have bachelors attempting to have sexual relationships with either the wives of other men or single women, would rather have the possibility of a third category – the Xanith – who protects the two primary genders from *zina* – illicit intercourse – and it is interesting to note that Xanith, although they adopt many of the mannerisms of women's dress, are specifically forbidden to dress *like* women because they are, in effect prostitutes, not an acceptable possibility for an Omani woman. 'For such a person to dress like women would be to dishonour womanhood.' (Wikan, 1977: 310) The Xanith, as Wikan states, form part of a triad which both reflects and supports the existence of the two dominant gender roles. In addition, there is the recognition that, for the health of society in general, sexual deviations are better acknowledged than driven underground; the Omani State 'acknowledges that transsexuals have utility: they act as a safety valve, and thus as a protection for the virtue of women'. (321)

Mark Johnson's *Beauty and Power* (1997), a study of transgendered male identities in two Muslim communities in the southern Philippines, also demonstrates how transvestite groupings can obtain a social space. Crucially, though, Johnson provides an example of how such a group has been able to adapt to the challenges of modernisation. In south-east Asian island culture, although the Americanisation of Philippine culture has brought significant changes to their role, gender-crossing has a history of association with the sacred and celebratory and those who choose this role have been seen as 'embodiments of and mediatory figures for, ancestral unity and potency'. (1997: 12) To some extent, this tradition has lent a degree of ambiguous acceptance to the group, as well as an allocated space of possibility.

Johnson comments that the *gays*, or *bantut,* as they prefer to be called, certainly constitute an ostracised group (they do not fit easily into traditional Muslim family structure) but are simultaneously admired as purveyors of style and for their beauty 'defined in terms of an imagined global American otherness'. (1997: 12) Johnson's study explores how inherited roles for transgendered men have changed over time, and also seeks to understand the inherent contradictions in the *bantuts'* situation. Above all, though, it illustrates the ability of a 'group' to transform itself in relation to modernisation, to find a new niche. The Philippines *bantut* may have transformed themselves but they have emerged from a traditional role of performing at weddings and births, a role also carried out by the hijras, perhaps reflecting a wider social belief that the place between the sexes conveys special powers regarding sexual relationships and procreation – one which is also found in other groups. Johnson comments on the recurrent anthropological tradition of selecting and 'valorising' a culture which esteems divergent sexualities in a way which is significantly different from the society from which the anthropologist comes, but he criticises anthropology for the delay in acknowledging the means whereby these are created and manipulated:

What anthropologists have been much slower to recognise are the shifting historical contexts and spatial fields in which such categories and practices have emerged not as sui generis but as the specific product of political and cultural entanglements. As others have argued, it is no longer either theoretically sound or empirically valid to treat various forms and formulations of gender and sexuality as isolated and self-perpetuating islands of desire. (13)

Johnson's argument that it is no longer valid to see sex and gender as 'isolated islands' is reflected in the positions of other transvestite groups and would seem to suggest that there are other cultural possibilities with regard to clothing and gender-changing than those prevalent in Western societies such as Britain. Paradoxically, as Westernised notions of consumer possibilities extend beyond the dreams of avarice, such cultural possibilities seem to be steeply on the decline.

While 'sacred status' is of importance, the Xanith demonstrate that it is possible for transvestites to be assigned a role which acts to support significant social values and in which a transgendered group is accepted even if viewed with some opprobrium. The *bantut*, also, are permitted to exist as an outsider community. By contrast, in a society such as Britain, transvestites have no social or religious role at all. They are thus perceived as a non-group of individual deviants. While there is a transvestite subculture, it is marginalised, generally derided and rarely visible to wider society. In short, UK transvestites occupy a non-space.

One further contrast needs to be made to balance this account. It appears that it is in those cultures in which transvestism is an honourable or expected activity that there have been generally greater personal and individual restrictions, particularly on gendered or sexual roles. This initially seems paradoxical but in the context of the concepts of socialisation and the freedom of the individual contrasted with the stronger hold of society, as discussed in the next chapter, it becomes explicable. The space of possibility also becomes the limits of possibility. Crucially, however, the restrictions themselves have stemmed from religious and cultural views that are in many cases being eroded as societies are experiencing modernisation.

This modernisation, though, is towards a global perspective in which the predominant cultural influences are those stemming from Western societies. It is in these societies that transvestism has no obvious role and is not just regarded with hostility but with derision. The *Bantut* show how it is possible to adjust and survive – and all such groups indisputably undergo change. During fieldwork in India it became very clear to me that the hijras are at a crossroads in terms of their position in Indian society; the honour and respect they have traditionally commanded is declining but there are other possible ways forward, some less attractive such as prostitution, others more hopeful such as politics and the media industry. The future for British transvestites is paradoxical: while growing societal freedom means they are unlikely to be subject to further restrictions, they will doubtless continue to be seen as individual deviants unless there are real shifts in the symbolic underpinnings and ongoing cultural discourses of sex and gender in Western societies.

Cross-dressing proves the glass through which both things – clothing and gender – are more clearly illuminated, and in some sense informs both. Perceptions of transvestites in some ways act as a metaphor for perceptions of the feminine: the UK shows itself to be a society where although women's roles may have changed, perceptions regarding masculine and feminine have altered very little – women are commended for 'masculine' attributes or actions, men are ridiculed or beaten up for acting 'female'. Why is this not true of other societies? I would propose four inter-linked reasons why men who want to act or live as women are regarded differently – why they do not have a place in the UK but they do in India and in some other cultures.

The first concerns society and differing concepts of individualism. Transvestites are primarily studied and treated in the West from a psychological perspective partly because, I would suggest, we perceive it to be their own choice and, thus, responsibility – whilst in India, this is much less the case. Linked to this is the second point which concerns notions of inevitability and 'destiny'. Both of these will be explored in greater depth in the next chapter. Thirdly, in some cases there is also the added value of sacred status which arises from being called by a higher being and thus, their acquisition of special powers. For the hijras, this is amplified by their symbolisation of 'divine union', or at least of the union of male and female within one person. This is aided by the existence of culturally supportive symbols, in particular, imagery of goddesses and gods, heroines and heroes who have crossed the gender divide or who display opposite-sex characteristics, combined with mythology which portrays the hijras themselves in a favourable light. Finally, there is the existence of a social role: in the case of some groups this is one of honour and respect; in it others does not necessarily convey any special status but does fulfil a social function, such as the Xanith, accepted as a safety valve by Oman society. Here again, the UK transvestites who have no role, neither social nor practical.

Within the Western context, it therefore starts to become very clear why transvestites have no place in the scheme of things. Women's economic and social position in the UK may have altered significantly in the last century, as paralleled by clothing changes, but not much has really changed for men – and underneath the surface improvements, at the level of structural symbolism (particularly regarding presumptions and truisms of what men and women do and are), little has changed for either sex. It would seem fairly clear that unless women acquire more status at this level within the cultural discourses, little will change for transvestites.

Marking Gender

If gender roles are purely a cultural construction and the options offered by cultural norms are limited to binary oppositions, it must surely follow that men and women would obligingly fit into these categories for the simple reason that they are all that exist – but in most cultures there seem to be a small but persistent group of people who deeply at odds with the gender they were born into, whatever their society construes that to be. There must therefore be a further element which is 'innate' or 'essential', which creates individual agency and the desire to challenge these norms, and which is a valuable part of our cultural diversity. Together, the range of responses to transvestism show that we do not live in a world constituted only of 'regularities'. Crossing gender boundaries is one aspect of this diversity and fully demonstrates the possibilities and variance allowed or created by some cultures and not others. As Geertz states regarding the 'empirical surprise' and 'cultural challenge' of intersexuality and crossed genders, 'if received ideas of the "normal" and "natural" are to be kept intact, something must be said about the rather spectacular disaccordances with them' (1983: 81).

There has been a flood of books about gender since the 1970s and – in Britain and America especially – an expansion from the 1980s onwards of books on self-exploration, many of them concerned with relationships. Both of these would suggest that these issues of sex, gender and sexuality have become mainstream – it is as if we recognise that major shifts can and must happen in this area – and yet two crucial points seem to have been missed. Firstly, that there are few signs of letting go of polarised, binary thinking with regard to sexes and genders and secondly, that unless the shift takes place at the level of the bedrock cultural discourses, nothing really happens and we continue to be diverted with surface appearances.

I began this chapter by asking whether transvestism was a sex move or a gender move. It seems clear that, while transvestism is primarily a gender phenomenon with a sexual components, the attempt to split sex, gender and sexuality confuses rather than clarifies. The examples of the UK transvestites suggest that these three cannot be divided, in the same way that a person cannot be divided. The contours of all three change not only within an individual but also in the broader world in which they live and find their ways of being, and this continual shift makes their geography a complex task. It also seems clear that the separation of sex and gender reflects Western cultural assumptions and does not form a satisfactory basis for cross-cultural studies, as notions of sex, sexuality and gender vary significantly across societies. In addition, because clothing is a form of communication within the discourses of sex in diverse societies as well as anchored material culture, transvestism seems to be a particularly helpful way of exploring these issues because it links them to observable items where the inner is reflected in the outer. When accounted for, not just in terms of how transvestites comprehend themselves but in how society perceives them, the prevailing models of sex and gender do not appear able to provide a fully grounded mode of explanation. To gain a fuller understanding of the discourses of sex in different societies, we need broader models which draw on fields such as material culture but also take into account the notions which, consciously or unconsciously, shape cultures.

Notes

1. (http://www.leaderu.com/jhs/rekers.html). Viewed November 2001.

2. The Naven ceremony may involve cross-dressing by men or women and takes place in relation to achievements within the extremely complex network of Iatmul kin relationships. It is not possible in this brief account to describe all of these in detail, although they are of significance to the performance of Naven and both familial and moietal relationships have a profound effect on behaviour between individuals and groups and how one individual treats or responds to another. The *wau* is a complex term used to describe not only the mother's brother but also, for example, the mother's mother's sister's son, whilst *laua*, primarily meaning sister's son, may also describe other similar classificatory relationships – and it is the relation between the two which forms the substance of the book. Bateson is very clear that the Naven is *not* a *rite de passage*, especially since it does not occur at the occasions of birth or death.

3. In *Self-Decoration in Mount Hagen*, the Stratherns' study of a further New Guinea society, they note that gender based dress codes are very marked and although there is no ritual context in which either sex is cross-dressed, it does take place and is tolerated with amusement. (1971:170 & 100 (fn))

4. This has an interesting parallel with Morphy's study of the Yolngu, natives of Northeast Arnhem Land in Australia, described in *Ancestral*

Connections (1991), where transvestism is used in the context of an initiation ceremony and in which all boys at a particular stage of their journey to manhood, are dressed as women. The Djungguwan ceremony is a regional ceremony which portrays the journey of the Wawilak sisters and other female ancestral figures but similarly, the point is to turn boys into men, not women.

5. 'Hysteria' is, after all, from the Greek, 'hysteros', meaning womb and is used in common parlance to describe the type of emotional expression which is generally attributed to women – and denied to men.

6. It is interesting – but perhaps too easy – to parallel the biological patterning of male and female within the body, an aspect of genetics which is as yet little known, to the 'mosaicism' as described by Hogan-Finlay and Witelson below. Although it is conjecture, it is interesting to consider that, as O'Connor states, 'If ... archetypes are innate behavioural patterns that have resulted from the endless repetition of specific experiences of human beings through time, then it seems ... highly probable that the anima and animus are mental representations or archetypal images of the minority of female genes in a man's body ... and the minority of male genes in a woman's ... Just as the body itself exhibits representations of the opposite genetic structure, so also it would seem reasonable to argue that the collective unconscious level, the anima and animus, are psychological or mental representations of the minority gene structure within each human being.' (1985:130)

7. Cornwall does not give a interpretation for the word *trottoir* and I have therefore assumed that the meaning is the direct translation, 'pavement'.

8. Although a different take on this is Rudd's adaptation of *Men are from Mars, Women are from Venus*. Rudd's book, *Who's Really from Venus?* aims to help male-to-female transvestites and their partners – wives or girlfriends – in an attempt to show that a man who cross-dresses is not a figure of fun but, through his combination of a strong 'Venusian' side combined with his 'Martian' characteristics has several very positive advantages as a husband or lover.

9. And, indeed, Moore was herself criticised for doing just this – ignoring the symbolic at the expense of the economic and social – in her 1988 text, *Feminism and Anthropology*.

7

Thinking of Themselves: Transvestism and Concepts of the Person

It was a diverse series of circumstances which led to the choice of transvestites as a research group, but one I regret not at all; few others could have turned out so rewarding. Transvestism, especially when explored cross-culturally, reveals an amazing kaleidoscope of possibilities – far more than it has been feasible to explore here – of behaviours and responses, as well as potential research avenues. Dress codes function as iconographic markers – particularly when plotted against the ever-shifting cultural models of sex, gender and sexuality. Gender is not the only factor, it is one of many which include class, age, sexual style and preference – and these with many permutations – but gender is the only one which is a binary divide and, perhaps because of this, the one for which the boundaries are so clearly marked. Why, in the cultural context of the UK or the US, where gender codes, particularly with regard to dressing, are so much more relaxed than India, are the penalties for reversing them are paradoxically so severe – and only for male to female transvestites? The sharp contrast between India and Britain doesn't just reflect issues of sex and gender; it is also informed by fundamental concepts of the person and the self. This final chapter will look at how the differences between concepts of the person and the self in the two different cultures focused on in this book contribute towards a holistic, cross-cultural understanding of transvestism and the wider issues which accompany it.

Transvestism as a Social Phenomenon

Despite the large amount of material concerning the discourses of sex, gender and sexuality, transvestism is surprisingly under-researched. Perhaps because it usually provokes derision or embarrassment and has risible rather than serious associations with sexual perversion and deviance, it has been shied away from, even in academic circles. In particular, transvestism has rarely been considered cross-culturally – and some important and thought provoking questions have remained unasked. The studies which do exist tend to be monocultural and some – Williams's study of the berdaches (1986) and, to a lesser extent, Nanda's of the hijras (1990), for example – have contained a distinctly polemical element. In a Western context, transvestism is perceived primarily as an individual phenomenon, and one which, at least until relatively recently, has commonly been viewed as a medico-psychiatric problem. Cross-cultural descriptions of transvestism demonstrate above all that there are other perspectives which can and should be considered, those which go beyond the psychological and individual. Not only is cross-dressing a global phenomenon, it is also subject to cultural forces.

In looking for explanations, it is interesting to consider Durkheim's work on suicide (1970). Although at first these two very personal imperatives – cross-dressing and the desire to take one's own life – may seem to form a strange companionship, they are in fact rather similar categories when viewed socially; the central locus of Durkheim's ideas was that suicide, much like transvestism, may appear to be an entirely individual phenomenon but it is also subject to cultural and social forces. Durkheim pointed out that the suicide rate was both enduring (it fluctuates considerably less than most demographic statistics) and sufficiently variegated for each society to be distinctive – and therefore worthy of sociological study as much as psychological:

> The individuals making up a society change from year to year, yet the number of suicides is the same so long as the society itself does not change. The population of Paris renews itself very rapidly; yet the share of Paris in the total French suicides remains practically the same … The causes which thus fix the contingent of voluntary deaths for a given society or one part of it must then be independent of individuals, since they retain the same intensity, no matter what particular persons they operate on. … If a way of life is unchanged while changes occur constantly among those who practise it, it cannot derive its entire reality from them. (1970: 307)

Transvestites, those who tempt social jeopardy by dressing in forbidden clothing, seem to appear as a relative constant throughout most human societies – like suicides – although the form varies and their numbers are considerably more difficult to measure. Each transvestite may be acting as an individual agent but s/he is also performing a social role for the whole of society, whether this is viewed as a social imperative, a transgression, or a striking out for balance and wholeness. (This may also be an interesting contributory explanation for why transvestism appears throughout history and widely varying cultures.) The secular cross-dressers of Western industrialised societies are consigned by their culture to a position which primarily bears disadvantages, marginalisation and disapproval. The hijras receive different treatment and their position, at least until recently, carried some respect. But although Western cross-dressers are in a very different position from those considered in contrast to them, their situation also grants certain benefits, particularly in terms of the range of options open to them.

Concepts of the Person, Individual and Society in India and England: Cultural Contexts of Transvestites and Hijras

Although the origin of ideas regarding the person and the self lie far back in religious and philosophical thinking, it was primarily Mauss and Dumont who introduced these concepts to anthropologists and social scientists, coupled with the need to understand that as a category, 'personhood' can be something very different according to context. Theories have shifted considerably since these early deliberations and, since the revival of interest in the 1980s, anthropology is one of many fields, including psychology and psychoanalysis, Marxism and feminism, waking up again to the significance of these issues to many areas of life and thought. Mauss's classic essay on 'The category of the person' (1938) did much to stimulate debate in this tricky and complex subject, in particular, distinguishing between the personal sense of self and the cultural concept of self – a distinction which is both interesting and important since it demonstrates the dichotomy between the two. The subjective and empirical sense of self may be anywhere on a given scale of possibilities but Mauss is very specific that he is dealing with the *concept* of self, the ideological construct which is in the hands of the élite.

Particularly in a Western context ideas about individuality are, as with transvestism and suicide, perhaps more likely to be seen as the province of psychology. As ethnography amply demonstrates, however, Western notions of the formation of 'personhood' and 'individuality' are by no means the only model. In a recent essay in *The Guardian*, Jonathan Raban points out that, regarding the conflict in Iraq, an understanding of such concepts seems rather important when 'setting out on such an ambitious liberal-imperial project to inflict freedom and democracy by force on the Arab world':

> The single most important thing that Wolfowitz [US Deputy Secretary for Defence] might have learned (had he read some of the classic texts on this part of the world) is that in Arabia, words like 'self', 'community', 'brotherhood' and 'nation' do not mean what he believes them to mean. When the deputy secretary of defence thinks of his own self, he – like me, and probably, like you – envisages an interiorised, secret entity whose true workings are hidden from public view. Masks, roles, personae (like being deputy secretary for defence) mediate between this inner self and the other people with whom it comes into contact. The post-Enlightenment, post-Romantic self, with its autonomous subjective world, is a Western construct, and quite different from the self as it is conceived in Islam. Muslims put an overwhelming stress on the idea of the individual as a social being. The self exists as the sum of its interactions with others. Rosen puts it like this: 'The configuration of one's bonds of obligation define who a person is … the self is not an artefact of interior construction but an unavoidably public act.' Broadly speaking, who you are is: who you know, who depends on you, and to whom you owe allegiance – a visible web of relationships that can be mapped and enumerated. (Jonathan Raban, *The Guardian Review*, 19 April 2003)

This 'interiorisation' of personhood, as Lukes and others have suggested, is particularly attributable to the combining of Christianity and classical thought, 'which suppressed altogether the sense that we are persons only as interlocutors and ends up generating the modern notion of the individual as monad, a movement that involves a significant loss of understanding.' (Lukes, 1985: 288) Something is gained but something is also lost. This difference between interior and exterior self was also extremely well demonstrated in an incident which occurred in Britain during late July 2002. A Zimbabwean government minister was deported from the UK while on his way through Britain to a conference on disability – he was on a list of sixty or so government members forbidden to enter the UK in demonstration of the UK's opposition to Zimbabwe's current policies. The BBC News reported the minister as being 'furious' and the Zimbabwean government as considering the UK officials 'quite mad'. Much of their fury and outraged astonishment can probably be attributed to the much clearer divisibility of an individual from his or her role in Zimbabwe society, and thus their bewilderment when he was arrested and deported while not in his role as a government minister but travelling as a disabled private individual. Ideologies of self are equally important when considering not just transvestism, and whether it is regarded as an instance of individual deviance or a social category, but also the much broader span of cultural orthodoxies regarding sex, gender and sexuality – which also contribute to perceptions of transvestism.

Roles are important because they demonstrate the ability to separate and to divide, to be a 'dividual' rather than an 'individual', to perceive each person as something separate and ultimately alone. They function as part of the network of relationships which allow the individual to act within society, albeit in different ways; the extent to which the amount of 'self' and the amount of 'role' which can be expected to be present in any individual's life changes in quantity and quality from one society to another. Sex, gender, roles and personhood have a strong relationship with each other and all are important for a cross-cultural study of cross-dressing. In most non-Western societies, roles are more clearly separated from the individual self; they exist in Western societies but are seen to function out of the individual self, to be closely bound up with the self, and to be subservient to notions of individuality, as the Zimbabwe example demonstrates only too clearly.

In the West, the self may be construed as an elastic and changing image which may be hard to pin down but is nevertheless a must in our society, something which we 'present' to others requiring construction and maintenance and effort. The UK transvestites demonstrate the construction of that self-identity more obviously than usual, in that they construct a female identity which is a counterpart to their male selves. When contrasted with the hijra narratives, it becomes clear, however, that there is more to it than this; UK transvestites feel the need to construct such an identity and to integrate it (evidenced by comments such as Pauline's in Chapter 5, 'there are two halves of me but they form a perfect whole'), particularly as a result of the cultural notion which dictates that we experience ourselves as a single and distinct entity, that 'self' and 'personhood' must be conflated into one individualistic whole.

The implications for hijras and UK transvestites follow through into significantly different pathways, particularly when looking at the sexed and gendered aspects of individuality. In most – perhaps all – societies, notions of the person are definitively and closely linked to conceptualisations of sex and gender, whatever their local variations. If gender is a constituent of roles, biological sex must also be part of individuality. Because in the West people are deemed to be – and are treated as – individuated selves, roles are seen as intrinsic to persons and, crucially, those persons are defined in binary terms. This is so fundamental that it could even be argued that in the UK and USA people are no longer seen as 'individuals', but as 'individual men' or 'individual women'. As Griggs (1999) notes in her account of a sex change, gender neutrality in Western society is not an option: over the years of shift from male to female, she was seen as man by some and woman by others, but never the possibility of something in between.

The problem with ideas which circulate absolutely routinely in a culture's thought and at such a subterranean level that they barely need to be spoken about or referred to, is that they are perversely difficult to access, usually necessitating a sideways approach. But this is what anthropology does so well, having a number of these at its disposal, gift-giving/reciprocity systems, for example, or kinship networks or, as in this case, ubiquitous items of material culture. Clothing is a 'way in' to notions of demarcation, in this case of one of the most obvious of binary divides to be found in any culture – male and female – and thus a way in to sex and gender. Having passed through this gate, it is also possible to progress towards ideas of the construction of the self, particularly since transvestites inhabit by choice at least two selves, a male and a female.

Crossing gender boundaries can be seen as a mirror of methods of construction of the self/individual/person. In the UK, where the ideology of individualism holds sway, the male and female self (which the transvestite often views as being 'two halves of the same whole') are conflated into one. The obvious assumption is that this construction makes sense to them and to the world in which they live. In India, however, where constructions of the self are much less predicated on the 'undivided' nature of the individual, the presentation of a unified 'two halves of a whole' format is unnecessary and, furthermore, the hijras' position within society has some element of cultural support.

For both groups – and probably for most societies – ideas about the self and ideas from religious and cosmological beliefs, social attitudes to morality and so on, can be seen to continually feed into each other, but also to be dynamic, to undergo major and minor shifts which reflect the cultural changes which are always taking place. Mauss suggests that human societies start with a much more 'sociocentric' notion of the person and evolve towards a more detached view – but, as Morris states, Mauss argues that:

> It is only with the coming of Christianity that the true metaphysical foundations of the person as a moral subject became fully established. A transition occurred between the notion of *persona*, of 'a man clad in a condition', to the notion of a person as an autonomous human subject. Of particular importance were the sectarian movements of the seventeenth and eighteenth centuries, for they 'posed the question regarding individual liberty, regarding the individual conscience and the right to communicate directly with God'. (Morris, 1994:4)

As Weber suggested in *The Protestant Ethic and the Spirit of Capitalism*, it is no accident that the modernist, consumer-capital driven society emerged in the West, where attitudes towards human competition and freedom were on a quite different level than in cultures such as that of India (and much of the rest of the world beyond northern Europe and America).[1] This cannot help but have profound implications which continue to echo each other in terms of the development of the 'rational individual' and the choices s/he makes.

Contrasting Concepts of the Self within the Hindu and Western Traditions

Compare Western ideas with the notion of self in India, where Hinduism posits a quite different set of ideologies and the background is not only the hierarchy of the caste system but also a binding family structure. Caste, which Dumont proposed eclipses all other aspects of organisation within Indian society, explained for him why Western notions of egalitarian opportunity for all had not developed in India.[2] Whilst caste may not be as all-explaining as Dumont would suggest, it certainly carries implications for the hijras, as does the Indian family structure – contrasting sharply with English society where, although the family certainly has a role, it is not generally expected to have such a tight grip on the individual as it does in India. The importance of this structure in India is reflected in the way in which hijras are organised: they live in groups which resemble a traditional Indian family.

Also, and most importantly in this context, notions of the need for individual 'freedom' and 'development' are less influential in India than in Great Britain. While this reflects differing concepts of personhood in each society, there is also a link to varying attitudes to the capacity for individual achievement. A society where many people see their destiny as being largely fixed from birth (for religious or other reasons), is likely to be more static than a society where there is a considerable emphasis on personal advancement. In the West, society is undeniably individualistic and as Morris states, has

a relatively inflated concern with the self which in extremes gives rise to anxiety, to a sense that there is a loss of meaning in contemporary life, to a state of narcissism, and to an emphasis in popular psychology on 'self-actualisation' ... The Western conception of the person is thus that of an 'individuated being', separate from both the social and natural world. ... [It] is materialistic and rationalistic. It reflects the thought of Western culture which has lost, Frank Johnson (1985) suggests, the sense of the mystical.' (1994: 16)

This is clearly not true of India, where the 'sense of the mystical' seems everywhere apparent, from the roadside shrines to the extensive belief in and use of astrologers and hand-readers (the practice of which also differs markedly from East to West being, in India, much more strongly linked to the belief that lives are governed by destiny and in the West, focused primarily on personality traits.) Whilst it could be said that many inhabitants of the Western world no longer have strong religious convictions and are largely unaware of the dogmas and precepts which have historically contributed to their cultural environment – and arguably, continue to do so – this is much less the case in India where religion, philosophy, culture and social systems seem inextricably connected. Hinduism as a social framework seems much more deeply entrenched and integrated into individuals' lives and experiences.

Consciously or not, concepts from Hindu religion and philosophy form a powerful influence on everyday thought and actions in the lives of most Hindus. As many authors have commented – and this is very noticeable when living in India – the relationship of caste to 'karma' (action), is all pervasive. This has strong implications for ideas of the person, particularly in respect of their being born with a history of performed actions, a 'slate' which is marked by the actions of previous lives, these being crucial in determining their position in this one. The caste system is not simply a social system but part of a divinely ordered and sanctioned scheme; the self, in Hindu thought, is identified more with the spiritual than the individual or social. Whilst Westerners see their strength of character as deriving from individuality, in Hinduism, the empirical self is a transient and flimsy article, since the real self is spiritual.

This is in strong contrast to the West, where a 'clean slate' is exactly what the individual is largely expected to have at birth, their life ahead being one of 'improving the shining hour', and their destiny very much of their own making. One example of this can be found in the different approaches between India and the West to yoga. It is interesting to note that the West has enthusiastically taken up the practice of yoga as a way of improving the self – the main yoga journal in this country is, indeed, named *Yoga for Life* – whereas in essence, yoga is conceived of within Hinduism as much more about transcending the self as an empirical experience – it is not, as Morris points out 'the key to life; it is ... the denial, the renunciation of it.' (1994: 92) It is as if, in order for the Western world to be able to embrace yoga, it must – at least partially – be formed into a product which is life-enhancing, a product which 'improves' the self, for the Western mind could hardly encompass the notion of a process which leads towards the expiry of meaningfulness on an individual level. The difference between the religious and philosophical under-pinnings of the two societies is very clear.

Religious thought would seem to be very important to this debate. For India, one does not have to completely swallow Dumont's arguments to observe that the caste system does not facilitate a view of the world as being one where infinite possibilities are open to the individual. This has very clear and important repercussions for the hijras, as the fieldwork shows. Questions about 'the operation', almost invariably received the categorical response 'I was born like this', thus identifying the hijras' condition as one of God's making, not their own, whilst in the UK, the transvestite's destiny is believed to be in his own hands and a matter of his choice.[3] It is interesting to observe that although in the UK, it would be perfectly acceptable for a vicar to say that his or her choice of career was a 'calling', i.e. s/he had been 'called by God' to do this, it is not even considered a possibility for a transgendered person to fall into the same category, in the way that a hijra or berdache does. For the transvestite, Dumont's comment – 'as Durkheim said, roughly, our own society obliges us to be free' (1980: 8) – would seem to apply; the transvestite has not been born like this but it is a matter of his own choosing and he must therefore be responsible for the consequences. Thus, for a transgendered person in India to say 'I was born like this' is completely conceded whilst in the UK, it is viewed with some cynicism. UK transvestites themselves would – and do – dispute their freedom of choice in this area, arguing that they have felt since they were old enough to be able to make such distinctions that they had strong female leanings, but it is arguably one reason why society regards them as strange – because it perceives this as a very odd choice.

The way in which each of these societies views diversity is also likely to be dissimilar. India has been characterised as a society where there is 'a place for everything and everything in its place'. If, as Jaffrey suggests, castism exploits difference but that difference is seen as more or less fixed it may, given elements of cultural support, be possible for a space to be created for a group such as the hijras (but only as a group). As Jaffrey states, the approach can be seen as one of 'you are not of us, we are not of you. In this paradox (lies) the paradox "identity". As critics of castism, the hijras had managed to form a "caste" of their own, the caste of "the excluded" and therefore "an identity" though equivalent to the untouchable.' (1997: 85)

Individuality and Identity

Mauss suggests that individuality and self-identity, so crucial to ideas of self in the West, may be seen as a cultural artefact in the same terms as anything else that we create. To some extent, we are all actors, demonstrating our ability to carry out our chosen or allotted role, and could thus be accused of 'conscious impression management'. As Eriksen makes clear,

> ... there are social conventions defining everything we do as social creatures. Even to express the most powerful and sincere emotions, one has to follow specific, culturally defined rules prescribing how to express such emotions. Even the most spontaneous of acts must be channelled through a socially defined mode of expression if it is to be comprehensible. (Eriksen, 1995: 42)

This has interesting implications for the transvestite in Western cultures. First, because transvestites clearly go against the social conventions of behaviour in choosing to dress at all, and second because one of the main reasons they state for wanting to do this is because they wish to express emotions which are not gender normative for males and thus dressing provides a sense of release. (As do the cross-dressed actors in the Naven ceremony described by Bateson. (1980))

Increased interest in and research into the ideologies of the self began to develop in the 1980s, following Mauss but distinguished by the idea that experience/empirical research is critical to understanding – and now 'experience' is seen by some as the rubric under which much research is going forward. (Carrithers et al., 1986: 422) If experience is the only reliable – or personally 'truthful' – way of accounting for the world around, then the UK transvestites' experience of their cultural world will inevitably provide a strong contrast to that of the hijras – and many others – because of the expectations and assumptions of that world regarding how identity is constructed and the notable differences of concepts of self and personhood in the West (or, more specifically, the UK and USA).

Clearly, there is a radical discontinuity between Indian and British societies. In Western (especially North Atlantic) societies, self, person and individual tend to be conflated and used almost inter-changeably, whereas in most societies a rather different construction obtains. This has repercussions for both of the groups studied here. First because, as the empirical evidence in this study demonstrates, whereas some UK transvestites verify their experience as being a matter of synthesising the 'sexed' and 'gendered' parts of themselves which they find at odds with cultural norms and thus strive to integrate – and, perhaps more importantly, to present as integrated – the hijras do not perceive the same necessity for the composite self, since the Indian model of self, personhood and individuality is crucially different in this regard. Second, some transvestites thus feel they have to merge the individual and the person, whilst hijras do not, and the hijras join a like community and leave the world they previously inhabited, whilst UK transvestites do not.

Personhood and Transvestism in Cross-Cultural Perspective

Hijras, like gender-crossers everywhere, are unquestionably a form of unorthodoxy. In Mary Douglas's terms, they 'spoil the pattern' of Indian life which is so focused on marriage and the production of children, since whatever their perceived sex, the thing that they can never do is bear a child. (1966: 64) But in Indian society, their role as both (and neither) male and female, has been made into a category, one which has – or has had – a number of favourable characteristics as well as the more obvious unfavourable ones. The contrast with Britain is very visible. Whereas the hijras must have an identity, British transvestites are denied one. In an individualistic society the transvestite is, not surprisingly, left to his own devices in terms of his desire to cross-dress, and it is of course never suggested that he should go off and join a particular group who share his interests, leaving all the rest of his life behind. One might question why the hijras must do this; if they are perceived in some sense as deriving a different – and more acceptable – place in society from their base within a culture with a greater emphasis on roles, why must they renounce their previous life and enter a separate community? The answer is almost certainly that it is these very roles which prevent them from staying within their original family, since they cannot fulfil the traditional role of husband and father. In order to withdraw from this part, they must withdraw entirely.

UK transvestites and Indian hijras each in their own way present a type of relationship of the individual to the collective – in both cases of individuals who deviate from a social norm through crossing fairly fixed gender boundaries, but each case demonstrating very differently constructed methods of how that relationship is neutralised (India) or controlled (UK). In addition, the fragmentary nature of the individual to the collective which exists in the UK would, arguably, not be tolerable within Indian society. UK transvestites are keen to portray themselves in a way which reflects both their individual identity and perspective and their view of the social position and experience of transvestites as a group. Because they seldom act or function as a group, however, their identity tends be much more varied. The hijras, by contrast, are very much a coherent group. They understand themselves as a defined community and have a settled place within the hierarchy of Indian society, one which is understood by its members and has culturally established boundaries. There are records of the hijras in mythology, folk tales and religious texts and they play a supporting role in some of the religious festivals and rites of passage, particularly weddings and childbirth. Their place, having been entered into, does not require further negotiation or re-negotiation with the boundaries of societal acceptance. The front they show to the world, their 'personhood', is fairly well formatted and is acknowledged as a way of being, 'the way hijras are'.

Also, human beings in all cultures seem to function as a cognising self (see, for example, Sokefeld, 1999). In general, human beings understand the process of continuing as an 'I' and maintaining a self that they cognise and re-cognise – as well as having a group identity which meshes with this: 'the cognising self (ego, I), certain of its existence through its own acts of cognition, becomes the warranty against an ambiguous and deceptive world of things.' (Sokefeld, 1999: 417) This 'warranty' that we are who we are only remains true if the ego continues in sameness of identity. This has different repercussions for UK transvestites and hijras: while transvestites have to take steps to integrate because they have more than one identity, hijras manage this by constructing a new 'identikit' self which is consistent with a different group identity. Whilst it has proved tempting for some to portray only Western cultures as champions of singularity, it seems likely that people will continue everywhere to interpret the world around them according to a model that could be interpreted in some fashion as individual – and to deviate from the norm. What they do with this variance of interpretation – or in Butler's terms, how they perform it – is distinctively modified by their cultural situation. Despite the general liberalisation of British society during the past forty years, where much individualism is not only accepted but affirmed, it may initially seem strange that transvestites are tolerated little better than they were half a century ago. The governing notions of an individual-directed – as opposed to a destiny-directed – culture go some way to explaining why in contemporary Britain although transvestism may be more widely discussed, it is still a matter of ridicule for the onlooker and embarrassment for the subject. The transvestite is still seen as a sexual deviant, while transvestism remains something to be discouraged and/or hidden.

Blurring the Boundaries: Deconstructing Theories of the Self

It is clear that ideologies of the person and their strong links with conceptualisations of sex and gender play a cellular part in what happens to transgendered men in India and the UK. But valuable as these theoretical constructs are, they are not without flaws. In particular, these are concerned with their 'monolithism' (dependence on a homogeneity which in many cases is seldom as entrenched as it might appear from many of the accounts given by some authors) and androcentrism. They may not invalidate the arguments above, but they both have implications for gender-crossers – and are of sufficient import, I believe, to call for a shift in the ways in which such notions are considered and applied by anthropologists and others working in these fields.

I am going to focus particularly on the androcentrism, since this has further implications for the subject of this study. Western philosophy – and thus many of the concepts which contribute to the Western comprehension of ideologies of personhood (and much more) – has had a strong male bias throughout its development. Not only have issues specifically connected with women's experience been excluded but also abstract concepts, such as reason and logic (very much associated with a male perspective, understanding and ordering of the world) have been privileged over other qualities such as instinct and intuition (often associated with 'the feminine'.) And yet this seems little recognised or acknowledged, as Morris points out: 'the concept of person, which is central to philosophy, is generally treated as without bias, and as referring to both men and women. Thus in such historical claims as "man is a rational animal" it is seen as only a simple matter of substituting "person" for "man" implying that it does not change its essential meaning. Feminists might well disagree with this assertion, and would argue that "man" implies precisely that, not the human person but the male gender.' (1994: 169–70)

This cannot but have influenced and modified much of the thinking concerned with concepts of the person, not only the ethnocentric view which is very difficult to stand outside but also the automatically assumed male perspective. In particular, the approach which emphasises personal freedom and autonomy tends also to shrink from and to disparage women and the themes which have come to be associated them such as physicality, nature, sex and the body. These characteristics highlight a number of the issues presented in this study and, in the West in particular, link directly to the attitudes which esteem male over female and thus cannot comprehend the desire of a male to become a part-time female.

Nancy Chodorow's work (1974, 1978), in the field of psychoanalysis and discussed by, for example Moore (1988) and Morris (1994) is of great interest to this discourse. Her studies deal primarily with gender identity differences between boys and girls, but the material becomes even more illuminating when considering the construction of Western philosophy and thus of ideologies of the person. Boys, she demonstrates, learn early to detach from the mother and this has implications for their ability to form relationships as adults. Girls, on the other hand, can remain attached and so are more likely to develop empathy and have less rigid 'ego boundaries', generally forming a more 'relational' way of being while boys advance their masculine identity through negation of connection or dependence and are more likely to experience themselves as detached, impartial and individuated. In consequence they gradually develop a style which is analytic and differentiated rather than empathic and associated. (1974: 56–7)

Chodorow's findings have two major strands of implication for this study. The first is of interest for theoretical conceptualisations of individuality in general, modes of abstraction into categories of thought which have, arguably, stemmed directly from a masculine, rationalist tradition. These are largely predicated on a Western, male perspective and thus are arguably much more applicable to men than to women in Western cultures. The second is pertinent regarding the fieldwork with UK transvestites themselves, who in many cases state that 'empathy' and 'association' are particular aspects of womanhood that they desire to emulate – the ability to form relationships more easily, converse in a less detached style, and abandon for a time the male attitude to the world which they perceive only too clearly as detached, analytical and competitive. Although it is obviously possible for them to converse with women while dressed as a man, it is the clothing and female appearance which enable these conversations to translate, in some crucial way, from being male-female conversations to female-female conversations.

UK transvestites exist in a society where the importance of individual self-expression could be argued to be paramount (although their particular form is strongly disapproved of), whilst Indian hijras exist within a social world where the bonds of relationships are generally considered to be placed above the needs or desires of the individual (and in Chodorow's terms is thus, arguably, a more 'feminine' culture). The hijras do not encounter the same problems in expressing their individuality – indeed they probably seldom consider it – but they are culturally supported in their life path by a number of linked philosophies and symbolic structures. The next section will consider these questions and the wider implications of theories of the person with regard to the fieldwork presented in this study.

Transvestites, Constructed Selves, and Issues of Sex and Gender

The interviews with UK transvestites indicate their conceptions of sex and gender and of themselves as individuals. Although a range of possibilities is presented, both from the replies to questionnaires and from the personal interviews, certain views clearly predominate – but they do not necessarily present the view one might expect. With respect to the issues of sex and gender, the outlook presented most frequently is that transvestites admire and often envy women, they seek to emulate them both in clothing and behaviour, and that they recognise that this is not well tolerated by the society in which they live (and they wish it were.)

With regard to concepts of the person, although the 'two halves of a whole' type of comment certainly exists, the majority of the feedback would seem to indicate that UK transvestites do not perceive this as a significant issue. It could be argued, of course, that their non-perception simply reflects the internalisation of such norms; that they are too deeply buried to be part of conscious awareness and that this is why transvestites automatically try to fit into a Western model of integrated individuation. But their statements would appear to contradict this, arguing instead for a model of instinctive separation of the dual male/female modes. For example John/Joy comments that he does, in a sense, do just the opposite of integrating the two halves of himself, in that he never allows himself to 'mix' the male and female sides of himself and clearly does not perceive the notion of having two selves as a problem.

Dan/Shelly similarly does not seem to consider the entirely separate male and female sides of himself as problematic: he may acknowledge the difficulties of being a transvestite (stemming mainly from cultural perceptions) but he 'loves the difference' – in lifestyle, movement, clothing, behaviour, conversation and so on – of being a woman. Gavin/Gina specifically states that he would be prepared to 'dump' the Gavin part of himself and has considered dressing as Gina full time but, arguably, this is simply that he feels considerably more comfortable with a female identity and with presenting that image to the world, rather than feeling that he has to integrate the two aspects.

This echoes Simon/Sandra's comment, 'as a man, I feel I am "me" as I *have* to be. I feel empty and not fully alive.' In response to the question, 'do you think/act/behave differently when dressed?', he does go on to say, 'I used to – but now feel much more synchronised. I love the transformation process', which could be read as implying that he feels inwardly comfortable with the separation but has bowed to the Western notion of integrated individuality in becoming more 'synchronised'. His comments regarding his train journey to Oxford (see Chapter 3), however, bear out the *differences* he feels rather than the integration between his male and female selves.

This would also appear to be true of the hijras; although one would not necessarily expect them to discuss notions of individuality versus holistic concepts of the self since they are as deeply internalised for Indian people as they are Westerners: their personal stories arguably demonstrate that they have a very clear and coherent notion of themselves as actors in their own lives. Unquestionably the hijras and the way in which they live their lives reflect concepts of the person, as well as concepts of sex, gender and sexuality, and the contrast with the UK transvestites shows that for both groups, these concepts are deeply inter-linked with the choices they make and the options open to them. Certainly it is crucial to perceive the social relations and the way in which these are culturally informed – but these are by no means as clear-cut as the initial core-thinking (put forward by, for example, Mauss, Durkheim, Dumont) might imply.

In addition to their having well-formed notions of a personal history, in the act of choosing to become a hijra, rather than having this option forced upon them, they indicate that they are acting as consciously individuated persons. This could be seen as bearing out Sokefeld's observations, based on his research in Pakistan, that 'there can be no identities without selves ... (and that this) is not about a cultural concept of the self. It is about whether we can discern something besides the changing identities of the 'empirical agent' (Dumont's term) – that is, whether we have to conceive of an acting self in addition to its identities.' (1999: 419) He further comments that his research, rather than conforming to the accepted dictates of notions of 'sociocentric' identities in non-Western groups, forced him to 'acknowledge the importance of acting individuals ... (and) is an example of the struggle to act and to present oneself as a consistent self in a situation of plural and contradicting identities.' (ibid.) I am suggesting that the hijras demonstrate that even in a situation where roles are pluralistic rather than dependent on notions of the individuated self, the sense of self as an individual is still present. Neither group in these two very different societies, therefore, completely bears out the hypothetical relationship with concepts of the self that one might expect, thus opening potential new avenues to be explored, both in ethnography and other fields – a potential which needs to be informed by real material rather than assumptions.

A Broader Conceptualisation of Transvestism

It is clear from the answers of UK transvestites that, for them, it is issues of sex and gender which are primary rather than concepts of individuality. UK transvestites who answered the questionnaires say repeatedly that their main reason for dressing as a female is to feel comfortable with displaying aspects of behaviour and personality they consider female. This would suggest, not surprisingly, that it is with concepts of masculinity and femininity that they are most engaged and that these are more the language in which the debate is conducted. This is hardly surprising, given the elusive and abstract nature of concepts of personhood. Whilst dominant, underpinning concepts of individuality and of the person are far-reaching and socially reified, they are also rather too abstract for everyday application.

Clearly, models primarily exist which reflect the dominant group of any society – in the West, undeniably still male and middle class – hence the emphasis on the primacy of the individual, a model which frequently does not adequately reflect other groups within Western society. Overall, however, it seems very clear that major shifts need to occur in this theoretical field and that they are as important to concepts of the person as they have been found to be in other branches of anthropological thinking, such as the now widely recognised 'double male bias' within much anthropological fieldwork. Notions of sex and gender and of the person are incontestably connected; as noted earlier, the dominant construction in Britain is that of gendered individuals. Beliefs, both in integrated individuality and in the binary nature of sex and gender, are so deeply rooted that they form part of the collective unconscious model; in practical and theoretical terms they are continuously and mutually reinforcing. Concepts of the person, though – formulated within the framework of the Western tradition of philosophy and added to by equally Western notions from other disciplines – have resulted in a set of conceptions (perhaps the same double male bias in a different guise), now being applied to non-Western societies.

By challenging the dominant social models, however, the hijras and the UK transvestites demonstrate that a further, personal construction is also possible, albeit one which is controlled through pigeonholing in India and suppressed into secrecy and embarrassment in the UK. One thing which becomes abundantly clear is that in both societies, any putative crossing, reversals, or 'neutering' in the sex and gender arena is one which provokes a strong reaction; the cultural insistence on conformity is deep-rooted, and the possibility of change in this area – especially in the Westernised cultures of the US and UK – continues to be something which induces anxiety and resistance; nor would this seem to be declining.

This raises again the question of why masculinity is still the 'must have' of crucial achievements for men and 'effiminacy' such an undesirable. Why, when so much has apparently changed in women's economic and social position in the West over the last century, is this still the case? (Arguably, more true for the West than for India.) Although it is fundamental to ask the question about the relationship between concepts of self and concepts of sex and gender, the answers still don't reach the conceptual issues underneath; we have to grasp the underlying cultural constructions which privilege the masculine over the feminine. Models of transvestism show up these issues with total clarity.

With reference to cross-dressers, it seems clear that concepts of the person seem to be less contrasted between the UK and India than is conveniently argued, whilst notions of splitting sex and gender appear to stem from a Western model (although there is a certain irony that Moore and others have often found their demonstration of such points within non-Western cultures.) If it is accepted that such notions derive from a Western model, the argument that the conflation of sex and gender merely reflects Western concepts of the person and 'individuality' begins to seem less cogent since concepts of the person are themselves inherently ethnocentric. In addition, the ideas put forward by UK transvestites themselves do not necessarily reflect the desire for integration of sexed and gendered selves one might expect.

Notions of personhood cannot help but inform issues of sex and gender and vice versa, and such conceptual frameworks are definitively of value to the issues discussed. There are, however, qualifications which need to be made – and which dent the apparent smoothness and solidity of such debates. The theoretical arguments regarding monolithism and androcentrism, coupled with the empirical research with transgendered men in the UK and Indian contexts, seem to demonstrate that some changes to the mould, in particular to the heavily weighted nature of these concepts and ideologies, are required. In addition, the ethnographic material here suggests first, that the UK transvestites do not necessarily conform to the notions one might expect of integrated individuality, and second, in the Indian context, in the most simplistic terms, hijras can become hijras because the category exists; it has cultural support and is (or at least, has been until recently) a position which commands some respect and honour.[4]

In addition, I would suggest that the tendency for academic discourses on sex and gender to concentrate on the economic, political and social worlds of cultures has led (with some exceptions) to a rather underdeveloped area of study and analysis of the imaginative and spiritual worlds which underlie the more obvious hegemonic structures. Although these have been only briefly discussed here, it would be much too simplistic to disregard the existence and influence of the religious, mythological and philosophical roots of cultural notions, since these crucially inform the situations regarding different perceptions of the see-saw of individuality and personhood – as well as sex and gender – which clearly obtain.

'This is an Absurd Ordination for People to Live in, in 2002'[5]

The complex, cross-cultural range of responses to transvestism soundly demonstrates that we are not locked into a world composed only of 'regularities' or even archetypes, constructed or otherwise. There will no doubt always be some elements which defeat comprehension and analysis. Whilst it is important that, as Whitehead comments, we do not simply replace the binary divide with points 'along any old axis' (1981: 110), it is equally essential that further possibilities regarding sex, gender and sexuality are taken on board. As Devor states in her lecture, *How Many Sexes? How Many Genders? When Two are not enough* (1996), we have begun to come to terms with the extraordinary bio-diversity around us in the world – together with an understanding of the need for its survival if the planet is to thrive – but,

> unfortunately, we have been very slow to generalise this concept to our understandings of gender, sex and sexuality. We tend to think of people whose genders, sexes or sexualities are unusual as 'mistakes' of either nature or of nurture. Our dogged insistence on thinking in terms of binary categorisations of male/female, man/woman, heterosexual/homosexual, either right/wrong serves to blinker our vision. It is time that we begin to … retool ourselves for the job of coming to see, appreciate and understand the value of human gender, sex and sexual diversity. (1996: 1)

Cross-dressing demonstrates this diversity and the possibilities which are – or have been – created by some cultures and not by others. The response to cross-dressing within the two very different cultures presented here is a fragment of the possibilities that exist but even just these two show up the analytic dichotomies and domains which stem from the binary divide of sex and gender.

The issues of gender become exciting when one goes beyond the debates which consider them either as opposite and completely separate camps or as either ends of a pole or, in postmodernist terms, a continuum with the shades of possibility which exist in between the far ends. As stated in the introduction, transvestism may at first appear to be an inconsequential subject matter, but deeper exploration reveals a great deal which contributes both to the sex and gender debate within social and cultural anthropology, to studies in material culture and to the issues which surround them.

Notes

1. Further than that, there is a strong argument (Morris cites Naomi Scheman, 1983: 226) that: 'the ideology of liberal individualism "is deeply useful to the maintenance of capitalist and patriarchal society and deeply embedded in our notions of liberation, freedom and equality".' (Morris, 1994: 184)

2. Although arguably, it was the British colonial period of administration which confirmed and systematised the caste system in India since they found it useful as a hierarchical tool for more effective government.

3. This is echoed in narratives regarding the role of a *berdache* – one which is not forced upon him but divinely ordained or called by 'destiny', as Schutzer describes: 'I was called through a vision, by *Anog Ite* (Double Face Woman) from out of the womb to be that which I am. She offered me a choice. Lakota deities never order. My gender transformation was called for by the Spirits. She blessed me with skills of a supernatural kind ... Winkte are men who dress like women, look like women and act like women. They do so by their own choice or in obedience to a dream. They are not like other men but *Wakan Tanka*, the Great Spirit, made them winktes and we accept them as such ... My people see me as multi-dimensional and I do not have to fight for a place in my society to be accepted ... Winkte are not branded as threats to a rigid gender ideology, but rather we are considered an affirmation of humanity's original pre-gendered unity – we are representatives of a form of solidarity and wholeness which transcends the division of humans into men and women. Winkte transformation was not, and is not, a complete shift from his or her biological gender to the opposite one, but rather an approximation of the latter in some of its social and ... physical aspects, effecting an intermediate status that cuts across the boundaries between gender categories." (Schutzer, 1994: 12)

4. As discussed in Chapter 6, it may be that the religious and mythological background have a greater influence than a straightforward application of concepts of the person allow. The existence of both male and female

deities within the cosmological structure and of gender-abrogating possibilities within the mythological world may create a culturally supportive
paradigm into which the hijras can fit whilst UK transvestites exist in an
entirely different culture in which there are few feminine core images.

5. Judith Butler, interviewed by Professor L Taylor, Radio 4, March
2002, discussing the continued cultural insistence on gender binarism.

Appendix A: Questionnaire

PART I

1. Are you aged 14–21 /22–28 /29–35 /36–42 /43–39 /57–63 /64–70 ?
   /70+ (Please circle)

2. Do you live in a village/small town /city /large town /suburb /other
   (please say)?

3. Your occupation?

4. When did you first realise that you wished to cross-dress? (Was it associated with anything in particular?)

5. How often do you now cross-dress (publicly and/or privately)?

6. Has the frequency changed during that time (more often? less often?)

7. Do you see or speak to other transvestites much? (Where, how?)

8. Have you talked to them much about why? *(e.g. Why some people
   need to cross-dress, why it should be you and no someone else,*

whether it is linked to childhood factors/upbringing or whether it is innate?)

9. Do their opinions coincide with yours or are they different (in what way?)

10. Have you ever considered gender re-assignment surgery?

11. Have you ever had psychotherapy/counselling?

PART II

12. What articles of clothing do you particularly like? (outer and inner wear)

13. Do they represent a fashion style? *(would they, for example, be the kind of thing that a woman your age would be most likely to wear? Or more glamorous/trendy/chic? Or more relaxed and informal? Are they what you would like your girlfriend/wife to wear?)*

14. Do you wear make-up? (always/sometimes?) and/or a wig?

15. Do you choose clothes particularly for their colour? texture? style? cut? comfort?

16. Where do you mainly shop for clothes/wigs/make-up etc.

17. Describe your favourite outfit (real or imaginary, but please say which).

PART III

18. Do you feel that dressing expresses an aspect of your personality? (Possibly one which is difficult to express in a masculine form?) Is there anyone who acts as a role model for your female self?

19. Which is more important, the *sexuality* of being dressed as a woman or the feeling of *being* a woman (personality aspect) ?

20. Does dressing make you feel that you have two possibilities of being you?

21. Is this an appealing factor? (One of the most appealing of it?)

22. Do you ever wish you had been born female. (Periodically? Often? Always?)

23. If so, why? What is it about being a woman that is so appealing?

24. How much of the (partial) desire to be a woman is appeased by dressing?

25. Do you feel that you act/think/behave differently when dressed?

26. Do you like the 'he' side more or the 'she' side?

27. Why do you think it is so important to us (/society) to be able to distinguish a man from a woman, for example if we walk past them in the street or sit next to them on a train. (e.g. is it because of sexuality? – or the kind of conversation one would have? – or is it just to be able to pigeon-hole them in a similar way to age-group?)

Please use this space to add any extra comments or to add to questions if there is not enough space underneath them.

If you would not mind me contacting you again, please put an identifying name or number and address or telephone number below.

Thank you very much for doing this. Please return the questionnaire to: Charlotte Suthrell, Trinity College, OXFORD OX1 4LF

Appendix B

Answers to Question 3 – Occupation

(10) marketing and production manager
(11) musician and teacher
(12) senior academic
(13) receptionist/post room manager
(14) student
(15) retired, disabled
(16) retired
(17) pharmacist
(18) marine engineer, retired
(19) business analyst
(20) retired
(21) unemployed
(22) computer analyst/programmer
(23) clinical prosthetist
(24) banker/representative/teacher, retired
(25) company co-director, semi-retired
(26) teacher and p/time astrologer
(27) charge nurse, retired
(28) foundry worker
(29) quality manager
(30) cartoonist
(31) degree level student cartoonist
(32) accountant
(33) database manager in civil service
(34) retired
(35) local govt. accountant, retired
(36) machinist
(37) retired
(38) airline pilot, retired
(39) consulting engineer, retired
(40) musician
(41) company director
(42) freelance photographer
(43) self employed (computers)
(44) mechanical engineer
(45) ex-soldier
(46) retired
(47) sales representative
(48) surveyor
(49) civil servant, retired
(50) insurance company official
(51) professional engineer
(52) retired
(53) paramedic services manager, retired
(54) RAF, retired
(55) –
(56) plasterer, retired
(57) engineer
(58) retired
(59) telephone engineer, retired
(60) –
(61) professional
(62) fire-fighter, retired
(63) office worker
(64) teacher/tree-surgeon, retired
(65) senior academic, retired
(66) store manager, retired
(67) college lecturer, retired
(68) chartered engineer

(69) proprietor of wholesale plant nursery
(70) holistic therapy student
(71) –
(72) senior buyer
(73) railway servant ('active retired')
(74) RAF, electronics design engineer, housewife, retired
(75) bank manager
(76) post office manager
(77) teacher, retired
(78) FE college manager
(79) none
(80) Home Office
(81) refinery operator
(82) physiotherapist, retired
(83) professional healthcare
(84) civil servant, retired
(85) lettings administrator
(86) self employed
(87) retired
(88) retired
(89) BT engineer
(90) retired
(91) fitter
(92) retired
(93) power station shift engineer
(94) retired
(95) lorry driver
(96) clinical psychologist
(97) civil servant (middle management)
(98) computer system designer
(99) retired
(100) accountant
(101) Pensioner (was car rectifier)
(102) Care worker
(103) police clerk
(104) teacher
(105) accountant
(106) teacher
(107) bank clerk, retired
(108) research scientist
(109) library assistant
(110) marine biologist in environmental science
(111) college lecturer
(112) in the transport business
(113) senior manager (banking and finance), retired
(114) retired
(115) company director
(116) electronic hardware designer
(117) retired
(118) on invalidity benefit
(119) design engineer
(120) writer
(121) student in caring professions
(122) manager
(123) lecturer
(124) disabled
(125) subject officer for exam board, retired
(126) retired
(127) quality assurance supervisor
(128) quality control in electronics, retired
(129) professor
(130) building surveyor
(131) managing director
(132) offshore
(133) systems engineer
(134) station assistant
(135) solicitor, retired
(136) accountant
(137) retired
(138) teacher
(139) manager in the printing industry
(140) administration assistant
(141) electrician, scenic designer and artist
(142) computer hardware engineer
(143) civil service
(144) chartered management accountant
(145) computer systems engineer
(146) legal executive
(147) marketing dealer/company director
(148) probation officer
(149) electronics engineer
(150) self-employed
(151) farmer
(152) –

(153) mental health community worker
(154) local govt administrator
(155) personnel and training officer
(156) teacher
(157) manager
(158) retired
(159) self-employed
(160) retired
(161) local govt officer
(162) carpenter, retired
(163) heating engineer/salesman
(164) teacher
(165) computer engineer
(166) BBC manager
(167) soldier and radar engineer, retired
(168) importer/distributor of engineering goods for research
(169) postman, retired
(170) engineer and training officer, retired
(171) tax inspector, retired, now engaged in full time research
(172) retired
(173) retired
(174) musician, writer, piano-tuner
(175) nurse (learning disabilities)
(176) Research Botanist
(177) –
(178) –
(179) sales manager

(180) –
(181) professional
(182) retired
(183) teacher
(184) manager (shop)
(185) clerk, retired
(186) computer engineer
(187) police, retired
(188) civil servant
(189) mature student
(190) engineer, retired

Some totals

30 in engineering/computing/ research science/aviation/ electronics
24 retired (no further information)
20 in teaching professions - teachers/college lecturers/ professors
28 admin & professional (civil service, local govt, accountancy, surveying, legal, police.)
17 trades including Plasterer, builder, lorry driver, foundry worker)
14 managers
12 health care workers (including pharmacist and clinical psychologist)
7 artists, musicians, writers

Appendix C

AGE AND FREQUENCY: Replies to questionnaire – questions 4, 5 & 6

Q4 (When did you first realise that you wished to cross dress?)
Q5 (Was it associated with anything in particular?)

Not everyone answered this and some only answered one part or the other – but of those who gave reasons, over a quarter (52) gave their mothers' or sisters' clothes as a crucial factor. Many of these mention the silkiness of their mother's underwear and how wonderful this felt (which makes one wonder whether Marks and Sparks cotton briefs will ever be remembered so fondly ...)

7 referred to icons of the screen or theatre such as Marlene Dietrich
10 could remember clearly incidents featuring the clothing of female childhood playmates
4 remembered their grandmothers' clothes and
3 remembered the illicit borrowing of articles of clothing from wives or
girlfriends.

For **Question 6 about the frequency of cross-dressing,** from the answers given, I decided on 6 categories – *less than once a month, once a month, two or three times a month, once a week, two or three times a week* and *most days* plus an additional division into three of *part time, full-time* and *almost full time*. Thus it is possible (and the most frequently encountered) to dress most days but still be part time because the part of the day spent dressed is in the evening after work. This also includes men who wear one or two items of female clothing almost all the time but combined with outerwear – or other components – of male clothing.

As I did chalk marks of five bar gates for the number of cross-dressers in each category, it rapidly became apparent that they were inversely proportional to the amount of time spent dressed in male clothing (i.e. the number of questionnaire respondents is proportional to the frequency of dressing in female clothing).

Only one man dressed less than once a month
11, approximately once a month
22, 2–3 times a month
32, once a week,
48, 2–3 times a week
64, most days
(total 178).

In the second set of divisions, 12 could be classed as full time
11 classed as almost full time and 165 as part time (total 180)
(The discrepancy between the two totals is due to 2 simply saying 'part-time'.)

$$\mathscr{Appendix}\ \mathscr{D}$$

The Construction of Femininity: An Archetype to Live Through

Adjectives used by UK Transvestites in Questionnaires
There seems to be a widespread opinion amongst the transvestites who answered my questionnaire that women are, for example, gentler and softer (these two attributes in particular were the most frequently recurring in the questionnaires). The adjectives given are particularly in response to the questions in Part III.

Below is a list of attributes taken from the questionnaires which were thought by the transvestites to represent the desirability of femaleness:

gentle, soft, yielding,
not – or less – aggressive (repeated many, many times)
graceful, elegant, delicate,
smooth, genteel,
dainty, beautiful
relaxed, tolerant, laid back,
at ease with self,
able to form close relationships
aware of sensuality,
fully sexual, sexy,
instantly attractive, wild
liberated, bold,
less inhibited (for example when dancing),
have more fun,
extrovert/outgoing
sympathetic, caring,
genuinely interested in others,
tender, loving, intimate
aware of movements and body,
having an aesthetic eye,

more appreciative of beauty
more expressive/having greater freedom of self expression
creative, imaginative,
magical, more colourful
friendlier, less aloof,
less stand-offish,
tidier, cleaner
petulant, silly, weak,
'think with their mouths',
vulnerable, the 'hunted'/desired
protected, looked after
coy, skittish, flirtatious,
glamorous, pretty
thoughtful, insightful, perceptive,
much more mature mentally,
have more fun/wider choices

Bibliography

Adler & Pointon (1993), *The Body Imaged: The Human Form and Visual Culture since the Renaissance*, Cambridge, Cambridge University Press.

Allen, Michael & Mukherjee, S. N. (1982), *Women in India and Nepal*, Canberra, ANU Press.

Appadurai, Arjun (1996), *The Social Life of Things: Commodities in Cultural Perspective*, Cambridge, Cambridge University Press.

Ardener, Shirley (ed.) (1981), *Women and Space*, Oxford, Berg.

— (1987), 'A note on Gender Iconography: The Vagina', in Caplan (ed.), *The Cultural Construction of Sexuality*, London, Routledge.

— (ed.) (1992), *Persons and Powers of Women of Women in Diverse Cultures*, Oxford, Berg.

— (ed.) (1993), *Defining Females*, Oxford, Berg.

Arthur, Linda (ed.) (1999), *Religion, Dress and the Body*, Oxford, Berg.

Backett-Milburn & Mckie (eds.) (2001), *Constructing Gendered Bodies*, Basingstoke/New York, Palgrave.

Baizerman, Suzanne (1992), 'The Jewish *Kippa Sruga* and the social construction of gender', in Barnes & Eicher, *Dress and Gender*, Oxford, Berg.

Bancroft, John (1989), *Human Sexuality & its Problems* (2nd Edition), London, Churchill, Livingstone.

Baring, A. & Cashford, J. (1991), *The Myth of the Goddess: Evolution of an Image*, London, Viking.

Barnes, Ruth & Eicher, Joanne B. (1992), *Dress and Gender: Making and Meaning*, Oxford, Berg.

Basilov, V. N. (1978), 'Vestiges of Transvestism in Central Asian Shamanism' in Dioszegi & Hoppal (eds.), *Shamanism in Siberia*, Budapest, Akademiai Kiado.

Bateson, Gregory (1980 [1958]), *Naven*, Stanford, Stanford University Press.

Baum, Rob Kim (1996), 'Forging Female Identity: the performance of metaphor and absence' unpublished thesis, California.

Beattie, John (1980), 'Representations of the Self in Traditional Africa', *Africa*, No. 50 (3) pp. 313–20.

Berger, M. Wallis, B. & Watson, S. (1995) *Constructing Masculinity*, New York, Routledge.

Berreman, Gerald D. (1971), 'The Brahmanical view of caste', *Contributions to Indian Sociology* (n.s.) 5: 61–23.

Beteille, André (1992), 'Caste and family in representations of Indian Society', *Anthropology Today*, Vol. 8, February 1992.

Bettelheim, Bruno (1955), *Symbolic Wounds: Puberty Rites and the Envious Male*, London, Thames & Hudson.

Bland, Jed (1993), *The Dual Role Transvestite: A unique form of identity*, Derby TV/TS Group.

Bogoras, W. (1909), *The Chukchee*, (ed. Boas), New York, Leyden.

Bornstein, Kate (1995), *Gender Outlaw*, New York, Vintage edition.

— (1999), interviewed in *Sex Sense* (Narrator, Tim Hardy), produced by Discovery Channel/Exploration Production.

Bowden, Ross (1983), Yena: *Art and Ceremony in a Sepik Society*, Oxford, Pitt Rivers Museum.

Briffault, Robert (1926), *The Mothers*, London, Allen & Unwin.

Broch-Due, Vigdis, Rudie, I. & Bleie, T. (eds.) (1993), *Carved Flesh/Cast Selves: Gendered Symbols & Social Practices*, Oxford, Berg.

Bullough, V. L. & B. (1993), *Cross-dressing, Sex & Gender*, Pennsylvania, Penn.

Butler, Judith (1990), *Gender Trouble*, London/New York, (Routledge) (1999 edition).

— (1993), *Bodies that Matter*, London/New York, Routledge.

Califia, Pat (1997), *Sex Changes: The politics of transgenderism*, San Francisco, Cleis Press.

Campbell, Joseph (1971), *The Portable Jung*, London, Penguin/Viking.

Caplan, Pat (ed.) (1987), *The Cultural Construction of Sexuality*, London, Routledge.

Carrithers, Collins & Lukes (eds.) (1986), *The Category of the Person*, Cambridge, Cambridge University Press.

Carrithers, Michael (1985), 'An alternative social history of the self', in Carrithers, Collins & Lukes (eds.) *The Category of the Person*, Cambridge, Cambridge University Press.

Chodorow, Nancy (1974), 'Family Structure and Feminine Personality', in Rosaldo & Lamphere (eds), *Woman, Culture and Society*, Stanford, Stanford University Press.

— (1978), *The Reproduction of Mothering: Psychoanalysis and the Sociology of Gender*, Berkeley, University of California Press.

Cohen, Anthony P. (ed.) (1986), *Symbolising boundaries*, Manchester, Manchester University Press.

— (1994), *Self Consciousness: An alternative anthropology of identity*, London/New York, Routledge.

Cole, Shaun (2000), *Don we now our gay apparel*, Oxford, Berg,

Collier, J. F. & Yanagisako, S. J. (1987), *Gender and Kinship: Essays towards a unified analysis*, Stanford, Stanford University Press.

Connell, R. (1996), 'New Directions in Gender Theory, Masculinity Research and Gender Politics', *Ethnos*, Vol. 61: 3–4.

Cornwall, Andrea & Lindisfarne, Nancy (1994), *Dislocating Masculinity: Comparative Ethnographies*, London, Routledge.

Craik, Jennifer (1994), *The Face of Fashion: Cultural Studies in Fashion*, London, Routledge.

D'Anglure, Bernard Saladin (1986), 'The Foetus of the Shaman: Construction of a third sex among the Inuit', *Inuit Studies*, 10 (1/2).

Daniel, E. Valentine (1984), *Fluid Signs: Being a Person the Tamil Way*, University of California Press.

David K. (ed.) (1977), *The new wind: changing identities in South Asia*, Chicago/Mouton The Hague.

Dean-Schulman, David (1980), *Tamil Temple Myths*, Princeton, Princeton University Press.

Devor, Holly (1996), 'How Many Sexes? How Many Genders? When Two Are Not Enough.' University Provost's lecture, University of Victoria, Canada.

Docter, Richard (1988), *Transvestites & Transsexuals: Towards a theory of cross gender behaviour*, New York/London, Plenum.

Douglas, Mary (1966), *Purity and Danger*, London, Routledge.

Dumont, Louis (1980), *Homo Hierarchicus*, Chicago, University of Chicago Press.

— (1985) 'A modified view of our origins: the Christian beginnings of modern individualism', in Carrithers, Collins & Lukes (eds.), *The Category of the Person*, Cambridge, Cambridge University Press.

Durkheim, Emile (1915), *Elementary Forms of Religious Life*, London, Allen & Unwin.

— (1952 [1989]), *Suicide*, London, Routledge.

Eicher, Joanne B. (1995) (ed.), *Dress and Ethnicity*, Oxford/Washington, Berg.

Ekins, Richard (1997), *Male Femaling*, London/NY, Routledge.

Elgood, Heather (1999), *Hinduism and the Religious Arts*, London, Cassell.

Eliade, Mircea (1958), *Patterns in Comparative Religion*, London, Sheed & Ward.

— (1964), *Shamanism: Archaic Techniques of Ecstasy*, London, Sheed & Ward.

Epple, Carolyn (1997), 'A Navaho Worldview and Nadleehi: Implications for Western Categories', in Jacobs, Thomas & Lang (eds.), *Two Spirit People: Native American Gender Identity, Sexuality and Spirituality*, Chicago, University of Illinois Press.

Eriksen Thomas, Hylland (1995), *Small Places, Large Issues: An Introduction to Social and Cultural Anthropology*, London, Pluto Press.

Errington, Shelley (1990), 'Recasting Sex, Gender and Power', in Atkinson & Errington (eds.), *Power and Difference: Gender in Island Southeast Asia*, Stanford, Stanford University Press.

The Evangelical Alliance Policy Commission (2000), *Transsexuality*, London.

Faithorn, Elizabeth (1976), 'Women as Persons: Aspects of Female Life and male-female relationships among the Kafé', in Brown & Buchbinder (eds), *Men and Women in the New Guinea Highlands*, Washington.

Fausto-Sterling, Anne (1992), *Myths of Gender*, New York, Basic.

— (2000), *Sexing the Body*, New York, Basic.

Ferris, Lesley (ed.) (1993), *Crossing the Stage: Controversies on cross-dressing*, London/New York, Routledge.

Foley, Helene P. (1994), *The Homeric Hymn to Demeter*, Princeton, Princeton University Press.

Foucault, Michel (1986), *The History of Sexuality*, London, Penguin.

Fuller, C. J. (1992), *The Camphor Flame: Popular Hinduism and Society in India*, Princeton, Princeton University Press.

Frazer, James (1914), *The Golden Bough*, London, Macmillan.

Frymer-Kensky, Tikva (1992), *In the Wake of the Pagan Goddesses*, New York/London, Free Press/Macmillan.

Garber, Marjorie (1992), *Vested Interests*, London, Penguin.

Garnsey, P. & Saller, R. (1987), *The Roman Empire*, London, Duckworth.

Geertz, Clifford (1973), *The Interpretation of Cultures*, New York, Fontana.

— (1983), *Local Knowledge*, New York, Fontana.

Gell, Alfred (1998), *Art and Agency: An Anthropological Theory*, Oxford, Oxford University Press.

Gilbert, S & Gubar, S (1989), *No Man's Land*, (Vol. 2: *Sexchanges*), Boston, Yale University Press.

Gillison, Gillian (1980), 'Images of Nature in Gimi Thought', in MacCormack & Strathern, *Nature, Culture and Gender* , Cambridge, Cambridge University Press.

Goffman, Erving (1979), *Gender Advertisements*, London, MacMillan.

Goulet, J-G. (1997), 'The North Athapaskan Berdache Reconsidered: On Reading More than there is in the Ethnographic Record' in Jacobs, Thomas & Lang (eds.) *Two Spirit People: Native American Gender Identity, Sexuality and Spirituality*, Chicago, University of Illinois Press.

Graves, Robert (1961), *The White Goddess*, London, Faber.

Gray, John (1993), *Men are from Mars, Women are from Venus*, London/New York, Thorsons.

Greenblatt, Stephen (1988), *Shakespearian Negotiations: The circulation of social energy in Renaissance England*, Berkeley, University of California Press.

Griggs, Claudine (1998), S/He, Oxford, Berg.

Grosz, E. & Probyn, E. (1995), *Sexy Bodies: the strange carnalities of feminism*, London, Routledge.

Guy, Green & Banim (2001), *Through the Wardrobe: Women's Relationships with their clothes*, Oxford, Berg.

Halperin, Winkler & Zeitlin (eds.) (1990), *Before Sexuality: The Construction of Erotic Experience in the Ancient Greek World*, Princeton, Princeton University Press.

Hamilton, Marybeth (1992), 'I'm the queen of the bitches: Female Impersonation and Mae West's Pleasure Man', in FERRIS (ed.), *Crossing the Stage: Controversies on cross-dressing*, London/New York, Routledge.

Harding, Jennifer (1998), *Sex Acts; Practices of Femininity and Masculinity*, London, Sage.

Harding, M. Esther (1981), *The Way of All Women*, London, Rider.

Hawley, John S. & Wulff, Donna M. (1984), *The Divine Consort: Radha & the Goddesses of India*, California, Berkeley Religious Studies.

Hays, H. R. (1966), *The Dangerous Sex: the Myth of Feminine evil*, London, Methuen.

Heelas, Paul (1996), *The New Age Movement*, Oxford, Blackwell.

Heelas, P. & Lock, A. (eds.) (1981), *Indigenous Psychologies: The Anthropology of the Self*, London/New York, etc., Academic Press.

Hendricks, M. (1993), 'Is it a boy or a girl?', *Johns Hopkins Journal*, Nov 1993; 10–16

Hendrickson, Hildi (1996), *Clothing and Difference: Embodied Identities in Colonial and Post-Colonial Africa*, London/Durham, Duke University.

Herdt, Gilbert (1982) *Ritualized Homosexuality in Melanesia*, California University Press.

— (ed.) (1993), *Third Sex, Third Gender*, New York, Zone.

Herodotus (1964), *The Histories* (Bk. I), [Tr.Rawlinson] London/New York, Dent/Dutton.

Hoch-Smith, Judith & Spring, Anita (eds.) (1978), *Women in Ritual & Symbolic Roles*, New York/London, Plenum.

Hodder, Ian (ed.) (1989), *The Meaning of Things: Material Culture and Symbolic Expression*, London, Harper Collins.

Hogan-Finlay, Mary (1996), 'Development of the cross-gender lifestyle and comparison of cross-gendered men with heterosexual controls', unpublished thesis, Ottawa.

Horton, David (1994), *Changing Channels: A Christian Response to the Transvestite and the Transsexual*, Nottingham, Grove.

Ingold, Tim (ed.) (1994), *Companion Encyclopaedia of Anthropology*, London Routledge.

Jaffrey, Zia (1997), *The Invisibles: A tale of the Eunuchs of India*, London, Weidenfeld & Nicholson.

Johnson, Mark (1997), *Beauty and Power: Transgendering and Cultural Transformation in the Southern Philippines*, Oxford/New York, Berg.

Jukes, Adam (1993), *Why Men Hate Women*, London, Free Association Press.

Jung, C. G. (1982), *Aspects of the Feminine*, Princeton, Princeton University Press (UK: RKP).

Kakar, Sudhir (1987), *Shamans, Mystics, Doctors*, London, Mandala.

Kearns, Emily (1992), 'Indian Myth' in Carolyne Larrington (ed.) *The Feminist Companion to Mythology*, London, Pandora.

Keenan, W. J. F. (ed.) (2001), *Dressed to Impress: Looking the Part*, Oxford, Berg.

Kessler, Suzanne & Mckenna, Wendy (1978), *Gender: An Ethnomethodological Approach*, New York, Wiley.

King, Dave (1993), *The Transvestite and the Transsexual*, Aldershot, Avebury.

Kondos, Vivienne (1985), 'Images of the Hindu Fierce Mother Goddess and Experiences of Mother', *Kailash*, 1985: 223–76.

Lamb, Sarah (2000), *White Saris and Sweet Mangoes: Aging, Gender and body in North India*, University of California Press.

Lampert et al (1982), *The Image of Man: The Indian Perception of the Universe through 2000 years of painting and sculpture*, London, Arts Council.

Lane Fox, Robin (1986), *Pagans and Christians*, London, Penguin.

Langner, Lawrence (1959), *The Importance of Wearing Clothes*, London, Constable.

Laqueur, Thomas (1990), *Making Sex: Body and Gender from the Greeks to Freud*, Harvard University Press.

Leach, E. R. (1961), 'Rethinking Anthropology', London.

Leacock, Eleanor (1981), *Myths of Male Dominance: Collected Articles on Women Cross-Culturally*, Monthly Review Press, New York.

Lechte, John (1994), *Fifty Key Contemporary Thinkers*, London, Routledge.

Lerner, Gerda (1986), *The Creation of Patriarchy*, Oxford, Oxford University Press.

Loizos & Papataxiarchis (1991), *Contested Identities*, Princeton, Princeton University Press.

Luhrmann, Tanya (1989), *Persuasions of the Witch's Craft*, Oxford, Blackwell.

Lukes, Steven (1985), 'Conclusion', in Carrithers, Collins & Lukes (eds.), *The Category of the Person*, Cambridge, Cambridge University Press.

Lurie, Alison (1981), *The Language of Clothes*, New York, Owl.

Lutz, C. & White, G. M. (1986), 'The Anthropology of Emotions', *Annual Review of Anthropology*, Vol. 15: 405–36.

Lynch, Annette (1999), *Dress, Gender and Cultural Change*, Oxford, Berg.

Macilvenny, Paul (1998), 'Talk is Sexy: Normalising Gender/Sex/Sexuality in a New Media', in Pedersen & Schener (eds.) *Sprog, Kon og Kommunikation* (proceedings of the 3rd Nordic Conference on Language and Gender), Copenhagen.

Madan, T. N. *et al.* (1971), 'On the nature of caste in India: a review symposium on Louis Dumont's "Homo Hierarchicus"', *Contributions to Indian Sociology* (n.s.) 5: 1–81.

Marglin, Frederique Apfel (1985), 'Female Sexuality in the Hindu World' in Atkinson, Buchanan & Miles, *Immaculate and Powerful, The female in Sacred Image and Social Reality*, Boston Mass.

Mauss, Marcel (1986), 'A Category of the Human Mind: The notion of person, the notion of the self', in Carrithers *et al*, *The Category of the Person*, Cambridge, Cambridge University Press.

Mead, Margaret (1949 [1962]), 'Male and Female', USA, Pelican edition.

Meigs, Anna (1976) 'Male Pregnancy & the reduction of sexual opposition in a New Guinea Highlands Society' *Ethnology*, 15: 393–407.

Mellen, Sydney L. W. (c. 1981), *The Evolution of Love*, Oxford/San Francisco, W. H. Freeman.

Miller, Daniel (1985), *Artefacts as Categories*, Cambridge, Cambridge University Press.

— (1987), *Material Culture and Mass Consumption*, Oxford, Blackwell.

— (1994), *Artefacts and the Meaning of Things*, in INGOLD (ed.), *Companion Encyclopaedia of Anthropology*, London, Routledge.

Miller, Virginia (ed.) (1988), *The Role of Gender in Precolumbian Art and Architecture*, Lanham, University Press of America.

Moir, Anne & Bill (1998), *Why Men Don't Iron: The Real Science of Gender Studies*, HarperCollins, London

Molloy, Ruth Lor (1997), 'Hijras, who are we?', Toronto, Think Asia.

Money, J. & Ehrhardt, A. (1972), *Man and Woman, Boy and Girl: The differentiation and Dimorphism of gender identity from conception to maturity*, Baltimore, Johns Hopkins Press.

Moore, Henrietta (1988), *Feminism and Anthropology*, Cambridge, Polity Press.

— (1994a), *A Passion for Difference*, Cambridge, Polity Press.

— 1994b) *Understanding Sex and Gender*, in INGOLD, *Companion Encyclopaedia of Anthropology*, London, Routledge.

— (1998), 'Is female to male as nature is to culture? Thoughts on making gender', *Social Analysis*, November, 42 (3).

— (ed.) (1999), *Anthropological Theory Today*, Cambridge, Polity Press.

Morphy, Howard (1991), *Ancestral Connections*, Chicago, University of Chicago Press.

Morris, Brian (1994), *Anthropology of the Self: The Individual in Cultural Perspective*, London, Pluto Press.

Morris, Jan (1974), *Conundrum*, London, Methuen.

Nanda, Serena (1990), *Neither man nor woman: the hijras of India*, California, Wadsworth.

Newton, Esther (1979), *Mother Camp: Female Impersonators in America* (2nd ed.), Chicago, University of Chicago Press.

O'Connor, Peter (1985), *Understanding Jung*, London, Methuen.

O'Flaherty, Wendy Doniger (1980), *Women, Androgynes, and other Mythical Beasts*, Chicago, University of Chicago Press.

Ortner, Sherry (1974), 'Is female to male as nature is to culture?', in Rosaldo & Lamphere (eds.), *Woman, Culture and Society*, Stanford, Stanford University Press.

Ortner, Sherry & Whitehead, H. (1981), *Sexual Meanings: The Cultural Construction of Gender and Sexuality*, Cambridge, Cambridge University Press.

Ortner, Sherry (1996), *Making Gender*, Boston, Beacon.

Ovid (1955), *Metamorphoses* (Tr. Innes), London, Penguin.

Parkin, Frank (1992), *Durkheim*, Oxford, Oxford University Press.

Peacock, James L. (1968), *Rites of Modernization*, Chicago, University of Chicago Press.

Pearsall, Judy (ed.) (1998), *The New Oxford Dictionary of English*, Oxford, Oxford University Press.

Phelan, Peggy (1993), 'Criss-Crossing Culture', in FERRIS, *Crossing the Stage: Controversies on cross-dressing*, London/New York, Routledge.

Piedmont, Ozmo (1996), 'The Veils of Arjuna: Androgyny in Gay Spirituality, East and West', unpublished thesis, San Francisco.

Poole, F. J. P. (1994), 'Socialisation, Enculturation and the development of personal identity', in Ingold, *Companion Encylopaedia in Anthropology*, London, Routledge.

Postma (dir.) (1995), *The Gender Bender*, (documentary film), London, Channel 4.

Pumphrey, M. (1989), 'Why do Cowboys wear hats in the bath? Style politics for the older man', *Critical Quarterly*, Autumn [31:3]

Quigley, Declan (1993), *The interpretation of caste*, Oxford, Clarendon Press.

Ramanujan, A. K. (1973), *Speaking of Siva*, London, Penguin.

Ramet, S. P. (ed.) (1996), *Gender Reversals and Gender Cultures*, London, Routledge.

Rapport, Nigel (1996), 'The Individual', in Barnard & Spencer (eds), *The Encyclopaedia of Social & Cultural Anthropology*, London, Routledge.

Raymond, Janice (1980 [1979]), *The Transsexual Empire*, London, Women's Press.

Reeves-Sanday, P. (1981), *Female Power and Male Dominance*, Cambridge, Cambridge University Press.

Rekers George (1985), 'Gender Disorders', (paper presented to) North American Social Science Network.

Richardson, Miles (1989), 'The Artefact as Abbreviated Act' in HODDER, *The Meaning of Things: Material Culture and Symbolic Expression*, London, Harper Collins.

Roosevelt, Anna Curtenius (1988), 'Interpreting Certain Female Images in Prehistoric Art', in V. Miller (ed.) *The Role of Gender in Precolumbian Art and Architecture*, Lanham, University Press of America.

Rosaldo, Michelle Z. & Lamphere, Louise (eds) (1974), *Woman, Culture and Society*, Stanford, Stanford University Press.

Robertson, Jennifer (1998), *Takarazuka : Sexual Politics and Popular Culture in Modern Japan*, Berkeley, Univeristy of California Press.

Rudd, P. (1998), *Who's Really from Venus? A tale of two genders*, Texas, Katy Press.

Schifter, Jacobo (1999), *From Toads to Queens: Transvestism in a Latin American Setting*, New York, Harrington Park Press.

Schutzer, M. A. Napewastin (1994), 'Winyanktehca: Two Souls Person', (Paper presented to the European Network of Professionals in Transvestism], August 1994.

Sedgwick, Eve Kosofsky (1995), 'Gosh Boy George, you must be awfully secure in your masculinity', in Berger, Wallis & Watson, (eds.) *Constructing Masculinity*, New York/London, Routledge.

Senelick, Laurence (1993), 'Glamour Drag and Male Impersonation', in FERRIS, *Crossing the Stage: Controversies on cross-dressing*, London/New York, Routledge.

Senior, Olive (1991), *Working Miracles*, Indiana, Indiana University Press.

Sharma, Satish Kumar (1989), *Hijras: The Labelled Deviants*, Delhi, Gian Press.

Shaw, Alison (2001), 'Gendering the genitals: the sex-assignment of the newborn', as yet unpublished paper, given in Oxford, October 2001.

Singer, June (1976), *Androgyny: Toward a New Theory of Sexuality*, New York, RKP.

Singh, Dyanita (1993), 'Altered States', in *The Independent*, London, 22.v.93.

Sinha, A. P. (1967), 'Procreation among the Eunuchs', *The Eastern Anthropologist*, Vol. 21, 2, 168–76, Delhi.

Sokefeld, Martin (1999), 'Debating Self, Identity, and Culture in Anthropology', *Current Anthropology*, Vol. 40, No.4.

Spelman, Elizabeth (1990), *Inessential Woman*, London, The Women's Press.

Srinivas M. N. (1997), 'Practising Social Anthropology in India', *Annual Review of Anthropology*, Vol. 26: 1–24.

Strathern, A. & M. (1971), *Self-Decoration in Mount Hagen*, London, Duckworth.

Strathern, Marilyn (1981), 'Some Implications of Hagen Gender Imagery', in Ortner & Whitehead, *Sexual Meanings*, Cambridge, Cambridge University Press.

— (1988), *The Gender of the Gift*, Berkeley, University of California Press.

Steinem, Gloria (1983), *Outrageous Acts and Everyday Rebellions*, London, Flamingo.

Tarlo, Emma (1996), *Clothing Matters: Dress and Identity in India*, London, Hurst.

Tayler, Donald (1996), *Embarkations*, Oxford, Pitt Rivers Museum.

Taylor, Gary (2000), *Castration; An abbreviated history of Western Manhood*, London/New York, Routledge.

Thomas, Wesley (1997), 'Navaho Cultural Constructions of Gender and Sexuality', in Jacobs, Thomas & Lang (eds.), *Two Spirit People: Native American Gender Identity, Sexuality and Spirituality*, Chicago, University of Illinois Press.

Torjeson, Karen J. (1996), 'Martyrs, Ascetics & Gnostics: Gender Crossing in Early Christianity' in Ramet (ed.), *Gender Reversals and Gender Cultures*, London, Routledge.

Turner, Victor (1982), *From Ritual to Theatre*, New York, Performing Arts Journal Publications.

— (1969), *The Ritual Process*, London/New York, RKP.

Ussher, Jane (1997), *Fantasies of Femininity: Reframing the Boundaries of Sex*, London, Penguin.

Warner, Marina (1996), *Monuments and Maidens*, London, Vintage.

Warwick, A. & Cavallaro, D. (1998), *Fashioning the Frame: Boundaries, Dress and the Body*, Oxford, Berg.

Weber, Max (2002 [reprinted from 1930]), *The Protestant Ethic and the Spirit of Capitalism*, London, Routledge.

Weeks, Jeffrey (1985), *Sexuality and its discontents*, London, RKP.

Weiner, James (ed.) (1994), *Aesthetics is a Cross-Cultural Category*, Manchester, Group for Debates in Anthropological Theory.

Weiner, A. B. & Schneider, J. (1989), *Cloth and Human Experience*, Washington, Smithsonian Institute Press.

Whitehead, Harriet (1981), 'The bow and the burdenstrap: A new look at institutionalized homosexuality in native North America', in Ortner & Whitehead, *Sexual Meanings*, New York/Cambridge, Cambridge University Press.

Wikan, Unni (1977), 'Man Becomes Woman: Transsexualism in Oman as a key to Gender Roles', *Man* (N.S.) 12, 304–19.

Williams, W. L. (1986), *The Spirit and the Flesh: Sexual Diversity in American Indian Culture*, Boston, Beacon Press.

Wilson, Elizabeth (1985), *Adorned in Dreams*, London, Virago.

Wood, Ed (Dir.) (1953), *Glen or Glenda?* (Film) USA.

Woodhouse, Annie (1989), *Fantastic Women: Sex, Gender and Transvestism*, London, Macmillan.

Woolf, Viginia (1928), *Orlando*, London, Hogarth Press.

Yorke, Michael (1991), *Eunuchs – India's Third Gender* (Film), London.

Zaehner, R. C. (1962), *Hinduism*, Oxford, Oxford University Press.

— (Tr.) (1966), *Hindu Scriptures*, London, Dent.

Index

adjectives (used by transvestites), 134

Ajmer, shrine of Baba Darga, 112(n)

Allah, 99

Allen, Michael, 106

'alter ego' (as category), 63

Anakreontic vases, 26

anatomy, and sexual difference, 151

androcentrism, in ideology, 175

androgyny, images of, 127

angels, sex of, 129(n)

anima and animus, 140–1

Anog Ite (berdaches and destiny), 181(n)

Anopura (village in Rajasthan), 103

Anthony/Suzanne, narrative, 42–3, 120

anthropology and fieldwork, 179

Antonopoulos, Katya, 90

'aparting', 60

Apollodorus, record of transvestism, 6

Ardener, Shirley, 15, 17, 18

Aristotle, 20

Arjun, 98, 127

artefactual importance, 69

Artemis, 129(n)

Atalanta, 129–30(n)

auto-gynephilia, 60

Baba Darga, Sufi saint, 112(n)

bantut (of Philippines), 6, 157

Barnes and Eicher (on clothing), 15, 122

Basavanna, 88

Bastian (colleague of Frazer), 6

Bateson, Gregory (*see* also *Naven*), 116, 137–39

bathroom, which one to use, 72(n)

Beaumont Society, 9(n), 34, 49, 60
  and heterosexuality, 146

Beaumont Society journal, 34

belief systems (role of), 5

belief systems, importance of, 123

berdaches, 6, 7
  and destiny, 182(n)
  etymology of, 149

berdachism as sex/gender role, 145
  as 'niche for homosexuals', 145

'best of both worlds' (as category), 61

Bhatt, Mahesh (director), 108

Bhatt, Pooja (director), 108

Bible, as mythology in Judaeo-Christian cultures, 85
  and binary nature of gender, 124

bichwala (middle sex), 110

binarism, notions of, 125

binary categorisation as 'common sense', 150

binary divide (sex and gender), 163

biological determinism, 20, 21

drag, 7, 107, 108
  and homosexuality, 146
  and gender codes, 163
  and individuation, 14
  as 'fun' activity, 39, 120
  contrasted with hijras, 121
dress, as mediator, 16
  as non-verbal code, 81
  as visual identificatory code,
  16
dress codes, as iconographic
  markers, 163
dressing as stress relief, 69
dual-sex-ism, 128
Dumont, L. (and 'the person'), 164
  on caste, 169, 171
Durkheim, E (on suicide), 164

Eicher, Joanne, 16
Ekins, Richard, 49, 55, 118
Elgood, Heather, 88
Eliade, Mircea and 'ritual
  transvestism', 141
Emma Peel, 42
endocrinological research, 40
Epple, Carolyn, work with the
  Navaho, 149
Eriksen, T. H., and social
  emotions, 172
Errington, Shelley, 24, 153
ethnographic fieldwork, 25
ethos and eidos (in Iatmul culture),
  137
eunuchs, 89
Evangelical Alliance, 131
Evans (UK High Street shop), 66
Evans-Pritchard, E., 112(n)

family structure in India, 169
Farrer, Peter, 73(n)
fashion, male and female, 31

multiplicity of Western styles,
  129(n)
Fausto-Sterling, Anne, 28(n), 151
female identity, construction of,
  167
female principle, role in ritual, 85
female sexuality, 'auspiciousness'
  of, 127
female to male transvestism, 16
feminine, as inferior or 'silly', 70
  devaluation of, 125
  projection of, 27
fieldwork, 3, 5,131
  comparisons, 115
  in the UK, 34
  poly-methodological approach,
  115
First World War, 73(n)
foetal development and sex
  attribution, 152
Foucault, Michel, 21
Frazer, James, 6

Galen, 17
Gandhi, M.K., 77
Garber, Marjorie, 20
Gaultier, Jean-Paul, 31
Geertz, Clifford, 22
  and intersexuality, 160
Gell, Alfred (inner and outer
  person), 142
gender as social construction, 19,
  21
gender codes in dress, 163
gender crossing and cultural
  diversity, 160
  and individual agency, 160
  as clothing choice, 146
  as occupational choice, 146
  conceptualisation of, 156
  less motivated by sexuality, 146